The New-Brutality Film
Race and Affect in Contemporary Hollywood Cinema

Paul Gormley

intellect™
Bristol, UK
Portland, OR, USA

First Published in the UK in 2005 by

Intellect Books, PO Box 862, Bristol BS99 1DE, UK

First Published in the USA in 2005 by

Intellect Books, ISBS, 920 NE 58th Ave. Suite 300, Portland, Oregon 97213-3786, USA

Copyright ©2005 Intellect Ltd

A catalogue record for this book is available from the British Library

ISBN 1-84150-119-0

Cover Design: Gabriel Solomons

Copy Editor: Julie Strudwick

Printed and bound in Great Britain by Antony Rowe Ltd.

Contents

5   **Acknowledgments**

7   **Introduction**
Torturous Cinema:
Questions of Affect, Mimesis and Race in The New-Brutality Film

43   **Chapter One**
Naïve Imitations:
Falling Down, the Crisis of the Action-Image and Cynical Realism

73   **Chapter Two**
Gangsters and Gangstas:
Boyz N the Hood, and the Dangerous Black Body

99   **Chapter Three**
Gangsters and Gangstas Part Two:
Menace II Society and the Cinema of Rage

137   **Chapter Four**
Miming Blackness:
Reservoir Dogs and 'American Africanism'

159   **Chapter Five**
Trashing Whiteness:
Pulp Fiction, *Se7en*, *Strange Days* and Articulating Affect

183   **Conclusion**

195   **Bibliography**

203   **Filmography**

207   **Index**

Acknowledgements

Although there are always too many people to thank in a project of this size, the following people deserve particular mention for their intellectual stimulus, and other support over the various stages of completion: John Beasley-Murray, The School of Cultural and Media Studies and Social Sciences and my Urban Film students at the University of East London, Haim Bresheeth, Jessica Edwards, Natalia Garcia, Jane Gaines and the Literature Programme at Duke University, Jeremy Gilbert, Andrew and Jessica Grierson, Laura Mulvey, Mica Nava, Luciana Parisi, Elaine Pennicott, Greg Santori, Ashwani Sharma, Mark Shiel, Sophy Smith and her family, Andrew Sneddon, Tiziana Terranova, Carol Watts, Paul Whelan, Nick Wilson - and my family.

This book is dedicated to the memory of my mother, Eileen Gormley (1947-1982).

Introduction

Torturous Cinema:
Questions of Affect, Mimesis and Race in The New-Brutality Film

One of the most striking scenes in 1990s' US cinema is filmed in ten minutes of real time and centres on a gangster's apparently meaningless mutilation of a cop in a disused warehouse. The infamous torture scene in *Reservoir Dogs* (Tarantino 1991) begins with a fixed shot of the gangster, Mr Blonde, sat on an abandoned hearse, and the cop tied to a chair in the centre of the room. From the cop's point of view, we see Blonde jump from his perch, with the sinister enunciation, 'alone at last'. As Blonde advances towards the cop, the shots start switching vigorously between both points of view, and we know that some sort of sadistic violence is about to ensue. After some verbal taunting, and the restless circular movement of the camera, the violence begins with a sudden slap to the cop's already swollen face. This blow is made more unsettling for the viewer, by a sudden switch in the camera's point of view which gives the effect of Blonde's outstretched hand coming towards the audience. The film then cuts to another shot of the gangster, standing behind the cop's head and gagging him with some sticky masking tape. As he silences the cop, Blonde makes the horrifying comment, 'I don't give a good fuck what you know or don't know, but I'm going to torture you anyway'. The gangster then pulls out his gun on a horrified cop, vainly struggling to escape the line of fire, and we know that knowledge or reason has no power to save the cop from the impending violence. This is echoed in the viewer's relationship to the scene. The bout of violence has no real narrative logic beyond the fact that we have been told by another member of the gang that Blonde is a 'fucking madman', and this lack of narrative cause and effect leaves the viewer without a clue as to what happens next.

The camera cuts to a close-up of Blonde's boot as he lifts it on to a table to pull out a razor, asking the bizarre question, 'Ever listen to K. Billy's Super Sounds of the Seventies?' The film then zooms in on the cop's beaten and anguished face, before it cuts back to Blonde dancing around him. Suddenly, Blonde lunges at the cop and the viewer with the razor. The changes in point of view become more frenetic, as the gangster sits on the cop's knee, and begins to slice his ear off with the razor. The camera then pans away, leaving the actual disembodiment unseen - although the acousmatic sounds of the cop's muffled cries of pain leave us with the impression of being visually present throughout the mutilation. Blonde then moves back into the frame, and while considering the organ, he alludes to the self-reflexive, sadistic and masochistic overtones of the scene with the question, 'Was that as good for you as it was for me?'[1]

After this torturous sequence, the viewer might reasonably expect some period of respite, with a cut away to another scene, but the film stays with Blonde, following him to his car. This escape outside of the claustrophobic confines of the warehouse is only temporary as the camera tracks the gangster, petrol container in hand, back into the building. In a slow tracking shot, he dances his way around the cop, to the sounds of Stealers Wheel's 'Stuck in the Middle with You.' The cuts between shots suddenly increase their pace, as Blonde begins to drench the cop with gasoline. The liquid also splatters the camera, threatening to splash through the boundary between screen and viewer. Finally the gangster pulls out a Zippo lighter, to torch the cop alive, when suddenly his chest explodes in a mass of red, with the sound of gunshots puncturing the soundtrack. The shot then cuts to the source of this gunfire, another, previously unconscious member of the gang, firing at Blonde, until the camera circles slowly around to Blonde as he slowly falls to the floor.

This particular scene contains a number of the features which mark the emergence of a new strand of Hollywood cinema in the 1990s, which I call in this book, the 'new-brutality' film. These films all signified a change in aesthetic - a new aesthetic direction in Hollywood film. *Reservoir Dogs*, *Falling Down* (Schumacher 1992), *Pulp Fiction* (Tarantino 1994), *Strange Days* (Bigelow 1995), *Se7en* (Fincher 1995) are all new-brutality films, and the one feature that they all share in common is their attempt to renegotiate and reanimate the immediacy and affective qualities of the cinematic experience within commercial Hollywood. There are other films we might include in this list but it is through these particular examples that I shall be exploring what we might mean by the notion of cinematic immediacy and affect in the context of the 1990s. All these films attempt to assault the body of the viewer and make the body act involuntarily in the sense that they all, as Linda Williams puts it, attempt to 'make the body do things'.[2] Most importantly, these films all make the viewer's body act in such a way that it imitates and mimics the actions of the cinematic body, or the bodies that the viewer experiences on the screen. They all contain images which cause a reaction based on immediacy and bodily affect which subordinates critical consciousness and awareness of the world or knowledge outside the image to its initial impact. Moreover the use of images of blackness and African American popular culture as a means by which to create a new cinematic affect and immediacy is a common strategy of all the new-brutality films of this book. It is also important to realise that African-American culture has historically been situated as a site of the 'new' in many of the important shifts in the economics and aesthetics of US cinema. Michael Rogin notes that 'each transformative moment in the history of American film has founded itself on the surplus symbolic value of blacks, the power to make African Americans stand for something besides themselves'.[3] This book will argue that the new-brutality film is another of these transformative moments and it is 'new' because of the particular ways in which contemporary black culture is used to produce affect. At the same time, the use of African-American culture to signal a new aesthetic direction in

1990s' Hollywood cinema also links this genre to wider questions of the construction of white American cultural identity.

These are sweeping claims and questions of affect are not readily associated with Hollywood-style cinema, caught up as it was in years of a narrative-centred tradition. They are also statements that depend on the notion of a viewer unsupported by empirical research and a 'balanced' reading. Nevertheless, these assertions are intended to raise some complex issues within the study of film theory and history, particularly concerning the ways in which meaning is made in the consumption of images.

Affect and Cultural Knowledge

One of the most important questions for contemporary film theory is the resonance between the bodily impact of the image and responses elicited by the cultural meaning or signification of images. Gilles Deleuze opens up this question in *Cinema 2* when he argues that 'the most pressing problem' in cinema is 'that of the relations between cinema and language'.[4] Deleuze's 'recapitulation of images and signs' explores the degree to which semiotic or what we might call a linguistic-based film theory has sought to reduce film to a series of signifiers and signifieds without taking into account that film does not fit exclusively into a language system. Steven Shaviro takes a broadly Deleuzian approach in his polemic, *The Cinematic Body*, arguing that the dominant paradigms of semiotic and psychoanalytic film theory is reductive and disavows the power of the connection between the cinematic image and viewer. Shaviro argues that the cinematic experience is primarily tactile and visceral, rendering the conscious and unconscious processes of signification to secondary level:

> In film...perception becomes a kind of physical affliction, an intensification and disarticulation of bodily sensation rather than a process either of naïve (ideological or imaginary) belief or of detached, attentive consideration.[5]

Barbara Kennedy's book *Deleuze and Cinema: The Aesthetics of Sensation* also seeks to explore cinema as a medium which is primarily an experience of non-cognitive senses. Kennedy's work is also part of a growing collection of research in contemporary film and cultural theory that seeks to explore the political and aesthetic qualities of the cinema through its affective powers. *The New-Brutality Film* is conceptually situated within the (false) binary of thinking about cinema as a mass of signs and meanings, and film as a primarily sensory and affective medium that signifies as a secondary process. Ultimately the book explores the resonations between affect and meaning, and argues that the politics and aesthetics of race in contemporary American cinema are too complex to be thought through in terms of either the signifying systems of cultural history or affect. The work of

Gilles Deleuze and later theorists critically engaging with his philosophies provides a useful prism through which to view some of these concerns.

For Brian Massumi 'affect holds the key to rethinking postmodern power', and his preliminary analysis of affect provides a means by which we can begin to think about the validity of reading *Reservoir Dogs* as distinct from what has been characterised as postmodern cinema.[6] Massumi argues for the primacy and autonomy of affect in the reception of images, but he also notes the importance of affect's relationship with other responses. He equates affect with intensity, suggesting that 'intensity is embodied in purely automatic reactions most directly manifested in the skin - at the surface of the body, at its interface with things', with vision being one of the most tactile of these surfaces.[7] Intensity or affect is disconnected from the signifying order or meaning, in the sense that it is a moment which is outside of the spatial coordinates of a linear narrative line:

> It is a state of suspense, potentially of disruption. It is like a temporal sink, a hole in time as we conceive of it and narrativize it. It is not exactly passivity, because it is filled with motion, vibratory motion, resonation. And yet it is not exactly activity, because the motion is not of a kind that can be directed (if only symbolically) towards practical ends in a world of constituted objects and aims (if only on screen).[8]

In other words at the affective moment when the image first assaults us, we are temporarily outside meaning. At the same time this moment of disruption also has an impact on the way in which we make meaning. Massumi is describing a body-first way of knowing in the sense that in the reception of images, we are subject to an affect in the first instance and this material bodily response subsequently becomes meaning. But according to Massumi the loop does not end there because meaning can also magnify affect. This is most clear in the distinction which he makes between *emotion* and *intensity* (affect) in image consumption:

> Emotion is qualified intensity, the conventional, consensual point of insertion of intensity into semantically and semiotically formed progressions, into narrativizable action-reaction, into function and meaning.[9]

Emotion is what we get from the content of an image, whether it be an emotion of joy, sadness, terror or ambivalence. At the same time emotion also feeds back into the intensity the image produces by enhancing its effect as if it 'resonates with the level of intensity rather than interfering with it'. There is a gap between an image's meaningful content and its immediacy, and the latter, argues Massumi, is connected to how affective or intense an image is. But this gap is not total in that the relationship between the meaning or content of an image and its affect is one of 'resonation or interference, amplification or dampening'.[10]

The torture scene in *Reservoir Dogs* is a particularly pertinent example of the ways cinema is both a mass of signs and a source of autonomous affect. An 'affective' reading might stress the strong mimetic connection between the body of the viewer and the actions and images of the torture scene. Like the cop tied to a chair, the viewer is subject to a torturous assault. Elaine Scarry argues that the objective of any given torturer is to create pain in the captive's body in order to rub out her or his conscious sense of place in the world. She asserts that 'brutal, savage and barbaric torture...self consciously and explicitly...acts out the uncreating of the created contents of consciousness'.[11] The torturer attempts to rub out the victim's conscious thoughts, and there is an analogy here in the cinematic experience of the assaulted viewer watching the torture scene. Like the cop, transfixed by the manoeuvres and incisions of the gangster, the viewer is also at the mercy of a scene which utilizes a number of cinematic styles and techniques to tie the viewer to her or his seat while being subjected to sudden changes in pace and action. The chief source of affect in the scene is apparent in the way it is played out in 'real time' with extended uses of the long take. There is a mimetic connection between the scene and the viewer in the sense that the 'time' of this episode is the same as that which the viewer experiences as the images unfold. This 'correspondence of time' between the viewer and the screen action bears a resemblance to the affect that Scarry discerns as the result of torture - the 'uncreating of the created consciousness' of the cinema viewer.

Yet, at the same time as being forced into this kind of relation with the situation and experience of the unfortunate cop, the film wants to force another reaction out of the viewer's body. At several points the viewer is invited to laugh. I would argue that this laughter is borne out of an initiated response to popular culture and cinema rather than a 'body-first' reaction to the images on screen.[12] Many critics have noted that the snappy allusions to Elvis, 'pop bubble gum tunes' of the seventies and various gangster films all demonstrate a highly developed ironic and playful sensibility, with Tarantino as the director who takes postmodernism to its ultimate conclusion.[13] As Umberto Eco says of George Lucas and Steven Spielberg, Tarantino is a 'semiotically nourished author working for a culture of instinctive semioticians', and the film uses well-chronicled postmodern techniques such as intertextuality and pastiche, which work on the viewer's ability to 'spot the reference' from her or his knowledge of popular culture[14]. One of the tasks of this book is to examine the difficult relations between reactions caused by an immediate assault on the body and those responses which depend on systems of meaning. The torture scene in *Reservoir Dogs* is a good place to start an analysis of such ambiguities.

Postmodern 'play' with the knowledge and memories of past popular culture is also evident in the formal devices that the scene uses to produce the mimetic connection of torture between the viewer and the cop. One of the problems with arguing that the immediacy of the torture scene in *Reservoir Dogs* is caused primarily by its use of techniques associated with cinematic realism (such as the long take and the tracking shot) is that these are methods which are familiar to contemporary audiences. The cinematography of the torture scene has been utilized throughout the course of Western cinematic history from Welles and Resnais, to Italian neo-realism, to the films of John Cassavetes, through to Martin Scorsese and Sam Peckinpah, and it belongs to what Andre Bazin calls 'the language of cinema'.[15] An important point to note here is that it is not easy to discern clear-cut divisions between images that have a bodily affect and those that operate through referencing structures of cinematic knowledge. *Reservoir Dogs'* appropriation of the techniques of realism is part of a much wider reference to the fundamental dynamic of aggression and masochism between cinema and the viewer. To fully understand what the affect of the torture scene might be, we first of all need to explore what it is *not*. Positioning the 'shock' of *Reservoir Dogs* within a history of the body relations between screen and viewer is vital to this understanding, particularly if we are to discern what, if anything, is *new* about the new-brutality film.

One of the major features of the torture scene is that it self-reflexively alludes to the viewer's vulnerability to an assault by the cinematic image, alluding to *Psycho* (Hitchcock 1960) and *Blue Velvet* (Lynch 1986) which, amongst other films, have also played around with the cinema's relationship to sadism and masochism. As Amy Taubin argues that:

> *What's transgressive about Reservoir Dogs is...the way Tarantino lays bare the sado-masochistic dynamic between the film and the spectator...the torture scene, far from being gratuitous, as many critics have asserted, is a distillation of the slap/kiss manip-ulation of the film as a whole. Mr Blonde, dancing around the frozen, fascinated cop (who is literally tied to his seat), changing rhythm mid-step, cracking a joke here, slicing off a bit of flesh there, is a stand-in for the director.[16]*

It is the way that this dynamic is so open in the film which makes it hard to analyze using established theories of cinema. An approach which uses ideology-critique might complicate what we mean by 'the director' and psychoanalysis would certainly be interested in what Taubin calls the sado-masochistic dynamic. But the fact that this power relationship is so open in the scene makes an investigation into it redundant. If repressive power is laid bare, what is the point of uncovering it? The film already assumes that this dynamic is part of the viewer's knowledge. If this is the case, and the film is self-reflexively displaying this knowledge and playing on the viewer's knowledge, can we label the viewer's response to the scene as affective? What this question, and this introduction has assumed so far, is that cinematic affect is something distinct and separate from (if related to) cultural and cinematic knowledge. In other words, cinematic affect has been situated as a site of the 'new', in terms of both sensation and of meaning.

This introduction will explore the tensions between affect and cultural knowledge in an attempt to make sense of a new-brutality film like *Reservoir Dogs*. The consideration of an affective contemporary action-cinema will aid an understanding of the aesthetic differences between the new-brutality film and other contemporary action films, most notably the postmodern blockbuster. This book will argue further that the tensions between affect and cultural knowledge are the most pronounced and defining features of the new-brutality film. These tensions distinguish the new-brutality film from other action film and are due to its mimetic engagement with 1990s' African-American culture and film. This is a an assertion which, of course, needs unpacking further and I will go on to argue that *Reservoir Dogs* and the other new-brutality films attempt to produce an affective shock by imitating the immediate and bodily response provoked in white viewers by images of black bodies. This response is experienced as immediate and bodily, but actually caused by racially organized systems of visual perception. The relationship between affect which produces meaning, and meaning which amplifies and resonates with affect can help illuminate the reasons why the torture scene both makes the skin crawl and tremble with laughter. We need to understand why (or if) affect is still possible, given that *Reservoir Dogs* makes cinematic and cultural knowledge and meaning an openly displayed component of the *content* of its images.

The inclusion of meaning and cultural knowledge as vital elements of the cinematic image is something which all the new-brutality films I discuss depend on, but it is not what makes them distinct from other Hollywood film in the 1990s. After all, virtually all Hollywood film since its beginning has depended on pleasure through knowledge as well as immediacy or affect. Much post-Screen film and cultural theory has concentrated on the audience pleasure gained through the knowledge of narrative, stars and the star system in the so-called Classical Hollywood era.[17] More recently postmodern film has, as Fredric Jameson notes, made our awareness of other versions of images 'a constitutive and essential part of the film's structure; we are now, in other words, in 'intertextuality' as a deliberate, built-in feature of the aesthetic effect'.[18] What is different about the torture scene in *Reservoir Dogs* and the images of other new-brutality films is the way in which they attempt to reanimate cinematic affect and the particular disturbances this affect causes in cultural signification - or the way meaning is made of these films. We need to ask what kind of affect was produced in Hollywood cinema of the 1990s? This is a question best explored in the context of a (selective) history of affect in film theory and history.

Shock, Thought and the Cinematic Body

The idea of the 'tortured viewer' is not a new phenomenon in film and film theory. For instance, Noel Burch argues that in certain films there are 'structures of aggression' between the film, filmmaker and the viewer, and it is worth quoting him in full:

> Every one of these forms of aggression...has its source in that very special, almost hypnotic, relationship that is established between screen and viewer as soon as the lights go down in a theatre...Whatever his level of critical awareness, a viewer, face to face with the screen is completely at the mercy of the filmmaker, who may do violence to him at any moment and through any means. Should the viewer be forced beyond the pain threshold, his defence mechanism may well be called forth and he may remind himself that 'it's only a movie'...but it will always be too late...the harm will already be done; intense discomfort, and perhaps terror will already have crossed the threshold.[19]

Burch suggests that film has the power to violently affect the cinema-goer, both physically and mentally. In the rest of the essay, he argues that both the form and content of certain films may cause discomfort or pain, either through the subject matter portrayed or through editing devices such as jump cuts or 'bad' eyeline matches.[20] The division that Burch makes between form and content enables him to argue that the films which have this violent impact on the viewer do not necessarily have to contain representations of violent actions.[21] The significant point is that the relationship of power between the screen, filmmaker and the viewer, has the potential to cause pain and discomfort to the viewer. These relations of power have had a huge influence in both the theory and practice of narrative film.

Alfred Hitchcock's films exerted a temporal bodily control over the viewer through suspense and this is elaborated on at length in a discussion Hitchcock had with the screenwriter of *North by Northwest* (1959), Ernest Lehman:

> Ernie, do you realize what we are doing in this picture? The audience is like a giant organ that you and I are playing. At one moment we play this note on them and get this reaction, and then we play that chord on them and they react that way. And someday we won't even have to make a movie - there'll be electrodes implanted in their brains, and we'll just press different buttons and they'll go 'ooh' and 'aaah' and we'll frighten them, and make them laugh. Won't that be wonderful?[22]

The Hitchcockian fantasy of unmediated directorial power over the body and thought of the spectator is not just about inflicting the affect of pain on the viewer. Rather, Hitchcock and Burch are (in different contexts) expressing the belief that film can have the power to completely absorb the film viewer and make her forget the world outside of the film - a similar effect to that which Scarry describes in relation to torture. Both express the belief/fantasy that film is capable of acting directly on the senses, body and thought of the viewer, in such a way that a conscious and critical awareness is forgotten or temporarily erased.

The idea of a moving-image which can alter conscious thought through a bodily shock was an immanent factor at the birth of cinema. Gilles Deleuze argues that the physical impact of cinema was the aesthetic impetus behind the work of the early makers of film, and that the immanent, automatic movement of the image in early cinema produced what he calls 'the nooshock' in the audience. The automatic movement of the cinematic image physically shocked in a way that changed the relations of thought between image and viewer. Deleuze defines the nooshock as a 'circuit' between the moving-image and the viewer which was initiated by 'the shared power of what forces thinking and what thinks under the shock'.[23] In early cinema the nooshock was achieved through the way these directors composed the relations of the newly acquired movement of the image:

> *Those who first made and thought about cinema began from a simple idea: cinema as industrial art achieves self-movement, automatic movement, it makes movement the immediate given of the image...It is only when movement becomes automatic that the artistic essence of the image is realised:* producing a shock to thought, touching the nervous and cerebral system directly.[24]

Deleuze points out that this kind of unmediated cinema of immediacy was dead almost as soon as it came into being, and that the early pioneers 'foresaw that cinema would encounter all the ambiguities of the other arts' with the pure power and immediacy of the nooshock being only, 'a pure and simple logical possibility'.[25] The shock of moving images wore off as audiences very quickly became accustomed to them. To produce an approximation of the early shock, development of formal considerations of cinema's potential to shock and affect thought would have to take place. To back up Deleuze's argument, and gesture towards one of the earliest and most simplistic examples of the nooshock initially affecting the thought of its audience, and subsequently dissipating, one only has to think of the early train movies which caused audiences to duck at shots of trains coming towards them, and which were almost immediately parodied in subsequent films (such as *The Countryman and the Cinematograph*) about audiences (or a particularly stupid individual) ducking before images of trains.[26] After noting the impossibility of the nooshock surviving in its pure form, Deleuze maintains that it is the drive towards the logical possibility of the immediacy or directness of the moving image which constituted the 'artistic essence' or aesthetic drive of classical cinema and its producers (which in his unorthodoxly viewed, but traditional canon, includes Gance, Vertov, Eisenstein, Murnau, Lang and Hitchcock).[27] We can see these shifts in the development of the practice and theory of cinematic aesthetics in Eisenstein's theories around shock and thought, and particularly the 'montage of attractions'.[28]

Deleuze's ideas are indebted to Walter Benjamin, and it could be argued that the latter is the one of the first theorists of cinematic affect. Benjamin's primary project is to explain the cinema as art form specific to the age of modernity. Within this historical framework, he is concerned about the ways in which cinema might potentially create a shock to the thought of the viewer. His work attempts to understand the contradictory situation where viewers are in an essentially passive and distracted state, but where she or he can also produce conscious and critical reaction. He notes that 'the spectator's process of association in view of these images is...interrupted by their constant sudden change', a direct response to the reactionary attitude of George Duhamel towards the early cinematic image. Duhamel argued that instead of changing the way the world is thought, the cinematic image prevented the individual's agency to think at all: 'I can no longer think what I want to think. My thoughts have been replaced by moving-images'.[29]

The key to Benjamin's notion of cinematic shock lies in the way he compares film to other art forms such as painting or sculpture. Perhaps the most influential aspect of his work is his conceptualisation of the cinema producing a 'withering away' of the aura of traditional arts such as painting and sculpture. Traditional art, according to Benjamin, acts like the commodity fetish in that it rubs out the concrete and sensual contact between the producer, object and consumer. The initial erasure of this material connection is caused by the cultural construction of 'the original' in the non-mechanical work of art. According to Benjamin, 'the presence of the original is prerequisite to the concept of authenticity' and signifying that, for a painting or sculpture to be considered as 'real art', it has to have the stamp of originality. The aura of a work of art is equivalent to the commodity fetish in that it grants the *objet d'art* a mysterious quality, or cult value, which has little to do with the processes that went into its creation.

Mechanical reproductions such as film have the ability to make the aura 'wither away' in two major ways. The mechanical reproduction can bring out details of the original which are not possible through manual reproduction and everyday vision. Cinematic manipulation of the duration and spatial properties of the image make the viewer perceive objects and people in different ways. Secondly the film can wither the aura of objects and artifacts because 'technical reproduction can put the copy of the original into situations which would be out of reach of the original itself'. This 'derealising' or 'deauthenticising' of the original is evident in the cinema's power to reproduce objects, such as buildings and paintings, in situations which are different to those habitually perceived.[30] Benjamin maps the effect on thought of the dissolution of the aura through the two polar opposite terms of 'distraction' and 'concentration'. He argues that the consumer who 'concentrates before a work of traditional art is absorbed by it'. In other words, Benjamin is alluding to the intense contemplation of the art gallery viewer, determinedly and consciously thinking of the origins of a piece of art, before getting lost in the unobtainable preciousness of such a concept. By contrast, the film is an art form where reception initially takes place in 'a state of distraction', where the aura or 'cult value' recedes 'into the background'. Film achieves this effect by placing the viewing public into the position of the critic, a position which, at the movies, paradoxically, requires 'no attention'. The fact that, at the time Benjamin was writing, cinema was not commodified as 'high art', and there was no developed conception of the 'original', (as in art criticism) added to the passive state of reception of film. At the same time cinema was also more susceptible to 'everyday' criticism in the sense that there would be no 'informed' reprisals from the custodians of the aura of 'high art'. But for Benjamin, the 'passive state' of the viewer was also undermined by the ability of the cinema to produce immediacy and affect which shocked the viewer into thought.

Benjamin compares the affective qualities of the cinematic image and the distracted experience of the cinema-goer to the habitual, tactile experience of our knowledge of the architecture which surrounds us. Our everyday use and perception of buildings 'cannot be understood in terms of the attentive concentration of a tourist before a famous building'.[31] We know our way around the buildings we frequently walk past or in, through a habitual and incidental touch and sight. As Michael Taussig points out, this habitual perception is 'where unconscious strata of culture are built into social routines as bodily disposition'.[32] Our physical relations to architecture manifest themselves through unconscious distraction. When walking through a familiar city street, on our way to work, we do not have to consciously think 'Which way now?', yet we still reach our destination through unconscious habit. Watching a film unfolding before us in a darkened cinema can initially reproduce this kind of perception. We perceive the objects and people on screen in a state of distraction, like the scenes we see in our everyday life. This conception of the cinematic experience is comparable with the psychoanalytic insight that there is a temporary loss of ego in the act of film watching, where the 'I' of the viewer goes missing.[33] But for Benjamin the revolutionary potential of the cinema lies in the way it shocks the viewer by displacing her or his everyday distraction with the different visualizations of the image. To put it another way, Benjamin is arguing that, even though we are caught up in the succession of images which constitute the film, the medium of cinema as mass art makes 'the critical and receptive attitudes of the public coincide' by provoking thought within the state of distraction audiences were supposed to have experienced.[34] The cinema for Benjamin has the ability to shock thought by shaking everyday perception, while the viewer consumes the images that unfold before her or him.

Benjamin's work retains certain compelling features. Film still consists of the onrush of different images which we are powerless to prevent from assaulting us in the cinema auditorium. But the assumption that Benjamin's analysis makes of cinematic affect is that we have no knowledge of what is coming next. It assumes that the cinema viewer enters the cinema without knowledge of both the particular narrative content of a film, but also the way that cinematic images are formally composed. The cinematic viewer very quickly became adept in positioning changes in the way that images assaulted them, and aware that these assaults came from the realm of culture in terms of the director's manipulation. One of the most striking aspects of the torture scene in *Reservoir Dogs* is that as soon as the gangster jumps down form the crate he is perched on we know exactly what is going to happen next. Benjamin does not answer the question of what role affect plays in cinematic response after the days of early cinema.

Gilles Deleuze offers an account of what happened to Benjamin's notion of cinematic shock once Hollywood narrative film achieved its dominance. He argues that the drive towards an affective cinema was corrupted in what he calls 'bad cinema', and what others have called Classical Hollywood film. Attempts to provide a physical and affective cinema,

> ...*would be confused in bad cinema, with the figurative violence of the represented instead of achieving that other violence of a movement-image developing its vibrations in a moving sequence which embeds itself within us.*[35]

When violence becomes a part of the narrative function in commercial cinema, Deleuze argues that the shock to thought which characterized the nooshock is lost. He goes on to declare that:

> *When the violence is no longer that of the image and its vibrations but that of the represented, we move into a blood-red arbitrariness. When grandeur is no longer that of the composition, but a pure and simple inflation of the represented, there is no cerebral stimulation or birth of thought.*[36]

One could read Deleuze's meditations on cinematic violence as a high cultural or even middle-brow critique of Hollywood's tradition of using representations of violence to attract audiences, taking the moralistic line that real violence is always bad and therefore so are the cinematic representations of it. The temptation to read Deleuze in this light increases when he starts using terms such as, 'bad cinema' and 'disgraceful works'.[37] Certainly there is a significant criticism of commercial cinema in the *Cinema* books. Yet, his argument is more complex than those of middle-brow film critics, in the sense that he is attacking represented violence because it loses the specific qualities of that which makes the violence of cinema, cinematic. The predominance of the representation of violence is 'bad' for Deleuze in the sense that it reduces the physiological shock of the image itself to another kind of shock, which can be defined and categorized in terms that are applicable to any other text or narrative. Deleuze is arguing from the point of view that in 'good cinema', narrative cinema is not an inevitability of the moving-image - 'narration is only a consequence of the visible [apparent] images themselves and their direct combinations - it is never a given'.[38] Cinematic narration only occurs when the images are structured in a certain way through techniques of montage and other processes. According to Deleuze, the image or sound should come first in the process of filmmaking. In this light the problem for Deleuze with representations of violence is that they only provide shock in the way that Hollywood uses them in the service of the narrative or story, and the violence of the images is only produced through the context of the narrative. For instance in a gangster picture, such as *White Heat* (Walsh 1949), the shock of the various images of violence is only produced by the character's narrative, and the narrative portrayal of Cody Jarret as a sociopath, not, according to Deleuzian thought, necessarily through the images themselves. Narrative representations of blood and violence in the cinema are still able to shock, but the shock they cause could just as easily be found in other texts - the descriptions of murder and sexual violence in Brett Easton Ellis' *American Psycho* spring to mind.

Hollywood cinema's attempt to achieve affect through narrative is 'bad cinema' for Deleuze because it depends on a belief in the ability of the actions of an individual to change the milieu in which that individual is situated. In other words the action-image cinema depends on a belief in the narrative structures of harmony, crisis, and closure which psychoanalytic theory describes as the reinscription of the Oedipal crisis. For various reasons, which echo recent theories about the postmodern crisis, Deleuze argues that this belief is no longer sustainable and the structures of Hollywood cinema became more distantiated as familiar cultural knowledge.[39]

The Crisis of the Action-Image

This loss of belief is manifested in what Deleuze calls the cinema of the 'crisis of the action-image', where a breakdown of the concrete relations between individual protagonists and the cinematic milieux they inhabit gets played out on screen. This is the cinema of Scorsese, Penn, and Peckinpah, where the characters become nomads wandering through what he calls the 'any-space-whatever' with no discernible connection to the world around them, or at least not a connection which enables them to act.[40] One can think of Travis Bickle in *Taxi Driver* (Scorsese 1976), or Charlie in *Mean Streets* (Scorsese 1973) as examples of this. But at the same time as these films play out the breakdown of belief in the action-image, they also attempt to produce new kinds of shock and affect. The violence in these films is not just an 'inflation of the represented' in the sense that they attempt to transform the nature of the cinematic image itself.

Sam Peckinpah's films are particularly striking examples of the tensions between a dependence on narrative meaning, and attempts to produce an immediacy through a stylization of the image. These pressures are particularly visible in the image which is violent in content. Peckinpah plays out the loss of belief in the individual to act in any definitive way on the milieu which surrounds him within the context of the narrative of his films. In *The Wild Bunch* (1969), the outlaws are no longer sure to which milieu they belong, an alienation which is encapsulated in the startling appearance of the motor car alongside the traditional iconography of the Western milieu. Consequently they can no longer be sure that the actions they take will have the desired effect on the world in which they exist. As Deleuze notes,

> *...there is no longer any grandiose action at all, even if the hero has retained extraordinary technical qualities. At the limit, he is no longer one of the 'losers', as Peckinpah presents them: they have no façade, they have not a single illusion left: thus they represent disinterested adventure, from which no advantage is to be gained except the pure satisfaction of remaining alive. They have kept nothing of the American dream, they have only kept their lives, but at each critical instant, the situation to which their action gives rise can rebound against them, making them lose the one thing they have left...In Peckinpah, there is no longer a milieu, a West, but Wests: including Wests with camels, Wests with Chinamen.*[41]

At the same time Peckinpah's films also reveal that it was no longer possible for the violence which previously was part of the narrative meaning in the Hollywood film to produce anything approaching affect or immediacy. This exposure of the affective redundancy of Hollywood's narrative violence is most apparent in Peckinpah's own aesthetics of cinematic violence and particularly in the combination of fast-cutting and slow motion to render action and violence which has become his trademark. Although Peckinpah's violent images are ostensibly part of the narrative content, they also go beyond it in the sense that the images themselves remain memorable, at least as much as the story to which they are attached. It is the 'crimson ballet of the slo-mo bullet-fest' which draws attention to the fact that it was no longer possible for violence to be contained within the narrative reality of individuals and still retain a shock value.[42] The actions of heroes within the narrative no longer have immediacy because the contemporary viewer of Peckinpah's films had seen the same narratives time and time again. And what is the aesthetics of Peckinpah's violence if not the mimetic power of the cinematic image, where the look of the viewer's eye is forced to slow down, and details, previously hidden, are revealed? It is not that more of everyday reality is revealed in Peckinpah's violence - it is rather that the slo-mo, fast-cut death has altered our habitual perceptions of what it is to be shot. 'Real people' do not die in slow motion any more than they die cleanly and quickly as part of logical linear narrative but this kind of imagery has created a new habitual perception of death.

The Postmodern Blockbuster

The relationship between meaning, knowledge and the attempt to provide an affective image is differently configured in the postmodern blockbuster film (a cinema which Deleuze does not engage with).[43] One of the important defining qualities of postmodern film is the in-built need for preconceived knowledge of other film. For instance the relationship between the viewer and films such as *Star Wars* (Lucas 1977) or *Raiders of the Lost Ark* (Spielberg 1981) is as equally defined by the knowledge of the western genre or Saturday morning serials, as it is by immersion in the fast-editing of the action sequences and narrative. It could be argued that in terms of the binary logic of distraction versus concentration, the postmodern blockbuster facilitates the kind of consciously focused reception which Benjamin ascribes to traditional art. The concentration required to 'spot the citations' in a postmodern film grants the film or genre, to which the reference is made, the status of 'the original'.

There is a strong strain of nostalgia in the postmodern film which grants the Hollywood productions of the 30s, 40s, and 50s, a quality akin to the Benjaminian aura. And this is partially due to the way that, at the heart of the postmodern film, there is a lack which creates a desire for something past and missing. This lack is the loss of the material, physical connection imagined to exist between the ideal spectator, and the screen, where the viewer would lose herself in the images of the Classical Hollywood film. Steven Shaviro notes this emptiness in *Blade Runner*, and suggests that,

> Blade Runner's *science fiction world is oddly permeated by nostalgia. The film composes its broken-down future, not out of elements of the past, but out of their absence. The desire for outmoded scenes and situations, for the easy legibility of conventions of genre and gender is validated - rather than frustrated - by the irrelevance and unattainability of such scenes and by the ostentatious artificiality of their postmodern reproduction.*[44]

The further irony of *Blade Runner*, and other postmodern films which take *noir* as their major point of reference, is that, even if it were possible to define *noir* as a coherent body of filmmaking, such a definition would stress the stylized nature of the cinematography of films like *The Big Combo* (Lewis 1955) or *The Woman in the Window* (Lang 1944).[45] The postmodern aesthetic of nostalgia is driven by an imagined situation where the contemporary viewer of 1930s and 40s Hollywood cinema was in a state of distraction, and more importantly, believed in the worlds or milieux which were presented in this cinema. For reasons which will be explored throughout this book, the postmodern film, particularly in its blockbuster form, assumes that the audience is no longer capable of taking the aesthetic form of the action-image seriously. Films like *Die Hard* (McTiernan 1988), *Lethal Weapon* (Donner 1987) and *Predator* (McTiernan 1987) base their narratives and action on the premise that there is no longer a relationship of belief between the viewer and the film. The intertexuality and self-reflexivity of these films with the stars almost telling the audience directly that 'it's only a movie', are symptoms of the imagined loss of a concrete, physical bond of belief between the screen and the viewer.

Yet, the postmodern film also employs another tactic to recreate some of the physical potential and pleasure of the cinema. The emphasis on 'the spectacular' in the *mise en scène* and the action of films such as *The Terminator* (Cameron 1984) is the second strategy that postmodern film employs to induce the viewer's distraction. Narratives in the form of character development tend to take second place to the special effect. The visual pleasures of the spectacular take precedence over narrative resolution, and the individual psychology of characters. The publicity slogan for *Terminator II* (Cameron 1991), 'It's Nothing Personal', sums up this decentralization of the narrative as the chief source of affect in the postmodern action film. This stress on the visual often centres on the image which is violent in content. In almost every instance, the spectacular in the postmodern blockbuster involves an attempt to move the content-based and individualized violence of Classical Hollywood film into the realm of the spectacular. The significance of the violent image is displaced from narrative interest in who is being killed and why, to the question of how extravagant the visual effects of such violence are. The viewer is no longer distracted or caught up in the narrative (which she has seen dozens of time before) but in the visual process. This focus on the spectacular is why mainstream critics, who have an interest in maintaining film as an auratic art form, often criticise films like *Twister* (de Bont 1996) for their 'bare plot' with 'little to hang on to' in the way of narrative interest.[46]

The way the postmodern blockbuster uses violence as spectacle, in order to recapture the imagined loss of cinematic immediacy, can be seen in the amount of bodies violently dispatched in the course of a film. The bodycount spectacle is evident in films such as *Rambo* (Cosmatos 1985) and *The Running Man* (Glaser 1987), where the action consists of the violent slaughter of dozens of 'characters'. This is the kind of violence which can be compared to that of a Tom and Jerry cartoon, with its techniques of fast-editing. But it is also the focus on the visceral nature and impact of the violent content of the image that marks the blockbuster's attempt to produce an affective reaction in the viewer. The concentration on the vulnerability of the body - any body - is prevalent in both the blockbuster and lower-budget form of the postmodern film. There are dozens of scenes that one could cite where the camera dwells on or implies excruciating violence. For instance, think of the scene in *Blade Runner* where Roy Batty (Rutger Hauer) breaks Deckard's fingers one by one, through a hole in the wall of the deserted L.A. apartment block, or the extended sado-masochistic scene between Frank (Denis Hopper) and Dorothy (Isabella Rossellini) in *Blue Velvet*, or again the squelch of the dead bodies in *Total Recall* (Verhoeven 1990) as Schwarzenegger is chased up the escalator. There is an attention to the detail of the physicality of the bodies on screen in this violence, which attempts to replace the immediacy lost in the processes of concentration required from the postmodern viewer.

The Deleuzian Time-Image

Deleuze would argue that, despite such demphasising of the narrative in favour of the spectacle, the blockbuster still represents an 'inflation of the represented', because at its heart the protagonist is still able to affect his milieu - even though such films hardly present this as believable. Deleuze argues that contemporary cinema is still capable of creating affect, but that this physiological response must be produced through images in and of themselves, without narrative structure to qualify them. This is the image which:

> ...make us grasp, it is supposed to make us grasp, something intolerable and unbearable. Not a brutality as nervous aggression, an exaggerated violence that can also be extracted from the sensory-motor relations in the action-image. Nor is it a matter of scenes of terror, although there are sometimes corpses and blood. It is a matter of something too powerful, or too unjust, but sometimes also too beautiful, and which henceforth outstrips our sensory-motor capacities.[47]

This kind of affect is evident in what Deleuze calls the 'time-image'. Time not space is the real marker of the specificity of cinema in post-Second World War film. The long-take represents one particular formal way in which the time-image may be created. As Jon Beasley-Murray notes, the specificity of the cinema remains in its unfolding of the image in the real time that becomes the lived time of thought and body. An affective cinema is possible in the way 'that the cinema viewer is maintained as part of an immanent functional and corporeal effect of the film's unfolding through time'.[48] For instance the extended use of the long take is one means of provoking this kind of bodily connection between the film and the viewer in the sense that cinematic time becomes the lived time of the viewer. Familiarity and recognition of the way cinema creates space means that film no longer has the power to affect the viewer in the ways it did in the early cinema. For Deleuze, it is only contemporary cinema's ability to manipulate time which produces affect before meaning. One of the problems for our purposes - the understanding of affect in a particular type of Hollywood film of the 1990s - is that the cinema which provides this affect for Deleuze is a very traditional canon of European Art cinema. The other major problem is that the formal techniques (such as the long take) which form the different 'time-images' defined by Deleuze are as familiar and clichéd as the narratives of Hollywood cinema itself.

Back to the Future

We need to take on board these different narratives of the affect of cinema to return to my original question of where the bodily impact lies in the torture scene in

Reservoir Dogs. This partial history of the affective image in Hollywood cinema offers some important clues in explaining why it is important to read the new-brutality film through an understanding of cinematic affect. We can only make sense of the torture scene by reading it as a particular moment of this history. The scene and the film in general openly displays the attempts that previous cinema has made at producing affect. *Reservoir Dogs*, and the torture scene in particular, contain remnants of the aesthetics of both the cinema of the crisis of the action-image and the postmodern Hollywood cinema. The narrative meaning of the scene is almost non-existent in the sense that there is no real diegetic reason for the gangster Mr. Blonde (Micahel Madsen) to attack the cop in the way he does, beyond the self-confessed and chilling rationale that 'I enjoy torturing cops'. The violent scenes, like those in Peckinpah, cannot be contained within narrative meaning - they are somehow beyond it. Blonde is also reminiscent of the nomads which populate Scorsese's cinema of the seventies. Like the rest of the gangsters, dressed in their strangely anachronistic and yet strangely new black and white suits, Blonde seems out of time within the milieu of 1990's Los Angeles, which surfaces occasionally in the flashbacks. The fact that most of the action takes place in the any-space-whatever of the abandoned warehouse serves to emphasize this lack of any concrete relations between the individuals and any definable milieu. The film almost cuts off any reference to any world outside that of the gangsters, and yet when that world does surface there is a feeling of discord and uncertainty.

The torture scene makes knowledge of the cinema of the crisis of the action-image as vital to the viewer's understanding of it as awareness of the fundamental dynamic of structures of aggression between film and viewer. The elements of the cinema of the crisis of the action-image as well as those of Classical Hollywood and wider popular culture are flaunted in manner which makes cultural knowledge a constitutive part of watching the scene, in a fashion which is superficially similar to the blockbuster. The power of the torture scene does not lie in the way it makes 'us grasp for meaning', or that we do not understand it, *but* that we know exactly what is going to happen when Blonde jumps down from the crates and are still powerless or unwilling to prevent it. This powerlessness in the face of Blonde's meaningless actions reverberates with memories of the cinema of the crisis of the action-image. This is a cinema which is also about knowing the futility of knowledge. In *Pat Garrett and Billy the Kid*, as in *The Wild Bunch*, we know the outlaw is doomed, and can no longer control the milieu around him in spite of the in-depth knowledge he has of that world. Yet, in *Reservoir Dogs* powerlessness in the face of knowledge is not just caused by the memories of the past powers of the individual (which is why Peckinpah's films are often described as elegiac), it also because there is an articulation - or more precisely, half-articulation - of a new site of aesthetic affect for white American film - contemporary African-American culture. The politics of race and the dynamics of mimesis may further an understanding of this.

Rodney King and the Dangerous Black Body

One of the charges often levelled at the films of Quentin Tarantino by film critics is that they represent the final triumph of style over content and that they are devoid of all political or any other meaning. James Wood, for instance, writing in *The Guardian* argues that Tarantino's films,

> ...*represent the final triumph of postmodernism, which is to empty the artwork of all content...only in this age could a writer as talented as Tarantino produce artworks so entirely vacuous, so entirely stripped of any politics, metaphysics or moral interest.*[49]

Derek Malcolm takes a similarly dim view of Tarantino's films calling him, 'a brilliant screenwriter...but with absolutely nothing to say' and describing *Pulp Fiction* as 'both empty and retrograde'.[50] In a sense it is understandable that these journalistic reviews stressed the lack of meaning in Tarantino's films because the critics are judging their cinematic value in terms of direct discursive and narrative content. These films are not 'political' in terms of narrative content in way that films like the recent *Bulworth* (Beatty 1998), *All The President's Men* (Pakula 1976), or any film directed by Oliver Stone are. But I would argue emphatically that Tarantino's films, from *Reservoir Dogs* to *Jackie Brown* (1998) are extraordinarily political in the way that they evoke and crystallize the sensations and affects around questions of 'race' that were embedded in 'the white cultural imagination' in the US of the 1990s.[51] Tarantino's films and their effect on the aesthetic shifts in Hollywood film should not be underestimated in the sense that they do represent a clear shift in Hollywood's cinematic engagement with race - which was (and still is) perhaps the most pressing political site in US culture. The torture scene in *Reservoir Dogs* illustrates the particular way in which the film invokes an affective shock through its engagement with the politics of 'race'. Before going on to explore this claim the new-brutality film must be contextualised within postmodern culture and its relationship to questions of affect.

The question of the affect of the new-brutality film cannot also be answered without reference to the idea that we live in a postmodern age characterized by an excess of images bombarding us everyday - to the point where there is no longer any difference between image and reality - a situation which Baudrillard famously referred to as 'hyperreality'.[52] Fredric Jameson argues that this surfeit of images has led to a 'waning of affect' in Western culture.[53] According to Jameson, the multiplicity of images and postmodern aesthetic techniques such as pastiche and intertextuality mean that we are no longer look for hidden truths or 'depths' in film or art. Images function as a sort of matrix of knowledge through which the postmodern subject makes links to other past and present aesthetic forms. This process of aesthetic consumption takes precedence over the power of the image, or work of art, to 'move' or affect the subject. We have explored this argument to some extent in the brief analysis of the postmodern blockbuster film above. In contrast

Brian Massumi argues that, far from producing a waning of affect, the postmodern condition is 'characterized by a surfeit of it'. He implies that the constant assault of the postmodern subject by many different images and media makes it impossible to assign meaning to them, before they have 'got under' the subject's skin. We cannot 'cognitively map' or assign significance to these images before they have entered our physiological being at some level.

This argument depends on the distinction that Massumi makes between emotion and affect discussed in an earlier passage. For Jameson, affect is synonymous with emotion, whereas for Massumi, 'emotion and affect...follow different logics and pertain to different orders'. This surfeit of affect makes the project of developing a 'cultural-theoretical vocabulary specific to affect' a vital undertaking for Massumi.[54] However for the purposes of this book, we also need to take on board the idea that different aesthetic and cultural institutions will produce different forms of affect. In other words the kind of affect produced by the particular environs and conditions of the cinematic experience will be different from that produced by multiplicity of images produced when flicking through the dozens of different channels available on cable or digital television. The cinema is a particular environment where we are confined to our chairs in darkness, and invited to 'gaze' rather than 'glance'. Within a culture where many images are bombarding us at the same time, the particular physical conditions of the cinema with its singular and large screen, film may be capable of provoking more powerful affective responses than ever.

The reason for dwelling on this particular point is that the torture scene in *Reservoir Dogs* seeks to emphasize the specificity of cinematic affect by evoking anxieties around the violence of black masculinity in the US. The scene produces a racialised affect by reversing the impact of one of the most notorious sequence of images seen in the history of contemporary media, the beating of Rodney King by the L.A.P.D. in 1991. The actual events of the Rodney King beating and trial occurred after the film's production but before its US and UK release, but the fears of black violence towards the forces of law and order were already engrained in the white cultural imagination. The imitation of a certain construction of 'blackness' - encapsulated in the Simi Valley jury's verdict of the L.A.P.D.'s non-guilt - is the defining constituent of *Reservoir Dogs* as a new-brutality film.

The actors playing the white gangsters in *Reservoir Dogs* produce performances which mime the language and gestures of the 1990s African-American figure of the 'gangsta'. Mr Blonde dances around the tied-up cop in a manner that calls to mind the stereotypical racialised discourse that white people have no rhythm, while black people are born with an inherent bodily, primitive grace. The much celebrated Tarantino dialogue also evokes the rhythmic style of rap with its intertextual references and quickfire pace. In other words I would argue that Blonde and the rest of the gangsters are coded as African-American. But this coding is not instantly recognizable and does not occur in the first instance because the viewer is unable to recognize the linguistic and cultural signifiers of African-American culture in the gangster's dialogue. In fact these signifiers are heavily obscured by the fact that most of the content of this dialogue is overtly racist, with constant references to 'niggers', 'coons' and 'jungle bunnies'. The association of the gangsters with the figure of the gangsta is rather produced through the cinema's power to force instances of, what Lesley Stern (after Proust) calls 'involuntary memory' in the viewer.

In a manner that echoes the earlier discussion of affect, Stern argues that 'involuntary memory pertains to sensation - the senses of touch, sight, smell, and hearing - rather than intellectual recognition'. She describes it as a process where 'some sensation in the present, summons an experience of the past'. Stern goes on to state that 'in the cinema it is not uncommon to experience involuntary memory,' and that 'it can happen that we are suddenly and unexpectedly seized, in the midst of the most seemingly mundane, by an overwhelming sensation of sensuous reminiscence'. Stern admits that many of these instances of involuntary memory occur 'within and across a constellation of largely personal and idiosyncratic associations'. But she also contests that the affective and sensual experience of involuntary memory is 'one of the reasons that people...continue to 'go to the movies' instead of just watching videos, for the physical conditions are well disposed to the activation of involuntary memory and receptivity to sensuous images'. She also suggests that films 'play in a quasi-structured way upon the memory of the viewer' in terms of memories of previous images in individual films, 'but also of film as a history of cinematic images'.[55] The association of gangsters with African-American - and particularly hip-hop - culture in *Reservoir Dogs* is a kind of quasi-structured activation of involuntary memory rather than an intellectual recognition.

The torture scene works as a particularly vivid example of involuntary memory because of the way it acts as a cinematic reanimation of the anxieties of the white cultural imagination around black masculinity. As I suggested above these fears were highlighted in the Simi Valley jury's reading of the Rodney King videotape. Judith Butler argues that the Rodney King episode is symptomatic of the 'racist organisation and disposition' of the visible around images of African-American masculinity.[56] Much of her argument is concerned with the way that the Rodney King video was read so differently by firstly, the people who interpreted it as the police assaulting Rodney King, and second, the white jurors of Simi Valley who saw the video as evidence of the threat of Rodney King to the thin blue (white) line of the L.A.P.D. What strikes Butler as particularly significant about the second reading is that the interpretation of the threat of Rodney King to 'law and order' was not framed as an interpretation or reading at all. The video was read by the jury as acquitting the officers involved but was still conceived as 'seen' rather than interpreted - as evident or evidence of the innate threat of African-American rather than a culturally constructed racialised assignment of meaning. For Butler, 'This is a seeing which is a reading, that is a contestable construal, but one which nevertheless passes itself off as a 'seeing', a reading which became for that white community and countless others, the same as seeing.'[57] Butler suggests - through the work of Franz Fanon - that images of the masculine black body in contemporary America activate a kind of immediate and affective response from audiences - and particularly white audiences. The Rodney King episode is symptomatic of the way that images of black male bodies tend to provoke a response which is couched in an immediate fear, anxiety and paranoia around the imagined primitivism, violence and authenticity of the masculine black body. Images of black male bodies provoked a body-first reaction in white audiences of the 1990s.

The torture scene in *Reservoir Dogs* plays with the involuntary affective responses, white audiences had when confronted with images of violent black masculinity. Blonde's mimesis of 1990s' images of black masculinity, coupled with the images of a cop who really is completely at the mercy of a random, meaningless violence evokes an involuntary recall of white fears around black violence. The scene also produces an extra dimension to media images of black violence. In his interpretation of Walter Benjamin's work, Michael Taussig argues that mimesis in the cinema is a 'two-layered process' where what takes place is both 'a copying or imitation, and a palpable, sensuous, connection between the body of the perceiver and the perceived'.[58] This sensuous, body-first connection between the bodies of the image and the bodies of those watching is caused by the fact that the copy attains an extra dimension lacking in the original. As Jane Gaines notes, 'the copy may, in fact, be seen as more powerful than what it represents because it derives its power from it without exactly being it'.[59]

In the torture scene's mimesis of fears around violence and black masculinity, the notion of the copy having an extra dimension and power is produced through the way the film plays with the resonance between immediate affect and cultural knowledge in the question of race. Even though Blonde is heavily associated with African-American masculinity, he is obviously played by a white actor - and just as obviously, he is also associated with the history of the white and classical gangster genre. In short there is a kind of racial confusion apparent in the scene which places the audience in the position where they have to think *differently* about the affective responses provoked by images of blackness in white culture. The seemingly immediate threat of the masculine black body is displaced by the involuntary memories of other images of white violence and power. The irony and paradox is that the immediate fear and paranoia that are provoked in white US culture by images of black male bodies are replaced by the affective immediacy of the cinematic copy. The disruption to thought and time (which Massumi characterizes as distinctive to an affective response) is caused in this scene by the resonance between the racist ideology that black masculinity is naturally prone to meaningless, criminal violence and the immediate response to images of the black body provoked by differences in physicality (skin colour etc.). The scene both plays on and disrupts the construction of blackness as the source of an affective violence by placing a white body and white genre as the centre and cause of violence.

American Africanism and the White Cultural Imagination

Toni Morrison argues that the situation and construction of African-American bodies and cultures within white American culture has been fundamental to the development of white American cultural identity. Using the American canon of literature as one of the most fundamental expressions of this cultural identity, Morrison notes that:

> *Through significant and underscored omissions, startling contradictions, heavily nuanced conflicts, through the way writers peopled their work with the signs and bodies of this presence - one can see that a real or fabricated presence was crucial to their sense of Americanness.*[60]

Morrison goes on to argue that every factor which constituted white American cultural identity within early American literature depended on, and was shaped by, the cultural construction of African-American slave population. The identity of the early white American settlers was formulated as one of 'autonomy, authority, newness and difference, absolute power' and could only be 'made possible by, shaped by, activated by a complex awareness and employment of a constituted Africanism'. Morrison goes on to note that, 'it was this Africanism, deployed as a rawness and savagery that provided the staging ground and arena for the elaboration of a quintessential American identity'. For Morrison, 'blackness has stimulated...notions of excessive unlimited love, anarchy and routine dread'.[61]

Affect plays a big part in Morrison's description of American Africanism. In the various examples of what she calls the 'white American literary imagination', blackness operates as a kind of symbol for what is beyond cultural knowledge, as a kind of sublime, or what Lacanians might call 'the Real'. Like the Real, blackness in the white literary imagination operates as 'the starting point, the foundation of the process of symbolisation' and at the same time blackness itself gets structured by the symbolic order itself 'when it gets caught in its network'. And like the Real, blackness in the white literary imagination is 'the product, remainder, leftover, scraps of this process of symbolisation, the remnants, the excess which escapes symbolisation'.[62] To put this in terms of the construction of identity in literature, Morrison argues that whiteness is constructed as the binary opposite of what it is imagined to not be. She argues that the great themes of American canonical literature - the creation of civilisation out of anarchic wilderness, 'individualism, masculinity, social engagement versus historical isolation; acute and ambiguous moral problematics; the thematics of innocence coupled with an obsession with figurations of death and hell' - exist because the white literary imagination has positioned African-Americans and African-American culture as an oppositional presence.[63] Consequently African-American culture becomes symbolised as the 'other' of the themes of American literature - as a site of savagery and primitive anarchism, which needs to be overcome. Yet, for Morrison this fabrication of African-American culture operates as more than just an othering of African-American culture. She suggests that American Africanism is 'reflexive' and:

> ...an extraordinary meditation on the self: a powerful exploration of the fears and desires that operate in the writerly conscious. It is an astonishing revelation of longing, of terror, of perplexity of shame, of magnanimity.[64]

The construction of African Americans as immanently violent, sexually licentious and primitive enabled the white literary imagination to 'articulate and imaginatively act out the forbidden in American culture'.[65] In other words, Morrison suggests that the very characteristics used to construct African-Americans, were key aspects of the formation of the 'self' of American white cultural identity. But they were elements of the self which could not be spoken - except in terms of projecting them onto African-Americans.

One of the key phrases Morrison uses throughout her argument is 'the white literary imagination'. Although she gives no absolute definition of what she means by this term, it represents a space where ideology, creative writing and affectivity combine and interact to enunciate and reveal a historically and socially located white American cultural identity. This identity is not fixed in any totalising or monolithic sense, but signifies a way of thinking and feeling which cuts across the essentialist conceptions of ethnic and national identity. The implicit drive behind Morrison's project is the reversal of the 'the invisibility of whiteness as a racial position in white discourse'.[66] This book will use the concept of a 'white cultural imagination' to describe a state where images of blackness are experienced in terms of affective shocks. The affectivity of African American culture manifests itself in the way the white cultural imagination both consumes images of black culture and in the processes which result in the mimesis of blackness in white cinema and other popular culture. The term signifies the historical, affective and creative processes which form white cultural identity, in the sense that the white cultural imagination suggests a 'white' way of thinking and feeling which is evident in every aspect of creativity and articulation in the production and the reception of culture. The white cultural imagination is often a state of paranoia, anxiety and desire generated by the threat of black violence when confronted with images of blackness. It is also the condition where those fears of black violence are experienced as immediate and affective even though they are produced and organised by what Judith Butler calls 'a racial disposition of the visible'.

The white cultural imagination is used in this book to signal a move away from psychoanalytic discourses which tend to construct the relationship between white viewers and images of blackness in terms of fetishism and disavowal.[67] The white films in this book are at times guilty of these practices. But the mimesis of black culture in the new-brutality film is less a matter of repressing the anxieties aroused by the 'other', than part of what Michael Taussig identifies as the mimetic processes of contagion and tactility where the differences between the white cultural self and the 'other' are always 'polluted' by that 'other'.[68] The book will argue that whiteness in the US is always affected and altered by the agency of black culture to the point where the racial boundaries between white and black have become blurred and difficult to determine. In discussing the torture scene of *Reservoir Dogs* I have already noted the way that Symbolic borders of race are being traversed in the film's mimesis of black imagery. The white cultural imagination can never be a fixed, essentialist state because it is always a result of a reaction to the agency of black popular culture, images of blackness, what black (masculine) culture signifies, and the way that black culture is mimed.[69] Using the term 'white' cultural imagination is to necessarily posit a difference between white and non-white ways perceiving the world and its images. As Richard Dyer notes there are many dangers in talking about whiteness as an identifiable cultural category, not least that such moves end up by reaffirming the 'centrality and authority' of white culture.[70] This is certainly not the intention of this book, nor is it going to be primarily concerned with the cultural studies project of analysing the new-brutality film's representations of different ethnicities and their politics. Yet, the white cultural imagination is a necessary term because both the African-American and white films of this book use constructions of race to produce a particular kind of contemporary affect which forces white culture to think through its dependency on African American culture. Chapters two and three of the book explore the genre of the 'hood film, and in particular, I will be arguing that films like *Boyz N the 'Hood* and *Menace II Society* are structured in such a way that they affect and produce meaning in different ways according to the Symbolic structures of different races. In the case of these films the white cultural imagination is an effect of the films.

The white cultural imagination is a shifting state where the cinema, other cultural artefacts it produces, and the fears and anxieties around blackness, change in relation to the fluid mimetic relations between white American and African-American culture. Morrison's work reveals that the white literary imagination of the eighteenth and nineteenth centuries tended to submerge, hide and disavow the way that blackness signified crucial constituents of white American identity. This book will argue that the so-called Classical Hollywood cinema used similar techniques of repression and marginalisation in its representations of blackness.

But the greater visibility and impact of contemporary black culture after the Second World War meant that the white cultural and cinematic imagination which came after could no longer disavow its dependency on images of blackness, and the book will explore how this initially manifests itself in the cinema of the crisis of the action-image, gets repressed within the nostalgia of the postmodern blockbuster, and re-emerges in the affective images of the new-brutality film.

This history is a necessary step to arrive at an understanding of the 1990s' white US cultural imagination and this book will argue that it was caught up within the chaos, simulation and emptiness which characterises 'the postmodern condition'. More specifically the predominance of intertextual nostalgia in postmodern film and culture highlighted white American cultural identity's reliance on constructions of the 'other' and its overriding tendency to mime other cultures. The realisation that popular white American culture and cultural identity is dependent upon mimesis and citation meant an aesthetic crisis in the white cultural imagination. This crisis manifested itself in the cinema through a desire to produce a new authenticity and substance missing from the nostalgia of postmodernism, and the new-brutality film is one of the symptoms of this process. One of the results of this crisis is that black culture has been, and still is, constructed as a site of desirable 'cool', and new and knowing authenticity. The new-brutality film paradoxically mimed these aspects of black culture in an attempt to overcome the emptiness and simulation of postmodern popular culture.

The Politics of Mimesis, Knowledge and Affect

Toni Morrison argues that one of the major features of American Africanism is the way an Africanist idiom is used to:

> *signal modernity...We should look at how a black idiom and the sensibilities it has come to imply are appropriated for the associative value they lend to modernism - to being hip, sophisticated, ultra urbane.*[71]

There is no doubting that Tarantino's films also use black culture as a means by which to authenticate and self-reflexively produce a certain 'hipness' and cultural cool around their consumption and reception.[72] This construction of blackness as cool (and Tarantino as a cool director) also exposes the tensions between affect and meaning in the contemporary cinematic experience.[73] People go to watch Tarantino films in order to become part of an initiated crowd for whom a knowledge of *Reservoir Dogs*, *Pulp Fiction* or *Kill Bill Vol1* (2003) is synonymous with a knowledge of 'what is going on' in contemporary popular culture. It is this aspect of the reception of Tarantino's films which also partially explains why the torture scene makes audiences laugh as well as providing a kind of affective shock. *Not* to laugh at the intertextual references to past 'cheesy' popular culture of the torture scene is to admit to not being versed and initiated within the smart self-reflexivity of postmodern culture and knowledge. A large element of the contemporaneity and hipness of Tarantino's films is the references they make to the aesthetic styles, politicised shock, cultural authenticity and 'coolness' of contemporary African-American popular culture. But at the same time the feelings of coolness evoked by the Tarantino phenomena are experienced as immediate - in the way they can make the skin tingle. Thinking about the differences between affect and knowledge/meaning in purely binaristic and totalising terms is impossible, and this is apparent in the different responses evoked in both the immediate bodily impact of Tarantino's films and the pleasures provided by hipness and knowledge-based pleasures of their intertextuality and self-reflexivity. But if it is difficult to distinguish between these two aesthetic elements, it is necessary to explore the way they interact in provoking viewer's responses because of the political questions around 'race' and cultural and cinematic identity that Tarantino's films raise.

Spike Lee's criticisms of Tarantino, and *Jackie Brown* in particular, point towards a need to engage with both affect and meaning/knowledge when thinking about the political significance of the new-brutality film's mimesis of African-American culture and its constituent American-Africanism. Lee has labelled Tarantino a 'wannabe' black filmmaker, who has appropriated the language and aesthetics of contemporary African-American culture to produce a kind of exploitative shock in the audience.[74] His major criticism centres around the liberal use of the word 'nigger' in all of Tarantino's screenplays and that it is impossible for a white writer and filmmaker to use it without evoking the history of white oppression and abuse that it carries with it. The word has been used widely by black artists such as Richard Pryor and by hip-hop culture in general as a 'signifyin'' strategy against white racist uses, but this, according to Lee is not possible from a writer who is white. The underlying critique of his comments is that Tarantino's dialogue is a kind of 'blackvoice' which like blackface, is a white symbolic construction based on 'the power to make African-Americans stand for something besides themselves'.[75] Without the empirical experience of being black, Tarantino's use of this term and his appropriative references to African-American culture as a whole are a cynical and exploitative attempt to cash in on the immediacy, cultural authenticity and 'coolness' which contemporary African-American culture signifies in the white cultural imagination. Tarantino's responses to these criticisms were firmly embedded within liberal ideology, and he argued that 'no one word should stay in prison'. He defended the various ways in which he used the word by claiming a kind of novelistic verisimilitude, expressing the belief that 'nigger' only appears in his dialogue, 'because it is a word that the characters would use' and that it is used to mean different things depending on the character using it.[76]

Lee's comments point towards questions of cultural property, where certain discourses and aesthetic strategies may only be employed by particular social groups. More importantly his criticisms also rest on the notion of the fetish, where black culture becomes a desirable 'other' which ultimately reaffirms white racist power relations. Tarantino's references to African-American culture are an appropriation from a position of imagined (white) knowledge which claims to be able to make black and white culture distinct and bordered entities. The fact that black culture is exalted as hip and as site of affect is illusory and does nothing to address the 'real' social and cultural relations between white and African-American culture which are those of exploitation and oppression. The problem with this position is that the authority to both knowingly appropriate black culture and maintain a clear distinction or border between white and black culture is missing (in different ways) from both *Reservoir Dogs* and *Pulp Fiction*. This book will argue that the authority and stability of white cultural and cinematic identity is precisely what is under the spotlight in these two films.

The gap in Lee's arguments is that Tarantino's films (and the new-brutality cinema's) mimesis of blackness is also wrapped up in a desire for an affective cinema in particular. This introduction has attempted to partially outline a history where a drive towards affect has been a constituent part of the different kinds of cinema which have emerged at different points in history. The affective qualities of the early classical cinema are different to those of the action-image and the crisis of the action-image and Deleuze offers a partial account of this history of cinematic affect. But the postmodern blockbuster and the new-brutality film need to be thought through in this context - as well as in terms of the politics of their representations. Affect is not outside of history, and the way that different affective properties of different cinemas have worked needs to place within this context. This book argues that the particular ways in which race and blackness is used as a source of a body-first reaction in the new-brutality films is specific to the time when they emerged in early 1990s. Indeed these films are themselves self-reflexively aware of their position in the history of cinema, and they are all 'films about film'.

Reservoir Dogs and *Pulp Fiction* show awareness of the crisis of the cinema of the action-image in their rootless protagonists, and the almost scatter-gun effect of their intertextuality is, on the surface, postmodern. At the same time both films position African-American culture as both the site of affect and as a site of 'hipness'. This dualistic American-Africanism is utilised as an alternative aesthetic to the knowing cinema of postmodernity because of the affective power of images of blackness on the white cultural imagination. But again both films also seem to demonstrate a self-reflexive awareness that their own impact and American white identity (and more specifically white American popular culture and cinema) has always depended on a mimetic relationship with African-American culture. In spite of this apparent awareness, both *Reservoir Dogs* and *Pulp Fiction* are unable to express their dependency on black culture through discourse or cultural knowledge. The relationship with American Africanism and African-American culture is only half-articulated by miming images which produce shocks in the white cultural imagination.

Reservoir Dogs and *Pulp Fiction* are different from *Jackie Brown* in this sense. The latter is quite open in its appropriation of the icons of the blaxploitation in the casting of Pam Grier and the way that the camera fetishises this black popular cultural icon. The impact of *Jackie Brown* depends on the open appropriation of iconic moments in black popular culture and the viewer's awareness of the 'hipness' of blaxploitation, and the association of blackness with 'cool'. *Reservoir Dogs* and *Pulp Fiction* depend on the affective shock of images which do not openly address or narrativize the importance of black culture in the white cultural identity, but nevertheless mime the immediacy provoked in the white cultural imagination by images of blackness. The torture scene emphasises the cinema's mimetic capability to produce affect, and activate involuntary memories, provoking an involuntary awareness in white viewers of the American Africanism endemic in white American culture *and* that the authority and meaning of white cultural identity is open to question. *Reservoir Dogs* tends to blur the distinctions between black and white identities and temporarily position them beyond ideological knowledge and recognition. This engagement with the mimetic relations between 1990s' white and African-American culture, through a reanimation of the affective power of the cinema is the way that shock is produced in the majority of the new-brutality films in this book. All of them suggest a desire to reanimate the affective potential of the cinematic experience which is at the same time dependent on using blackness as a potentially affective disruption to the certainties of white cultural identity.

Chapter 1 explores a film which attempts to address the impact that contemporary black culture has on the white cultural imagination by emphasising, a contingent, but ultimately more powerful, degree of authority in white culture. *Falling Down* (Schumacher 1992) is a film which, like *Reservoir Dogs,* is aware of the crisis of action-image cinema, in the sense that it constructs this kind of cinema as anachronistic and incapable of providing the structures of belief between the screen and the viewer which are necessary for an affective cinema. The film tries to avert this aesthetic crisis by initially miming, through the central character of DFens (Michael Douglas), the sensations of immediacy and authenticity provoked in the white cultural imagination by the genre of New Black Realism.[77] Films like *Boyz N the Hood* (Singleton 1991) and *Menace II Society* (Hughes) contain a politicised 'black rage' at the way that white cultural identity and the American Dream has been founded on the marginalisation and oppression of African-Americans. The films express this rage by miming and signifyin' the aesthetic structures of white Hollywood cinema in a way which reanimates the affective impact of the action film. *Falling Down* initially replicates this rage by suggesting that the American Dream has also failed its founders, the white middle-class male. Eventually, through a series of different shifts in identification and focalization, the film imposes on the viewer a position of cynicism, where the corruption and failure of the American Dream and its cinema are revealed, but where its illusions are allowed to continue - albeit in a limited and contingent form. By adopting this position, *Falling Down* constructs both New Black Realism and the affective responses it provokes in the white cultural imagination as primitive and naïve.

But in Chapters two and three, I will suggest that *Falling Down*'s response to the New Black Realism is itself naïve because the film does not fully grasp the sophistication and complexity of the aesthetic and political impact of this genre. Chapter two examines *Boyz N the Hood*, to explore the root moves of New Black Realism in the genre's drive to provoke a politicised affective shock to the white cultural imagination, and to provide a cinematic expression of 'black rage'. The chapter argues that there were three different affects of *Boyz N the Hood* in the white cultural imagination. The first of these involves the critical reception of the *Boyz*, which talked in terms of the film's 'raw power' and ability to assault the senses. This critical response was permeated with the fear and paranoia evoked by images of black violence and the 'dangerous black body', as well as anxieties around the imagined tendency of black audiences to copy representations of violence. The second response to the film was almost the opposite of the first. Once white viewers and critics had contextualised the narrative of *Boyz* within the familiar aesthetic structures of the action-image, it became regarded as 'safe', in the sense that critics focused on the film's overt messages of black self-help and anti 'black on black' violence. This response acted as a denial and repression of the most significant affect of the film. In its miming of the aesthetics of the cinema of the action-image, and particularly the gangsta's mimesis of the gangster, *Boyz* reveals the anarchic violence which lies at the heart of the white cultural imagination and the American Dream, and it is this affect which is manifested in the shocking images of the white new-brutality film.

Chapter three focuses on *Menace II Society* which is much more aggressive in its assault on the authority of the white cinematic and cultural identity. The film mimes the aesthetics of images, which range from the gangster film, to *noir*, to Scorsese to 'True-Crime' TV, all of which have been regarded as affective and authentic at some point in the history of their critical reception. In this mimesis, *Menace II Society* suggests that a white racial rage permeates the history of the image-making of the white cultural imagination. The film also reveals that it is this racial rage which has led to an aesthetic crisis in the ability of white cinema to produce a bodily response in the viewer, while at the same time celebrating African-American cinema's ability to reanimate cinematic affect by inflecting and recasting the old genres with a politicized black rage.

It is at this point that the book will be in a position to 'make sense' of a film like *Reservoir Dogs*. This film marks a turning point in the aesthetics of Hollywood action cinema. Like *Falling Down*, *Reservoir Dogs* is aware of the crisis of the action-image cinema and the postmodern blockbuster, and *like Falling Down*, the film responds by miming the affective shock which images of blackness and the genre of New Black Realism, and the aesthetics of rap provoke in the white cultural imagination. But *Reservoir Dogs* is not cynical like *Falling Down*. As I suggested above the white cultural imagination's dependence on African American culture and American Africanism is not directly spoken as cultural knowledge in this film. The film does not articulate a position of cultural authority from which white cultural imagination can reaffirm its own identity. *Reservoir Dogs* shocks the white viewer because it uses the mimetic and affective capability of the cinematic image to mime the images of blackness and American-Africanism which are experienced as immediate and violent by the white cultural imagination. The film, like the genre of New Black Realism, effectively reanimates the affective potential of the cinema. *Reservoir Dogs* also frames this reanimation within another kind of American Africanism which fabricates white culture as a space of dead, empty simulation, caught up in the chaos and uncertainty which has been categorized as 'the postmodern condition'. By contrast, African-American culture and particularly rap, is constructed as having the knowledge to provide culture and a cinema which is authentic, affective, and with a depth beneath the surface simulations of postmodernity.

The association of white cultural identity with the tropes of postmodernity, and contemporary African-American culture as a knowing source of cultural authority, cinematic affect and authenticity is also present in the three films discussed in the final chapter. *Pulp Fiction* (Tarantino 1994), *Se7en* (Fincher 1995) and *Strange Days* (Bigelow 1995) all demonstrate that *Reservoir Dogs'* mimetic engagement with contemporary African-American culture, American Africanism and cinematic affect is not an isolated case. All of these films are marked by their attempts to move away from the knowledge-based pleasures of the postmodern blockbuster, and to provoke a 'body-first' response in the viewer. *Pulp Fiction* marks a continuation of the mimetic relations between cultures in *Reservoir Dogs* in that it foregrounds the construction of white popular culture as a blank meaningless surface, where African-American culture is the site of a controlling cultural authority and an affective shock to the white cultural imagination. But *Pulp Fiction* is also more explicit than *Reservoir Dogs* in the way that it imbricates the affective power of 1990s' African-American culture, and what Carol Clover refers to as the symbiotic relationship between the assaultive and reactive gaze of the cinema and viewer.[78] The film constructs whiteness as a state of both voyeurism and masochism, and as desiring a depth in the image which can affect. Blackness is situated as both a barrier to the voyeurism of white culture and the place where the assaultive gaze is turned back on the viewer.

Se7en also positions white culture in this way, and in its cinematography and *mise en scène*, it performs a mimesis of the shock provoked by images of blackness, while laying bare the impulses of the white cultural imagination to seek that shock in that affect in both contemporary African-American culture and the fabricated immediacy of the 'dangerous' black body. At the same time blackness is also constructed as a site of omniscient, but impotent knowledge. *Strange Days* is slightly different from both of these films. It is much more explicit in narrativising the perceived crisis in white cultural identity and white action cinema. It openly refers to the masochistic desire of an empty, artificial white cultural identity, while directly evoking images of blackness which the white cultural imagination has fabricated as immediate and affective. And more than any of the other films in this book, *Strange Days* attempts to articulate a politics of identity around the white cultural imaginations dependence on African American culture and the fabrications it builds around blackness. In this sense *Strange Days* marks a shift from the affective power of the new-brutality film and films like the recent *Bulworth* (Beatty 1998) which attempt to symbolize this mimesis as a political and cultural discourse.

The book begins with the question of mimetic relations between white and African-American cinema of the early 1990s and an exploration of *Falling Down*'s attempt to articulate these relations with a 'naïve' imitation of the 'hood film.

Notes

1. The fact that it is an ear that is cut off alludes to the famous opening of *Blue Velvet* (Lynch 1986), where the main protagonist, Jeffrey (Kyle Maclachlan) discovers an ear in some wasteland. The sado-masochistic themes of *Blue Velvet* are directly referenced here.

2. Williams, *Film Quarterly* (1992: 14).

3. Rogin, *Critical Inquiry* 18 (1992: 417). Rogin cites *Uncle Tom's Cabin* (Porter, 1903), *The Birth of a Nation* (Griffith 1915), *The Jazz Singer* (Crosland 1927), and *Gone With the Wind* (Fleming/Cukor/Wood 1939) as the four most prominent examples of American film's transformative moments.

4. Deleuze (1989: 25).

5. Shaviro (1993: 21).

6. Massumi in Patton ed. (1996: 235).

7. *ibid.* (219).

8. *ibid.* (220).

9. *ibid.* (221).

10. *ibid.* (219-220).

11. Scarry (1985: 38).

12. Throughout this book I will be using the term, 'body-first' to describe those films which 'make the body do things' before conscious awareness or emotional involvement mediate the viscerality of the image.

13. For instance, see the reviews in *The Guardian* (12 November 1994: 31 and 20 October 1994: 11).

14. Eco in Lodge ed. (1988: 454).

15. Bazin (1967: 23-41).

16. Taubin, *Sight and Sound* 2 (1992: 5).

17. See for instance, Dyer (1979 and 1987). I am using the term Classical Hollywood in the formalistic sense defined by Bordwell, D., Staiger, J. & Thompson, K. (1985) and Maltby, R. & Craven, D. (1995) amongst others.

18. Jameson (1991: 20).

19. Burch (1981: 124).

20. *ibid*. (122-5).

21. In order to illustrate this point, Burch argues that George Franju's 1949 film, '*Le Sang Des Betes* is certainly not a film for children, but neither is *Last Year at Marienbad*' *ibid*. (124).

22. Spoto (1984: 440).

23. Deleuze (1989: 156).

24. *ibid*. (156). For an interesting essay on the relations between the shock of early cinema and modernity, see Singer in Schwarz & Charney eds. (1995).

25. Deleuze (1989: 157).

26. See Kirby in *Camera Obscura* 17 (1988: 112-31).

27. See the chapter called 'Thought and Cinema' in Deleuze (1989: 148-173).

28. Eisenstein (1986: 181-4).

29. Benjamin in Mast, Cohen & Braudy eds. (1992: 678).

30. *ibid*. (667). A quite self-conscious example of the 'out-of-placeness' of an original piece of art restoring a physical contact between the consumer and the commodified object can be found in the 1945 film version of *The Picture of Dorian Gray* (Lewin). The relationship between the portrait and the subject is of course fantastically physical, something which the film attempts to reproduce between the viewer and the film, by only showing the portrait through Technicolor inserts in the predominantly black and white film.

31. *Ibid*. (667 & 679).

32. Taussig (1994: 25).

33. Metz (1982: 42-58).

34. Benjamin in Mast, Cohen & Braudy eds. (1992: 679).

35. Deleuze (1989: 157).

36. *ibid*. (164).

37. *ibid*. (16).

38. *ibid*. (26).

39. Deleuze lists various socio-political and aesthetic reasons for 'the crisis which has shaken the action-image' including:

    the war [Second World] and its consequences, the unsteadiness of the 'American dream' in all its aspects, the new consciousness of minorities, the rise and inflation of images both in the external world and in people's minds, the influence on the cinema of new modes of narrative with which literature had experimented, the crisis of Hollywood and its old genres... (1986: 206).

    Chapter 1 of this book explores these factors in more detail, and the idea of the 'crisis of the action-image' is engaged with throughout.

40. *ibid*. (111).

41. *ibid*. (167-8).

42. Seydor, *Sight and Sound* 5 (1995: 20).

43. This book uses the term, 'postmodern blockbuster' to describe what has elsewhere been called

the 'High-Concept movie' (See Wyatt (1994)). Despite the fact that the term 'postmodern' has often been overused in contemporary cultural and film theory, it is preferred here because of its aesthetic and historical connotations. The films placed under the label are by no means homogenous, but they are included because of their emphasis on the spectacular image and for their nostalgia for the affective power of the so-called Classical Hollywood cinema. I suggest that the term can only be applied to big-budget blockbusters after *Star Wars* (Lucas 1977) and before *Speed* (de Bont 1995). See also Fred Pfeil's essay, 'From Pillar to Postmodernism' for an exploration of the formal qualities which allows films such as the *Die Hard* and *Lethal Weapon* series to be labelled postmodern (Pfeil in Lewis ed. (1998: 146-186)).

44. Shaviro (1993: 3).

45. The list of material attempting to define *noir* as genre is virtually endless. But the standard beginning article for a negotiation of *noir*, in terms of its cinematography, is Place, J. A. & Peterson, L. S., *Wide Angle* 10: 1 (1974: 30-35). For an effective deconstruction of *noir* as a useful cinematic term, see Vernet in Copjec ed. (1992).

46. Francke, *Sight and Sound* 6 (1996: 65).

47. Deleuze (1989: 18).

48. Beasley-Murray, *Iris* 23 (1997: 39).

49. Wood, *The Guardian* (12 November 1994: 31).

50. Malcolm, *The Guardian* (20 October 1994: 11).

51. The 'white cultural imagination' is a term which will be used frequently in this book and its meaning will be addressed later in this introduction.

52. Baudrillard (1983: 23).

53. Jameson (1991: 10). Jameson's analysis of the place of affect within postmodernity in this chapter as a whole is pertinent for my argument.

54. Massumi in Patton ed. (1996: 221).

55. Stern (1995: 39).

56. Butler in Gooding-Williams ed. (1993: 18).

57. *ibid*. (16).

58. Taussig (1994: 21).

59. Gaines (1994).

60. Morrison (1993: 6).

61. *ibid*. (44 & xii.).

62. Zizek (1989: 169)

63. Morrison (1993: 5).

64. *ibid*. (17).

65. *ibid*. (66).

66. Dyer (1997: 3).

67. See for instance the discussions around fetishism, disavowal and race in Hall ed. (1997: 264-269). Also see the bibliography (277: 279).

68. Taussig (1993: 25-25).

69. When discussing black culture, this book is referring almost exclusively to contemporary black male culture. To some extent this means that the book is open to the charges levelled by Deborah McDowell around the tendency of academic criticism to romanticize the 'bad boys of gangsta rap' (McDowell in Stecopolous and Uebel eds. (1997: 379)). McDowell is one of a number of critics who argue that 'sexual anxiety is...the real subject of rap', and that the establishment of struggles against white cultural racism and constructions of blackness is often accompanied by black male fears of feminization (361-365). The misogyny of gangsta rap and

the 'hood film is obviously a subject which needs close attention, and the affective potential of the 'hood film and rap cannot be read outside of their frequent content of sexual violence. This book implicitly recognises McDowell's argument that race and gender 'must be read together' (381), but it is also concerned with those aspects of black culture which provoke the greatest anxiety within the white cultural imagination. As McDowell points out 'nobody wants to talk about (black) girls' problems because they don't have the thunderclap of a gunshot' (380).

70. *ibid.* (10).

71. *ibid.* (52).

72. This is certainly the case in Britain where *Reservoir Dogs* was initially publicised as an independently produced 'art-house' film. Various newspaper and magazine articles also emphasised the cult status of Tarantino as a star director or 'new auteur'. For instance see Pulver, *The Guardian G2* (19 September 1994: 8-9).

73. See Lawson, *The Independent* (4 February: 28) for a description of Tarantino as a 'rock and roll director'. See also Corrigan (1991: 101-37) for an interesting essay about the auteur as cult and the commerce of 'auteurism'.

74. For the history of and discussion provoked by this criticism see, Carter, *The Independent* (3 December 1998: 32).

75. Rogin, *Critical Inquiry* 18 (1992: 417).

76. Bauer, *Sight and Sound* 8 (1998: 8-9).

77. A term coined by Diawara in Copjec ed. (1993: 261).

78. Clover (1993: 191-202).

Chapter One

Naïve Imitations:
Falling Down, the Crisis of the Action-Image and Cynical Realism

This movie shows the way things really are, not the way they should be.[1]

For better or worse, Falling Down *is one of those films that has hit an American nerve.*[2]

Falling Down is the tale of one day in the life of two white middle-class men, Bill Foster (Michael Douglas), known as DFens through most of the film, and a cop, Martin Prendergast (Robert Duvall). Both live in 1990s' Los Angeles, and in the opening scenes both are caught in the same traffic jam. The story begins when DFens, frustrated with the traffic jam, walks away from his car, telling irate drivers he is going home. This sets off the beginning of a picaresque series of violent encounters between DFens and a carefully contrived and largely hostile multi-cultured LA populace as he begins a quest to reach the house of his estranged wife, Beth (Barbara Hershey), and daughter, Adele. Beth has placed a restraining order on him for fear of the domestic violence he might inflict. In fact his real home is with his mother, and he has been made redundant from his job as a defence worker. The resolution of Dfens' journey occurs when he is finally tracked down by Prendergast on Venice Beach pier, where he is holding Beth and Adele hostage. Prendergast relieves him of his gun, as he asks in disbelief, 'I'm the bad guy?' He states that he has nothing left to live for, and challenges Prendergast to a duel, which ends with him being shot as, unknown to Prendergast, he is armed only with a water pistol.

But this is not the film's resolution, because alongside DFens' havoc-wreaking odyssey, there is another focus of attention in the parallel story of Prendergast, told through parallel montage, and under the guise of the generic framework of the police procedural thriller of pursuer and pursued. As the action unfolds we learn that Prendergast is also beset by obstacles and frustrations in his everyday life. He is taunted by his colleagues who regard him as a 'desk-jockey', not 'man enough' to face the violence and danger on the streets. We learn that Prendergast accepts this situation because of his wife's fears over his safety. His wife (Tuesday Weld) is pressurising him into retiring early, and move to Lake Havasu, a retirement town in the Californian desert, and constantly disrupts the process of his work and the narrative, nagging him about domestic matters. She was a former beauty queen, who has never recovered emotionally from the fading of her good looks and the loss of their infant daughter to Infant Death Syndrome. As DFens' rampage progresses throughout the day, Prendergast is the only cop who recognises that there is a pattern in the seemingly random violence across LA, and gradually, with the help of his former partner, he regains an authority both in the department by tracking down DFens, and with his wife, telling her to 'shut up' on the phone, and changing his retirement plans.

Falling Down is a Hollywood film which seeks to mark itself as different from the formulaic Hollywood blockbuster or high-concept film - despite the fact that it stars Michael Douglas and is directed by Joel Schumacher, 'journeyman' director of films like *Batman Forever* (1995) and *Flatliners* (1990). The film attempts to establish itself as an authentic, immediate and contemporary portrayal of the social problems facing the 'average white male' in the LA metropolis, and offer an alternative viewing experience to the nostalgia-based spectacular pleasures of the postmodern blockbuster. Joel Schumacher's avowed intention to 'show the way things really are' signals this difference in the sense that the fantastical worlds of films like *Total Recall* (Verhoeven 1988) and *The Terminator* (Cameron 1984) would never attempt to claim such access to the 'truth' of contemporary American culture. On one level *Falling Down*'s departure from the blockbuster can obviously be explained in terms of genre. The film could be described as a 'social-problem' movie which deals with the contemporary social realities of a carefully configured Los Angeles, whilst even non-science fiction blockbusters such as *True Lies* (Cameron 1994) could not claim to have any concrete grounding in the social world. The question still remains of how the makers of *Falling Down* felt it was still possible, in the early 1990s, for a Hollywood film to provoke a response in the viewer which depended on such outmoded concepts as 'reality' and 'truth'? In addition, how did *Falling Down* manage to be 'one of those films that has hit an American nerve' resulting in spontaneous, wide scale outbreaks of American audiences cheering at DFens' every move?[3]

The answers to these questions lie beyond the formal generic differences between *Falling Down* and the postmodern blockbuster, and in the way that the former seeks to manipulate both the affective potential of the cinematic experience and the discourses of convention and tradition which permeate Hollywood film. *Falling Down* attempts to control its viewer's responses, and more particularly the white cultural imagination, by provoking a body-first affective response, and at the same time, directing the thoughts and reactions that such a response evokes. The film wants to situate its viewers within a framework of knowledge where they imagine they have seen the truth of 1990s' white American identity - and a viewing position from which there is very little scope for manoeuvre outside of the movie's own logic and imagined knowledge. Moreover the film seeks to do this by initially stimulating an affective response based on the fabrication of African-American culture as site of affect which the film also equates with truth and the real. This attempted manipulation of the viewer's responses is produced through a tight, schematic hierarchy of three viewing positions which develop over the course of the action. The first of these is an immediate identification and focalization with the actions and situations of DFens. This position is eventually undermined by the way the film makes DFens and his actions objects of nostalgia. By the end of the film the viewer is encouraged to assume a position of what I want to call 'cynical realism' which ultimately associates African-American culture with primitivism and a childlike naivety.

Throughout *Falling Down* there are tensions between the impossibilities of a purely affective Hollywood cinema and the pleasures of knowing Hollywood's traditions and histories, and these are apparent in the opening scene. The film begins with a black screen with the acousmatic sound of heavy breathing, followed by a long take which moves in turn from a close-up of clenched teeth, to tense bespectacled eyes, and then a sweaty knotted brow. In the same shot the camera draws back to reveal the whole figure of Michael Douglas (DFens) sitting in a car. This is not a familiar Michael Douglas however. Gone are the designer suits, executive hairstyles and cars that made him such a familiar middle-class icon in films such *Fatal Attraction* (Lyne 1987) and *Disclosure* (Levinson 1994), to be replaced by a fifties-style, buzz-cut hairdo, horn-rimmed glasses, 'working-stiff' short-sleeved shirt and tie and small Japanese saloon. The strangeness of this Michael Douglas is accentuated by the fact that his body is shot from a high angle and through the windows of the car giving a distorted effect, comparable to a circus mirror. After this detailed examination, the long take shifts its position from exhibiting Michael Douglas as the object of its gaze, to one where his point of view becomes dominant. The camera focuses on the objects and bodies in his immediate field of vision. An overbearing soundtrack of horns, children screaming, and coke-fuelled yuppies swearing into mobile phones accompanies the camera as it pans around to view obnoxious bumper stickers, 'a Garfield suction doll leering like a gargoyle from behind a windshield, and a busload of repellent kids'.[4] This long take is then followed by a series of fast edits which switch from more close-ups of DFens' frustrated sweating body - most notably when the camera catches an irritating fly crawling over his sweaty neck - to the angry anarchic scenes of other motorists caught in the same jam. By the end of the scene, the discomfort caused by the fast-editing and the rising soundtrack places the audience in a mimetic relationship with the figure trapped in the car, and it comes as huge relief when DFens ends both his, and the audience's discomfort, by getting out of the car, and telling other drivers he is 'going home'.

The connection between the viewer's and DFens' situation and body provides the chief source of affect in this particular scene. Like DFens, the viewer is trapped in a confined space, subject to the various images which assault us though the screen and hit DFens through the distorted screen of the car window - which, incidentally, he is unable to open. The close-ups of DFens' body emphasize this bodily, mimetic link between himself and the limited mobility and freedom of the viewer, stuck in the cinema seat. But as well as operating in this affective, immediate way, the scene is also opening up the relationship of belief between the viewer and the Hollywood narrative film, and more particularly on the belief in the ability of the individual protagonist to act in a concrete manner within the cinematic world in which he is situated. More precisely the film evokes the theories of space and action that dominated the Screen tradition of film theory in the 1970s and 1980s, and most famously delineated in Laura Mulvey's seminal essay, 'Visual Pleasure and Narrative Cinema'.

The presence of this self-reflexive tendency in *Falling Down* is most apparent in the way DFens is positioned and figured in relation to the spatial dimensions of the opening scene.[5] Despite the fact that the close-ups of DFens/Michael Douglas's face and neck are filmed as a long take the effect is one of fragmentation as the camera moves around various parts of the visage. The different angles and depths of field that the camera takes when filming emphasize the fragmentation of DFens' body, as well as accentuating its confinement and lack of mobility. The comparisons with 'Visual Pleasure and Narrative Cinema' are worth noting. One of the central arguments in Mulvey's essay concerns the paradigmatic and gendered relations between the male and female protagonists in Hollywood narrative cinema of the 1930s, 40s and 50s. The argument runs that, in general, 'the active male figure' of these films demanded a three-dimensional, naturalized space, within which he carried the active and masterful look of the camera, and, by proxy, the look of the viewer. Images of women produced an opposite effect where female stars were often broken up into images of body parts through close-ups of legs, faces and so on. Such fragmentation according to Mulvey's essay 'destroys the Renaissance space, the illusion of depth demanded by the narrative...'[6] These differences in the cinematographic construction of male and female roles made the woman star less real, with 'the quality of a cut-out or icon', in contrast to the active, narrative and look-bearing male protagonist.[7]

The concern here is not to engage with old debates concerning the validity of Mulvey's essay but that the opening scenes of *Falling Down* seem to be engaging with the theory of space and action/activity outlined in 'Visual Pleasure and Narrative Cinema' and the Screen tradition in general.[8] The fragmentation and confinement of DFens' body in the opening scenes is a reversal of the active, controlling look and movements of the 'Classical Hollywood' hero (which formed the basis of the Screen critiques of Hollywood), in the sense that he is figured as a victim of the cinematic world around him from the start. This reversal operates at the level of discourse and meaning rather than affect in the sense that the cinematography which figures DFens as a victim of cinematic space corresponds to the overall 'meaning' the film attempts to convey. Throughout the first half of the film, DFens is constructed in terms of 1990s' discourses of masculinity in crisis.

His lack of a job and relationship problems figure him as a victim, and in the course of his journey across Los Angeles, what would have once been instant respect for the authority of the white working-class male, turns into hostility, misrecognition and confrontation in the film's representation of a contemporary LA.[9] In other words, the film presents a representation of an emasculated white American male subject which seeks to counteract the feminist and African-American discourses, critical of the authority of white male identity, by representing a white male 'everyman' for whom that authority and power no longer exists.

The film is working primarily here at the level of cultural and political knowledge and discourse rather than at the level of a body-first affective response - despite the physical connection between DFens and viewer in the opening scene. This tension becomes even more acute because DFens is played by the iconic figure of Michael Douglas. Douglas has made a career out of playing 'victim-heroes' in films such as *Fatal Attraction* and *Basic Instinct* (Verhoeven 1991), and as Carol Watts notes, 'Michael Douglas is encoded as a star in terms of the crisis in masculinity he enacts'.[10] 'Douglassic Man' starts out from a position of harmony and authority which is threatened by femme fatale figures, such as Glenn Close in *Fatal Attraction* and Demi Moore in *Disclosure*.[11] The narratives of these films tend to unfold in an orthodox linear fashion to the point where Michael Douglas is allowed to restore a lessened, more contingent, degree of authority by vanquishing these contemporary *femme fatales*. In addition, Michael Douglas evokes the almost involuntary comparison with his father Kirk Douglas, who was able to play the uncompromised action-taking hero of Classical Hollywood.

Although *Falling Down* is addressing and contributing towards the 'backlash' discourse of the 1980s and early 90s, the film is also gesturing towards a more fundamentally cinematic question - that of the apparently declining role of affect and belief in the images of Hollywood narrative film.[12] The film undermines the cultural familiarity of the discourses it engages with a self-reflexive awareness of what Gilles Deleuze calls 'the crisis of the action-image', and the crisis of Hollywood realism.[13] This awareness is most apparent in the spatial and temporal relationship between DFens and the milieux in which he finds himself, and this is worth exploring through Deleuze's ideas concerning the action-image and its crisis.

The Action-Image and the Crisis of Realism

Gilles Deleuze argues that belief in the individual actions of the protagonist in a coherent filmic space was vital to the realism which was the underlying aesthetic and philosophy of the Hollywood form of the action-image - or what others have called Classical Hollywood.[14] He argues that, 'what constitutes realism is simply this: milieus and modes of behaviour, milieus which actualize, and modes of behaviour which embody'.[15] He goes on to state that:

The milieu and its forces incurve on themselves, they act on the character, throw him a challenge and constitute a situation in which he is caught. The character reacts in his turn (action properly speaking) so as to respond to the situation, to modify the milieu, or his relations with the milieu, with the situation, with other characters. He must acquire a new mode of being (habitus) or raise his mode of being to the demands of the milieu and of the situation. Out of this emerges a restored or modified situation, a new situation. Everything is individuated: the milieu as a particular space-time, the situation as determining and determinate, the collective as well as the individual character.[16]

Deleuze's analysis of the structural properties of Hollywood realism is in some ways similar to the analysis of action and space predominant in the Screen tradition of the 1970s and 80s. Both paradigms theorize the action of the individual protagonist as crucial, in that he acts to resolve a disruption - or in Deleuzian terminology, a 'challenge' or 'situation' - which is produced by the milieu of the film. For Deleuze there must be a concrete sensory-motor link between the protagonist and the situations that the milieu throws down - 'that the sensory-motor link must be very strong' and that, 'on the one hand the situation must permeate the character deeply and continuously, and on the other hand the character who is thus permeated must burst into action at discontinuous intervals'.[17] The viewer's belief in this link then enables Hollywood realism to provoke an affective response.

The sensory-motor connection between protagonist and milieu must be believable in order for there to be a concrete bodily relation between the viewer and the film.[18] At the same time there must be a level of cultural recognition between the individual protagonist and the cinematic world in which he is situated. The hero can only act with any degree of authority when he is recognised and known by the milieu in which he moves and vice versa. Thus even in *film noir*, which Deleuze points to as the genre of realism where the sensory-motor links are verging on fragile, the hero/anti-hero possesses the cultural and social knowledge to deal with the everyday and act decisively upon it.[19] This is despite the often hidden criminal forces and twists of fate that sometimes govern his fate. In a film like *The Big Sleep* (Hawks 1946), Marlowe can easily manoeuvre his way around the everyday world and is able to discern the reality and appearances of most situations, handling them with tough, smart quips and appropriate physical violence - despite the hidden machinations of Eddie Mars.

The strong sensory-motor links of situation and action between the individual protagonist and milieu can only survive if it remains possible to believe in a cinematic world which presents itself as a totality - where the viewer is immersed in the film as a global situation. In other words, Deleuze is arguing that in order for Hollywood cinema to exist as affective immediate art, the viewer must be able to believe in the illusion that for the film's running time, the cinematic world of Hollywood realism is, a real and total situation where the viewer's body and mind is mimetically connected to the world of the film, and where the film becomes the world. The viewer must be capable of believing in the action-image as totality (even partially), otherwise the strange, almost hypnotic relationship, which Noel Burch makes fundamental to the relationship between screen and viewer, is replaced by distanciated extracinematic knowledge interrupting the mimetic connection.[20]

Deleuze argues that, after the Second World War, the realism of the action-image suffers a philosophical and aesthetic crisis where belief in the action-image as a totality is more difficult. This crisis is not a financial one as 'films of this type go on being made for a long time yet' and 'the greatest commercial successes always take that route', but it is rather a crisis of aesthetics and belief.[21] In the cinema of the 'crisis of the action-image' the links between protagonist and milieu and the belief in these connections have become dispersed and weakened because of several factors, 'some of which were social, economic, political, moral and others more internal to art, literature and to the cinema in particular'.

We might mention, in no particular order, the war and its consequences, the unsteadiness of the 'American dream' in all its aspects, the new consciousness of minorities, the rise and inflation of images both in the external world and in people's minds, the influence on cinema of the new modes of narrative with which literature had experimented...[22]

This particular extract is interesting not least because it is one of the few places that Deleuze suggests explicitly ideological and historical reasons for shifts in the kind of cinema that Hollywood was producing. The crisis of the action-image is implicitly connected to the crisis of the American Dream in the sense that 'we hardly believe any longer that a global situation can give rise to an action capable of modifying it - no more than we can believe that an action can force a situation to disclose itself, even partially'.[23] In a vein which echoes crises around 'the postmodern condition', Deleuze implies that the extracinematic world has become too fragmented and uncontrollable for individual action to make any fundamental difference beyond the local. It is the ability of the individual to take action within a local situation which has universal and global effects that is one of the basic foundations for the myth of the American Dream. In the cinema as well, the local can no longer stand in for the global - as it does for one of the last times, (and under great duress) in the relationship between George Bailey (James Stewart) and Bedford Falls in *It's a Wonderful Life* (Capra 1946).

The two great principles of the American Dream - the ability of the individual to act and achieve, and the simultaneous effects those actions have on the community at large - are no longer taken seriously:

> *The most 'healthy' illusions fall. The first things to be compromised everywhere are the linkages of situation-action, action-reaction, excitation-response, in short, the sensory-motor links which produced the action-image.*[24]

Deleuze's reasoning also provides justification for the argument that *Kiss Me Deadly* (Aldrich 1955) marks the end of classic *film noir*. Ralph Meeker's Marlowe is the ultimate in action-image protagonists. His whole being is directed towards achieving his goals through violent verbal or physical action, and to changing the film's milieu through that action. But Meeker's Marlowe becomes an oafish clown instead of the smart controlling Bogartian figure, because of the intrusion into the *noir* totality of the unsymbolisable and uncontrollable violence of nuclear holocaust. *Noir* as violent global situation is not viable because it is no longer possible to believe that an individual - no matter how disposed to action - can credibly alter that milieu. Nor can we believe that Marlowe's actions can force the situation to reveal itself - until it is too late and 'Pandora's box' is opened at the end of the film.

Deleuze goes on to argue that 'a new kind of image is born' out of the crisis facing the action-image and can be identified in 'the post-war American cinema outside of Hollywood'. There are 'five apparent characteristics' of this new cinematic image: *'the dispersive situation, the deliberately weak links, the voyage form, the consciousness of clichés, the condemnation of plot'*.[25] The multiple narratives of the 'dispersive situation' contrast sharply with the enclosed narrative realities and singular milieu of Hollywood realism. Deleuze points towards Robert Altman films such as *A Wedding* (1978) and *Nashville* (1975), ('with the multiple soundtracks and the anamorphic screen which allows several simultaneous stagings') as examples of this new cinema.

The deliberately weak links between protagonist and milieu occur because of a break down in clearly defined cause and effect structures in narratives. The protagonists in this new kind of cinema are subject to what Deleuze calls 'white events, events which never truly concern the person who provokes or is subject to them, even when they strike him in his flesh'.[26] Thus Travis Bickle in *Taxi-Driver* (Scorsese 1976):

> *wavers between killing himself and committing a political murder and, replacing these projects by the final slaughter, is astonished by it himself, as if the carrying out concerned him no more than did the preceding whims... The actuality of the action-image, the virtuality of the affection-image can interchange, all the more easily for having fallen into the same indifference.*[27]

In other words there is the appearance of holes in the diegetic reality, and the links between protagonist and milieu become deliberately weakened as 'chance becomes

The New-Brutality Film

the sole guiding thread'.[28] *Taxi Driver* is also a good illustration of third property of the new image, where 'the sensory-motor action or situation has been replaced by the stroll, the voyage and the continual return journey' through the 'any-space-whatever', which Deleuze argues is the 'undifferentiated fabric of the city - in opposition to action which most often unfolded within the qualified space-time of the old realism'.[29]

Fourthly, the 'consciousness of clichés' points towards the multiplication of intertextuality and increased parodying of the old genres in post-war American cinema. To continue with the *Taxi Driver* example, Travis Bickle's journey through the city and his rescue of Iris can be read as a reworking of *The Searchers* (Ford 1956) - which can itself be seen as displaying some of the symptoms of the crisis of the action-image.[30] Deleuze's argument is that the cinema of the crisis of the action-image deliberately used clichés to highlight the fact that it was no longer possible to believe in the old genres as affective cinema. If the viewer has seen these images elsewhere the belief in the individual film as enclosed, affective totality becomes less and less tenable. Familiar situations, actions and narratives become clichéd, and distanciated as part of cultural knowledge. The proliferation of cinematic images in other media such TV and video adds to this sense of cliché.

Finally the condemnation of plot, which Deleuze identifies as the fifth characteristic of the cinema of the crisis of the action-image, is evident in the lack of a centre to the milieux of these films. Whereas in *film noir* the criminals would be distinguishable by their actions, there is no recognisable milieu which the protagonist can act against or even with in the crisis cinema of post-war America. For instance in *Point Blank* (Boorman 1967) Hunter (Lee Marvin) rampages around Los Angeles trying, in vain, to find the centre of the organisation responsible for stealing his money. This lack of a centre undermines the narrative plot that drives the film from the outset, which is ultimately revealed to be empty. The conspiracy film of the 1970s is a clear example of the removal of realism's narrative drive and centre. Films such as *The Parallax View* (Pakula 1974) go through the motions of a noir-like mystery plot, without ever reaching the point where the centre of the criminal conspiracy is revealed. The conspiracy is everywhere without a definable central milieu. The old genres are parodied to the point where belief in them is impossible.

According to Deleuze the incorporation of these five elements in post-war American film was a limited endeavour to free itself from the properties of the action-image. The attempts of Scorsese, Altman and Cassavetes to produce a new kind of affective American cinematic image were unsuccessful (according to Deleuze) because:

...the rage against cliché does not lead to much if it is content only to parody them; maltreated, mutilated, destroyed, a cliché is not slow to be reborn from its ashes. In fact, what gave the American cinema its advantage, the fact of being born without a previous tradition to suffocate it, now rebounded against it. For the cinema of the action-image had itself engendered a tradition from which it could now only extricate itself negatively. The great genres of this cinema...collapse and yet maintain their empty frame.[31]

This passage echoes the Benjaminian distinction between the immediacy of the early cinema compared to the concentrated knowledge required for art with a tradition. The revisions and parodies of the old genres leave the action-image intact, but without the affective substance and concrete connections between viewer, ideology and image which made belief in them possible. The films of Altman and others become themselves part of the tradition of the action-image - because of their parodic imitations - and not a new kind of affective image.

The Postmodern Blockbuster, Noir, and *Falling Down*

It is worth bearing Deleuze's analysis in mind while considering the state of Hollywood action cinema at the time of *Falling Down*'s release and the film's attempt to produce affect. *Falling Down*'s difference to the commercially successful postmodern blockbuster of the late 1970s and 1980s has already been noted and these films can be read as another kind of response to the loss of affect and belief in American cinema that Deleuze detects in the crisis of the action-image. The idea that the 'great genres' of American cinema 'collapse and yet maintain their empty frame' resonates with the aesthetic and commercial strategy of the Schwarzenegger/Stallone/Willis blockbusters of the 1980s and early 90s. Unlike the cinema of the crisis of the action-image, films like *Total Recall* (Verhoeven 1988), *Rambo: First Blood Part II* (Cosmatos 1985) and the *Die Hard* trilogy reference the tradition of action-cinema through pastiche rather than the critical parody of an Altman film.[32] The intertextuality of the blockbuster and the near winks to the camera from its stars serve to distance the viewer from any illusion of belief in the enclosed world of the film. In fact these films tend to emphasize their 'non-believability' through an exaggeration and inflation of both the individual protagonists and the milieux and situations they act against and within. A film like *Die Hard* directly references the Western genre (specifically Howard Hawks' *Rio Bravo* (1959)) but blows it up to the point where any sensory-motor link between viewer and action is self-reflexively taken apart. The heroes are over-muscular superheroes and the criminals are mock-evil super villains carrying and extending all the characteristics of the protagonists, action and milieu of the classic genres.[33] These are not 'individuated' protagonist or milieux any more, but overblown and empty composites of previous images in action cinema.

In spite of this, there remains a nostalgic yearning for immediacy in these films, as well as a residual visceral, bodily impact on the viewer. But their affective power depends on overloading their spectacularity. Like the heroes and criminals, the situations in a film like *Die Hard* are also inflated to the point where what counts is how big the next explosion will be, and how impressive the next special effect is. These films act like a rollercoaster and the viewer's body is often strongly tied to the visual peaks and troughs of such films.[34] *Speed* (de Bont 1995), where the situation is everything, marks a turning point in the blockbuster's engagement with physical affect. It deliberately limits and scales down the confines of the situation in an attempt to reproduce and reanimate the sensory-motor links between the viewer and the action. The bus becomes the enclosed qualified space-time totality in a similar fashion to the community or world in action-image cinema. The difference here though is that the affect of the film is supplied through the way this particular milieu constantly threatens to collide with other 'any-space-whatevers' (the airport, freeway etc.).

A Deleuzian reading would critique the blockbuster's affective impact because of the lack of new thought produced by its visceral images. Deleuze' primary project is to detect in cinema 'the upsurge of the new thinking-image' which engages with the idea that the specific ontology of cinema is produced in its experiments with time.[35] By extending and over-inflating the properties of the action-image, the postmodern blockbuster is, according to Deleuzian thought, maintaining the empty structures of the action-image, long after the belief in these films as totalities has waned. There are many holes in Deleuze's history of the philosophy and aesthetics of post-war American cinema - not least the fact that he makes no mention of the blockbuster and its visceral pleasures. But his argument does make a suggestive starting point from which to engage with the attempt by *Falling Down* to reanimate the affective structures between Hollywood film and the viewer. *Falling Down*, unlike the blockbuster, does not seek to provide bodily impact through an inflation of the powers of its protagonist to act in a decisive fashion to change or modify the milieu and situation in which he is caught. Indeed, one of the most striking aspects of *Falling Down* is that DFens' series of adventures is marked by the constant misrecognition of both DFens and the particular milieux he moves through. DFens demonstrates a remarkable level of naivety in thinking that the Korean shopkeeper should respect him because of US foreign aid policy; that fast food hamburgers should look the same in reality as they do in advertisements; that the 'customer is always right'; and that the Hispanic graffiti marking gang territory should be written in 'fucking English'. The film even makes a direct reference to the difference between the super-knowledge and power of the blockbuster hero and DFens in the sequence where he attempts to blow up a freeway construction site. Unsure which button to press on his portable rocket launcher, DFens asks the advice of an African-American child, who thinks he is playing a role in an action-movie called *Under Construction*. Even after instruction, DFens is still unable to aim the launcher correctly.

This naive understanding is at its most intense in his belief that his 'home', and the goal of his quest, is still with his estranged wife and child, after she has placed a restraining order on him. Misrecognition also dominates the milieux' perception of him: the Korean shopkeeper calls him a thief when he just wants change; the Chicano gang see him as easy pickings when he wanders onto their land; the neo-Nazi shopkeeper mistakes him for a vigilante with the same political beliefs as himself; the geriatric golfers think he is a groundsman; and the family, having a surreptitious barbecue in the house of their employer, think he is a security guard. This process of misrecognition, and the resulting gap between the world of DFens and that of the milieux of the film, means that any action DFens takes is ultimately pointless.

The film also contains other characteristics of the crisis of the action-image. The situations and confrontations that DFens encounters are 'white events' in the sense that the only thing that truly concerns him is his final destination. His journey across the various neighbourhoods of Los Angeles is reminiscent of the Deleuzian stroll, as he becomes the nomad who has no connection to the spaces he moves through.[36] There is also the lack of centre to the criminal conspiracy that DFens believes is at the heart of his troubles. At the end of the film he bemoans the fact to Prendergast that 'they lied to me', whereas Prendergast knows that 'they' lie to everyone - including 'the fish'. This difference between the two protagonists is vital to the way that the film constructs its viewing positions and we need to look at this in more detail later. But one final element of the crisis of the action-image that *Falling Down* incorporates is the consciousness of cliché that Deleuze refers to. We have already touched on the major example of this in the discussion of the iconic status of Michael Douglas, where his association with the 'backlash' cycle of movies has become a distanciating element of his performances.

But although *Falling Down* may be responding to the crisis of the action-image, it is also clear that in the first half of the action the film is also seeking to reanimate the affective links between the protagonist, action, milieu and situation. It is almost as if the film is seeking to imitate the cracks and fissures opened up by *Taxi-Driver* and plaster over them with the more traditional qualities of the action-image and Hollywood realism. Moreover the film tries to transcend the distanciation caused by its awareness of the crisis of the action-image by making links between its own diegesis and familiar, recognisable situations in the extracinematic world. Both of these factors are evident in comments made about the intention behind the film from its director and star. Joel Schumacher argues that the purpose behind the film was 'to give a face and a soul to the six o'clock news story we see all the time, the one about the seemingly ordinary man who's worked hard all his life, who's been a law-abiding citizen, who snaps suddenly'.[37] Michael Douglas stated that being in the role of a creator of action was one of the reasons that persuaded him to take the role of DFens: 'Coming off the kind of reactive role I played in *Basic Instinct*, which can be frustrating, I was looking to do something where I initiated action or created things'.[38] The question we need to ask again at this stage is how both Douglas and Schumacher felt it was possible to make a Hollywood action film which could provoke affective links between the action, protagonist and some notion of authenticity. Perhaps more interesting than this question is the fact that, judging by audience responses in the US, there *was* a kind of spontaneous affective response to DFens' actions.[39] It could be argued that such responses formed part of an expected response to Michael Douglas' association with the 'backlash' cycle. Certain audiences could have been responding to DFens/Douglas' reactionary rampage around LA because they expected the movie to provide the same kind backlash-inspired catharsis as they experienced when Alex Forrest (Glenn Close) is finally vanquished in *Fatal Attraction*.

I want to suggest that *Falling Down* is a rather different film from *Fatal Attraction* in this respect and that the initial bodily connections between DFens and the audience go beyond the discursive limits of backlash politics. As I noted above there is a tactile affective engagement in the opening frames of the film with the mimetic connection between viewer and the trapped, unfamiliar-looking figure in the car. This link also goes beyond the identificatory structures of the gaze outlined in psychoanalytic theory where the lead protagonist carries the desires of the audiences through their active look. As we have already seen, DFens' is figured as much a victim of the cinematic space and situations as he is an action-taker within them.

Part of the reason for the affective link between the viewer and the film is the fact that the spaces which DFens inhabits and comes into conflict with are configured as more real than the character himself in both their banality and universality. As Carol Clover notes:

> Many of the irritations and social ills in Dfens' awful day are indeed things that can affect and offend anyone; the traffic jam, the annoying bumper stickers, the ludicrous uniforms and protocol of the Whammyburger restaurant, the shopkeeper's refusal to give change, the general rudeness of all towards all. These are Everyone scenes, and they provide some of the film's most trenchant moments.[40]

Falling Down echoes anxieties around the postmodern condition by displaying a metropolis which can no longer be imagined as a whole or a totality. The space of this Los Angeles is fragmented and consequently anarchic. Moreover, the anarchy is banal, with conflicts over traffic jams, territory, and shop prices. It is the fantasy of being able to act against the seemingly uncontrollable and fragmentary spaces of banal urban existence which provides the first viewing position of *Falling Down* - identification with the actions of DFens. This is also the fantasy of reversing the crisis of the action-image where an individual attempts to make sense of the whole again through brief violent bursts of action.

Yet, this identification with the seemingly spontaneous actions of DFens is not as immediate as first appears. The affective power of the film is partially provoked by its evocation of memories of *film noir* - and more importantly, the ideological structures which were at the heart of the genre. Marc Vernet has produced a reading of *noir* that contradicts the critical orthodoxy which has interpreted *film noir* as a 'leftish' film genre, which seeks to expose the flaws and fissures of the American Dream by displaying a 'down and dirty' USA, riddled with crime and corruption. Like Deleuze, Vernet reads *noir* as the action genre where the dream is at its most vulnerable, but he also argues that *noir* represented a renewal of two of its ideological principles:

> *The first was the repetition of the citizen's allegiance to national principles, but according to which national institutions can only maintain their power through the individual, through the simple citizen apparently lost in the immensity of the country...The second thing (but intimately tied to the first) that was brought up-to-date by film noir was the renewal of the jeremiad, that half-political, half-religious discourse operative from the very foundation of the United States, which allows the fundamental values of the nation to be recalled by accentuating all the deviations in the nation's history that followed their not being respected.*[41]

Vernet argues that a large proportion of *noir* films featured a 'simple citizen' attempting to reinstate the belief in the direct connections between the individual and community by granting a power to that individual to right the wrongs that were present in the system. *Noir* presented 'overtly vast systems' (including 'the justice system and the police as well as the Mafia, unions, Nazi networks within the country, and later, communists'.[42]) as betraying the populist version of the American Dream which stressed individual responsibility and action as well as freedom. His central point is that these films cut across traditional generic differences (i.e. the detective film, gangster films, or propaganda films) to present 'a fight to the death between an individual and a network which threatens fundamental freedoms'.[43]

Taking just a few of the instances of DFens' proclamations of what he believes to be his 'fundamental freedoms', it is easy to see the comparisons with Vernet's reading of the righteous individual in *noir*. Indeed the basis of DFens' anger is that he has been lied to by the very institutions which were supposed to guarantee his rights as an individual American. DFens' struggle can be read as the individual exposing the flaws and corruptions of the system that promised happiness and security to the citizen that upheld its values, and failed to deliver those promises. In the fast food joint he stands up for the right of the individual consumer against the multi-national conglomerate food chain, backing up 'the customer is always right' philosophy with a machine gun. He tells the rich (arguably Jewish) geriatric golfers that their private golf course should be a public park where families should be free to roam and go for picnics. His former job as a defence worker, where he helped to 'protect America', and his desire to reclaim the utopian family life he believes he once had, could be said to lie at the heart of the white American male's ideological existence. As bell hooks argues, 'there is a way in which *Falling Down* is about a white man who's saying, 'I trusted the system. I did exactly what the system told me to and it's not working for me. It's lied to me'.[44]

If *Falling Down* represents an updating of American populism and the jeremiad, it is hard to see how such a renewal could have the kind of bodily and affective impact that I am claiming that the film, in part, has. If, as Vernet argues, these two basic tenets of the American Dream already needed revising in the *noir* films of the 40s and 50s, the figure of the 'righteous individual' with a responsibility towards his milieu is already part of cultural nostalgia of the US. This point is partially demonstrated by the way that *It's a Wonderful Life* (Capra 1946) has become a regular Christmas feature shown innumerable times on network and cable TV. This film takes the ideological structure of the individual (George Bailey) fighting to keep the community and individual's rights intact against the impersonal corporate forces of big business (Potter) to its fullest - and most strained - expression. As we shall see the next viewing position which *Falling Down* imposes on the viewer does indeed attempt to make DFens' and his actions things of nostalgia. But in the first instance there is one more crucial point we have to explore in analyzing why DFens, the milieux he confronts, and the actions he takes, provoke an affective immediate response.

The White Negro

Falling Down, like the other new-brutality films in this book, is directly responding to the short-lived but important genre of African-American film which Manthia Diawara has labelled 'New Black Realism', and particularly 'hood films such as *Boyz N the Hood* (Singleton 1991) and *Juice* (Dickerson 1991).[45] One common link between these films is their images of the violent lives of (mostly) male African-Americans in 1990s' USA. Interestingly Diawara also calls these films '*noir* by noirs' and many of them also mime the ideological structures that Vernet identifies in the classic *noir*. But in films like *Boyz N the Hood* the allegiance expressed through characters like Furious (Laurence Fishburne) is not to the national principles of the USA but to African-American people. As we shall see in the next chapter, this is particularly marked in the black separatist speech he makes to two of the film's protagonists, Tre and Rikki. And when the deviations in the institutions of the USA are displayed in these films, it is not to recall the 'fundamental values' on which they were based, but to express what Diawara interprets as the 'black rage' at the heart of New Black Realism.[46] Diawara takes black rage to mean 'a set of violent and uncontrollable relations in black communities induced by a sense of frustration, confinement and white racism'.[47] The two films that I shall be looking at in detail, *Boyz N the Hood* and *Menace II Society* (Hughes 1993), both express this politicized anger in their images and narratives, and it is clear from comments by Schumacher that *Falling Down* attempts to visualize a comparable fury:

> *Movies reflect society, and there have been several movies in the US about anger in the street but they had all been by African-Americans. Well they're not the only angry people in the United States.*[48]

There are several points of interest in Schumacher's comments - not the least that he imagines a black cultural dominance in the production of movies which are able to 'reflect society'. But what is more striking is the way that anger is taken to be a universal violence which can be expressed, regardless of the specific political situations and conditions which produce it. Although New Black Realism has its own cultural and historical grounding, *Falling Down* attempts to transfer that anger to white situations through simply changing the representation of the character expressing rage.

Throughout the film there are many explicit parallels drawn between DFens and African-Americans. There is the scene where an African-American, dressed in the similar attire of white shirt and tie to DFens, is staging a sole individual demonstration against a bank which has told him, like DFens, that he was 'not economically viable'. The connotations of the 'individual against the system' and the connections between DFens and this figure are made even more explicit as the African-American gazes forlornly towards DFens, mouthing 'don't forget me', as he is carried away by the police. These connections between DFens, 'blackness', and authenticity are also displayed in two scenes with African-American children. In the Whammyburger restaurant it is a black kid who puts his hand up to respond to DFens' questions concerning the authenticity of the burger advertised on the wall, and it is another who teaches him how to use the rocket launcher that DFens has procured from the dead neo-Nazi.

One of the reasons for this association of DFens with African-Americans is the film's cynical desire to not alienate the black audiences who make up a disproportionate percentage of the cinema-going American public. Throughout the course of his conflicts with the different ethnicities and sexualities of Los Angeles the one significant group DFens leaves alone is the African-American community. But there is also another motive for this association with DFens and African-Americans and this is to do with the way that blackness provokes both an immediate, affective response, and operates as a site of authenticity and the real in the white cultural imagination. Judith Butler argues that there is a 'racist disposition of the visible' around images of the bodies of African-American males.[49] In the paranoia of the white cultural imagination images of male black bodies are experienced with a sense of immanent and immediate danger and violence by white viewers. Part of the success of the widespread 'True-Crime' shows such as *Cops* (which is referred to directly in *Falling Down*) were the predominant images of black men suspected of being the perpetrators of violent crime. What is striking about these programmes is that very rarely does any violence occur - except in the staged reconstructions - but they still provide a visceral thrill through the immediacy white viewers experience when faced with the imagined violence of black bodies. Immediacy and viscerality becomes associated with authenticity, the real and blackness.

As Mike Davies notes in relation to Los Angeles, black violence had replaced the Red Menace as the 'satanic other' of white middle-class ideology - both before 9/11 and the increasingly visible 'other' of the Hispanic.[50] But in *Falling Down* DFens' association with blackness is more than just an othering, and is closer to what Toni Morrison calls American Africanism. Morrison argues that 'a real or fabricated presence' of African-American culture was crucial to the formation of American white cultural identity and the white cultural imagination.[51] Two crucial aspects of this American Africanism involved the construction of African American culture as both a primitive savagery and as a sign of urban modernity and hip. In the next two chapters I will be exploring in some detail the way that New Black Realism has been consumed by the white culture in terms of both of these aspects of American Africanism. Indeed *Boyz N the Hood* and *Menace II Society* have been discussed in terms of their immediacy by both journalistic and academic critics. This is despite the fact that both of these films use cinematic structures which Deleuze would equate with both the action-image and the crisis of the action-image. Despite the cultural familiarity of these kind of films, New Black Realism has been described as a genre which is raw and savage and assaults the senses first.[52] It is this immediacy which *Falling Down* seeks to appropriate and which forms the film's own attempts to reanimate the affective links between Hollywood action film and the audience.

Yet, while it seeks to appropriate the immediacy and affect which the white cultural imagination associates with African-American culture, *Falling Down* also seeks to depoliticise black rage and primitivise it. This is made clear if we look more closely at the detail of the encounters that DFens has with the African Americans in the film. The two black children that he meets are the closest that DFens gets to an encounter with hip-hop culture. The dress and attitude of the kid who helps him launch the grenade is particularly reminiscent of the gangstas who inhabit the 'hood in *Boyz N the Hood* and *Menace II Society*. He is knowledgeable in a 'streetwise' fashion about the weapon DFens is carrying having learnt how to use it from watching TV and films. The scene where the black kid in the burger joint is the only one who can tell the difference between the image and the reality of the burger that DFens purchases also evokes the association between blackness, authenticity and the real. But the fact that it is only black children that can bond with DFens on his violent rampage negates the political causes behind black rage. If, as Schumacher claims, DFens is the white version of the angry black man and his representations in the 'hood films, then the link between him and black children who know about guns seems to suggest a certain primitivism and naivety both in the 'real-life' violence of black rage and the images of black anger on screen. This association of black rage and naivety is even stronger in the scene featuring the placard-waving, 'non-economically viable' demonstrator outside of the bank. The black individual cuts a pitiful figure, displaying the same kind of naive understanding of the 'real' contemporary world as DFens, as he takes on the might of a corporate America backed up by the institutional forces of law and order. At this stage this anger and the kind that DFens displays are not condemned outright by the film, but it is the point that the film begins to draw back from the visceral immediate pleasures that the film initially offers in the reanimation of the action-image.

The Last Classic Spectator

The second position that the film actively encourages the viewer to take is one of cultural nostalgia, and it is where the film also accepts that the crisis of the action-image is a terminal state. The figure of the sole black demonstrator evokes memories of the collective black political action found in the civil rights actions of the 1950s and 60s. By displaying this figure as a sole individual taking futile action, the film suggests that this kind of action is no longer possible in 1990s' Los Angeles. In the same way DFens is also shown to belong to another era. In the first instance the viewer is encouraged to read DFens as a victim and product of 1990s' America - 'the seemingly ordinary man who's worked hard all his life, who's been a law-abiding citizen, who snaps suddenly'. His initial appearance can be read to signify his ordinariness with his unfashionable 'buzz-cut' hairstyle, horn-rimmed, large-lensed glasses, and overweight body, clothed in a 'working-stiff's' white shirt and tie. But as the film goes on it becomes clear that this appearance is less a signifier for his 1990s' banality, and more a marker for ideologies and actions that have their place in another era - particularly the 1950s. His clothing becomes not so much a sign for his 'ordinariness', but one which marks him as the retro-conformist. He would not look out of place as the patriarch in one of the many ephemeral films produced by the state department in the 1950s and which presented moral propaganda on the way 'decent' American families should live.[53] The ideological thrust of DFens' action and words signal him as a figure from the past, and particularly as someone who would be more at home in the post-war years up to the mid-sixties. His desire to roll back prices to pre-1965 levels in the Korean shop signal this almost at the outset of the movie, and the emphasis placed on his role in helping to 'protect America' by building missiles and the yearning for comfortable suburban existence with patriarchal small-town values as ideological cornerstones make DFens the perfect Eisenhower subject.

The renewal of populism and the jeremiad found in *film noir* and other films of the action-image were already part of a cultural nostalgia, and DFens himself reminds us of the *noir* hero, battling his way through a world that seems stacked against him. He is even more reminiscent of the noirish nightmare sequence in *It's a Wonderful Life* where George Bailey is transported to a Bedford Falls community where he never existed - as well as the more obvious comparisons with Travis Bickle. Consequently he is not recognised by the milieu in which he has formerly played such a vital part through his enacting of the American Dream, and where he consequently becomes anachronistic in the face of the big business which has taken over. The analogies with DFens' are clear here as he travels around communities and milieus which do not recognise him.

But having made this point, the nostalgia created around the figure of DFens is less for a 40s and 50s Hollywood hero than for the people who it is nostalgically imagined were watching these films at the time of their making. Fredric Jameson argues that US nostalgia for the 1950s is produced predominantly through that period's representation of itself - as opposed to 'deeper realities of the period'.[54] He argues that it is those 'TV series - living-room comedies, single-family homes menaced by *The Twilight Zone*, on the one hand, and gangsters and escaped convicts from the outside world, on the other - that give us the content of our positive image of the fifties in the first place'.[55] The significance of the cultural representation of the fifties, produced through the period's own mass cultural representations of itself, is complex in considering DFens. DFens can be read as a figure of the fifties, but at the same time he must also be read as a representation of that period's own representations. The recognition of this double-construction of DFens (who in this light is doubly-removed from any idea of contemporary immediacy and authenticity) contributes towards a distanciation in the relationship between the viewer and his actions.

But the fascination with DFens remains because of the nostalgia for, and fascination with, those 'classic' spectators who 1990's viewers imagined watched the images of the fifties with a degree of affective response and belief - and who exist only because of the 1950s' representation of itself. Slavoj Zizek argues that our contemporary nostalgia for classic *film noir* is predominantly based on an enchantment with those people we believe to have watched these films when they were first released:

It is clear that we can no longer identify with it [classic noir]. The most dramatic scenes from Casablanca, Murder, My Sweet, *or* Out of the Past *provoke laughter today among spectators, but nevertheless, far from posing a threat to the genre's power of fascination, this kind of distance is its very condition. That is to say, what fascinates us is precisely a certain gaze, the gaze of the 'other', of the hypothetical, mythic spectator from the 40s who was supposedly still able to identify immediately with the universe of film noir. What we really see, when we watch a* film noir, *is this gaze of the other: we are fascinated by the gaze of the mythic 'naïve' spectator, the one who was 'still able to take it seriously', in other words, the 'one who believes in it' for us, in place of us. For that reason, our relation to a film noir is always divided, split between fascination and ironic distance: ironic distance towards its diegetic reality, fascination with the gaze.*[56]

Thus, according to Zizek, the belief in the filmic world, which 1970s' film theory assumed of its ideal spectator, is no longer at the basis of the cinematic experience. Because we, as contemporary viewers, cannot believe in, or be affected by, the situations, actions, and individuals of the action-image, we form a nostalgic fascination for those who supposedly could. Zizek's theory, like that of the 1970s, presupposes an ideal spectator, except that instead of the spectator who does not know enough (about the workings and contradictions of ideology), in this case the spectator knows too much and yearns for a 'lost innocence' - before the contemporary viewer's wide-scale knowledge of Hollywood cinema and its formulas created a postmodern self-reflexivity.

The film encourages our fascination with DFens in this light because he is ultimately constructed as the last of these 'classic spectators' of the 1950s, transported to a world where what he takes seriously is regarded as anachronistic by the milieux he encounters. After his initial status as a protagonist whose actions and frustrations evoke a spontaneous identification in the viewer, DFens becomes a viewer who cannot believe the world around him refuses to recognise him. He still believes that the city he wanders through is an enclosed totality which will recognise and modify itself according to his actions. He still believes that he forms an important part of the community and the nation, even though it is clear to the viewer that these beliefs are no longer tenable. DFens is like Truman in *The Truman Show* (Weir 1998) where the world which the protagonist inhabits is a very different place to the one he thinks it to be - or believes it should be. This is why DFens tells Prendergast at the film's end, to 'Take a look at this town. That's sick'. He is the last classic spectator who cannot believe that his illusions have fallen down.

The Truman Show differs from *Falling Down* in the sense that our identification is supposed to remain with Truman, whereas the nostalgia for DFens, the action-image, and the American Dream which the film initially reanimates is blown apart as *Falling Down* progresses. This is where we need to discuss the third and final viewing position of the film which seeks to place the viewer in a position of all-seeing knowledge of 1990s' urban existence. It is important to realise that the immediate bodily connection of the first viewing position and the cultural nostalgia evoked by the second viewing position are not easily distinguishable or clear-cut during the first half of the film's action. Indeed blurring the boundaries between affect and nostalgia is important to the way that the film works towards its final, monolithic, viewing position. The film encourages a viewing position where the viewer must experience both the immediate impact of DFens' actions and the nostalgic distancing of those actions in order to achieve the complete knowledge that the film makes a necessary precondition to perceive what it prescribes as the final true reality. We can analyze this final position by exploring the ways in which the first two are broken down.

There are several points in *Falling Down* where DFens and his status as the last classic spectator are registered as kind of cultural psychosis. More importantly these are also the places where the film signals to the viewer that belief in DFens and his actions, and identification through nostalgia are kinds of false consciousness. At the outset of his encounter with the neo-Nazi shopkeeper identification with the nostalgic gaze of DFens is at its strongest. As DFens is shown around the backroom of the shop and the shopkeeper begins his racist rantings, the camera's view becomes that of DFens as it scans around to discover the Nazi literature, uniforms and other paraphernalia. This identification becomes even stronger when DFens tells the Nazi that 'I am not the same as you', begins a monologue about the freedom of speech in America, and becomes victim to the Nazi's violent assault. What follows is a series of close-up shot-reverse shots between the leering Nazi, bent over behind DFens, repeating the words 'give it to me', and the latter, fumbling around for the switchblade knife in his pocket. The cumulative effect of this action on the viewer is the desire to see the Nazi stabbed by DFens.

But as the scene moves on, the viewer is forced to confront the nature of this desire, in a twist of identification which is analogous to a key scene in *Psycho* (Hitchcock 1960), analyzed by Slavoj Zizek. Zizek starts from the Metzian assumption that, before identifying 'with persons from diegetic reality, the viewer identifies with him or herself as pure gaze'.[57] He goes on to argue that in the scene in *Psycho* where Norman Bates has pushed the car containing Marion Crane's body into the swamp, 'the viewer is forced to face the desire at work in his or her seemingly neutral gaze'. When the car stops sinking, the camera moves to Norman's face and the viewer is suddenly reminded that 'his/her gaze is identical to Norman's'.[58] The viewer has a traumatic realisation that she or he has been identifying with the psychotic which, in the Lacanian/Zizekian revision of Freud, is outside of the limits of Symbolic reality. Like the scene in *Psycho*, there is a stage in DFens' encounter with the Nazi where the viewer becomes aware that they have been identifying with the psychotic. DFens, whilst still espousing good Americanisms such as 'freedom of religion', unnecessarily kills the Nazi with a pistol - unnecessarily in terms of the logic of the action since the Nazi is already fatally incapacitated with a knife sticking out of his shoulder. The fact that DFens has finally 'cracked' is signposted when, after killing the Nazi, he shoots the mirror reflecting himself, shattering and fracturing both his and the viewer's gaze. Because of the complexity of the relations of viewing DFens the significance of this recognition is not in regarding DFens as an individualized madman, but in seeing the nostalgia he bears for the mythical TV America of the 1950s as psychotic. If the viewer recognises DFens as emblematic of fifties ideology and culture (as film encourages), then his psychosis must be read as more than a matter of the 'sick' individual in the sense that it is the nostalgia for that period which comes to be signalled as a kind of collective cultural psychosis. In the film's ultimate schema of realism, any attempt to renew the jeremiad and a populism which sees the individual as capable of taking direct action against the 'system' becomes as removed from reality as psychosis. The film also attempts to associate the nostalgic desire to see this fight against the system played out on screen with a state of delusion. The film seems to say that for the viewer to indulge in such a nostalgic viewing position is to see the world through a fractured deranged vision which, in an even more obvious display of symbolism than the shooting of the mirror, is signalled through the cracked lenses on DFens' glasses after his encounter with the Nazi.

Confirmation that DFens is deranged happens towards the end of the film when he begins to watch a video of one of his daughter's birthdays. Like DFens' discourses of his idyllic family life, the video starts by painting a rosy nostalgic picture of the event. But then, in a manner analogous to the shift away from the nostalgic mode in the scene with the neo-Nazi, the viewer is presented with a picture of DFens as abusive husband and father, as his wife and daughter refuse to fit into his (literal and metaphoric) picture of family behaviour. There are several interesting points to note in this video revelation. The appearance of DFens in the video is marked in its contemporary banality. As opposed to the retro-figure he appears as in the rest of the film, here he looks like Michael Douglas normally does in all the victim-hero films I mentioned above. His hair is middle-class executive length and gone are the fifties large-framed spectacles. In one sense this reinforces the idea of nostalgia for the fifties as a cultural psychosis. Despite the warnings that family life in the video is not in a state of harmonious balance, the appearance of DFens in the video signifies him as more 'normal' in contemporary terms, and the subsequent change in his appearance as the kind of regression associated with psychosis.

The fact that it is a video that captures DFens (in his pre-psychotic state) within the film reinforces the gap between 1990s' reality and nostalgic psychosis that the film evokes. Chris Darke argues that video images go a stage further than film in producing realism in the mechanical reproduction of the world. Both Darke and Bellour argue that, after photography which produced 'the first image to be invested with a "quantity of analogy"', and cinema which added 'the analogy of movement', video 'supplements' this with 'a new analogy, that of the image without any delay':

> *As a simultaneously degraded and clinical presence within the well-mastered film image, the video image has come to replace the grain of 8mm and newsreel with its own zero-degree realism. That (film) was then, this (video) is now.*[59]

If film is then and video is now, the film uses the video of DFens at home with his family to suggest that this figure was more in tune with the 'now' of reality, and that the figure we have been following for most of the film's action is again displayed as belonging to another, past, time - because of the formal qualities of the narrative film that this figure is situated in. The irony here is that the video, in the logic of the film's plot, was shot before the action we have been caught up in.

Cynical Realism

This breaking down of the nostalgia around DFens is a prerequisite for the emergence of the film's final and dominant viewing position. This final position is what the film prescribes as the final true reality of 1990s' urban existence. It encourages the viewer to accept this 'truth' by shifting the viewer's identification from the nostalgia and psychosis of DFens to the pragmatic figure of Prendergast. In many ways Prendergast is directly comparable to DFens. Like DFens, he is portrayed as a similar average white male, suffering from the metaphorical castrations of the contemporary world. He too is no longer a father, is harassed by his overbearing wife, and is about to retire from work where he is treated with contempt by his boss and most of his colleagues. The connections with the 1950s are also apparent in his domestic set-up. His wife was a former small-town beauty queen who lost her looks because she had a child that was wanted more by him than her. The fact that this wife is played by Tuesday Weld, who starred in many late 50s' and early 60s' feelgood movies as the small-town beautiful 'girl next door', adds to the symbolism.[60] The film makes it clear that Prendergast is the alternative locus of identification to DFens - almost to the exact moment when the viewer's shift is supposed to take place. After DFens shoots the mirror-image of himself, the film immediately switches to a shot of Prendergast, arguing with his boss in the men's room, in front of a mirror, producing a Chinese-box effect, and making the image of Prendergast appear to stretch back to that of DFens. From this moment Prendergast assumes the role of action-taker in his quest to find DFens, and eventually confront him. But because of the way the film has shifted both traditional and nostalgic expectations of the relations between the viewer and the hero, Prendergast cannot be articulated in either of these modes.

Instead, Prendergast's situation within the diegesis is analogous to the final viewing position. Prendergast is the only character who recognises and 'knows' DFens as the relic of the past the film ultimately portrays him as. Prendergast is the only one who can see the pattern in DFens' actions, signified in the way the former can plot the latter's next move on the office map of LA. Like the final viewing position, Prendergast 'sees' things as they really are, eschewing the naivety of the action-image hero and the psychotic dangers of nostalgia. Instead he admonishes DFens for his struggle against the imaginary 'they' of the system: 'you're mad because they lied to you? They lie to everybody! They even lie to the fish!' Prendergast is not a naïve classic spectator who still believes that individuals can still modify milieux and maintain the American Dream through individual action. Instead Prendergast believes that actions are always individualised and local rather than global and encompassing. He accepts that his contemporary urban existence is one of anarchy, chaos and fragmentation on the ground while not fundamentally challenging the 'they' who have lied to those people about the death of the American Dream. Prendergast 'knows the score' in the sense that he realises and accepts that, behind official declarations of the healthiness of the American Dream from the institutionalised powers that run the US, the individual's ties to the community are no longer strong enough to maintain that dream as a reality.

Prendergast's philosophy is a mixture of individualized pragmatism, and what Slavoj Zizek and Peter Sloterdijk have termed 'cynical reason'.[61] Zizek notes that,

> *The formula as proposed by Sloterdijk would be 'they know very well what they are doing, but still they are doing it'. Cynical reason is no longer naïve, but is a paradox of an enlightened false consciousness: one knows the falsehood very well, one is well aware of a particular interest hidden behind an ideological universality, but still one does not renounce it.*[62]

The film's political and philosophical position is the same as Prendergast's because of the way it breaks down DFens and his actions as both a site of immediate, affective identification and as site of cultural nostalgia. Prendergast's position is made the only viable choice. Consequently he is seen as more 'real' than DFens - and the extreme position to the right of DFens found in the fantastical character of the neo-Nazi. Consequently the fragmented, violent and banal LA which DFens moves through is also seen as authentic and the real, because it also misrecognises DFens. But it is only Prendergast who has the knowledge to recognise both the milieux of the film and DFens. Consequently it is only through him that the viewer can gain access to the full knowledge and the cynical reality that the film has to offer has to offer as 'truth'. The film, like the cinema of the action-image, still bases its realism on the actions of an individual, but that individual no longer believes in the 'illusions' of the American Dream, and at the same time will not renounce the institutions which still produce the ideological universality of the Dream.

The film belongs to a cinema of cynical realism. Its acceptance of the corruptness of the American Dream enables it to let Prendergast keep many of the attributes of the action-image protagonist but with degree of contingency. It is no longer possible for any one individual to have a completely decisive affect on a unified and global milieu, but it is still possible for many of the characteristics of the cinema of the action-image without the total belief in them that the classical spectator was imagined to have. Belief is tempered by knowledge, but this is not a knowledge that threatens the aesthetic structures and affective power of the action-image. Rather it is a knowledge which allows this cinema to perpetuate itself.

Cynical Realism and the 'hood' Film

The consequences of *Falling Down's* philosophy are complex in the extreme, and needs to be thought through in terms of both its cinematic and political significance. On one level it is clear that *Falling Down* attempted to regenerate a Hollywood action cinema which cannot be categorized in the same way as either the Hollywood blockbuster or the kind of thriller that has been called neo-*noir*. Miriam Hansen notes that the blockbuster film no longer attempts:

> to homogenize empirically diverse viewers by way of unifying strategies of spectator positioning (as 1970s film theorists claimed with regard to classical films). Rather the blockbuster gamble consists of offering something to everyone, of appealing to diverse interests with a diversity of attractions and multiple levels of textuality. All this is not to say that the classical mode of spectatorship has vanished without a trace, on the contrary, it makes powerful returns in the nostalgia mode. But it becomes one of a number of options, often contextualised and ironised, and no longer functions as the totalitarian norm it is supposed to have been during the 1930s and 1940s.[63]

Hansen's comments are similar to the 'Deleuzian' reading of the action-image and the blockbuster outlined above - despite the residual notions of 'spectatorship'. Clearly the blockbuster belongs to the tradition of action-image cinema, but at the same time it is generally self-reflexive enough in films like *Total Recall* and *Die Hard* to realise that this cinema can no longer provide the same kind of affective connections and belief that it is once believed to have done. Individuals and situations are inflated to the point where they implode. The viewer can either go along for the spectacular ride that these films provide visually or maintain a distance produced by nostalgia for the imagined impact of classic action-image cinema.

Falling Down displays a kind of realism, which is distinct from the immediacy of cinema that produces the classic spectatorial position, and also the distanciated pleasures of the Hollywood blockbuster cinema. The film sets up various positions from which to view DFens and the film. But these positions are not 'options' in the same sense as Miriam Hansen identifies as symptomatic of the blockbuster. The fluidity of agency, which Hansen's reading of the blockbuster implies, is absent in *Falling Down*. In other words, on one level the film appears to be knowing and self-reflexive in the postmodern sense, but it actually produces a more monolithic viewing position than that which was imagined to be the case with Hollywood film of the 1940s and 1950s. The cynical reason and realism of the film becomes the overriding ideology and affect that the film produces.

But this cynical realism is produced in direct competition with the affect and immediacy that 1990s' African-American film produced in the white cultural imagination. The film appropriates what it sees as the affective power of African-American culture, but then dismisses such immediacy as primitive and childlike. *Falling Down* is an attempt to be 'smarter' than the new Black Realism, by breaking down the heroic status of its angry violent man, and turning him into a regressive psychotic. The association of DFens with black culture and black rage means that his naivety is directly comparable to that displayed in New Black Realism. Anger and violence is made the equivalent of regressive nostalgic psychosis, and it is only those on the side of the law, like Prendergast, who have developed beyond these 'childish' responses to their situation. In many ways DFens is the 1990's equivalent of Norman Mailer's 'White Negro' - except that, whereas Mailer's surrogate Black man was exalted for his regression, DFens is ultimately broken down. DFens in all his retro-conformity is the 'anti-hipster'.[64]

The film's connection between DFens and the 'hood film fails to understand the specific cultural, historical, political and aesthetic moves that New Black Realism made. As we shall see in the next two chapters, these films are highly complex in their strategic play with the immediacy, affect and paranoia which images of black bodies produce in the white cultural imagination. *Boyz N the Hood* and *Menace II Society* both reveal the American Africanism and racial rage which lies at the heart of the US white cultural imagination's perception of white cultural identity. These films suggest that that the very attributes which are used to other African-American culture both constitute, and are desired by,

Notes

1. Joel Schumacher, director of *Falling Down*, interviewed in Fuller, *Interview* 23 (1993: 112).

2. Clover, *Sight and Sound* 3 (1993: 6).

3. *ibid.* (6-9).

4. Doherty, *Cineaste* 20 (1993: 39).

5. Throughout this book I will be using the term milieu or milieux in the Deleuzian sense. A milieu is the particular space-time of the film in which the character acts - in other words, the particular world or community of the film. Milieu is also a philosophical term that Deleuze uses frequently in other work, most notably in his collaborations with Felix Guattari. Brian Massumi

argues that, 'in French, milieu means 'surroundings', 'medium', and 'middle'. In the philosophy of Deleuze and Guattari, 'milieu' should be read as a technical term combining all three meanings'. (Deleuze 1987: XVII). In this chapter, I am using milieu to suggest a space in the film which takes into account the ideologies of subjects present within the *mise en scène*, and which are recognisable as subject positions and thought in the extradiegetic world.

6. Mulvey in Easthope ed. (1993: 117).

7. *ibid.*

8. There many critiques of Mulvey's essay, but for the most useful summaries see Clover (1991), Shaviro (1993) and Fuery (2000).

9. See Davis & Smith eds. (1997: 31-8) for a discussion of *Falling Down* as an example of identity politics for white males.

10. Watts, *Women: A Cultural Review* 6 (1995: 282).

11. *ibid.*

12. This is a term coined by Susan Faludi to describe a growing number of cultural productions in the West which react against feminist discourse and politics. See Faludi (1991).

13. Deleuze (1986: 187-217).

14. Deleuze argues that there were five 'great genres' of the cinema of the action-image, including the American comedy, the 'psycho-social' film, *film noir*, the Western, and the 'historical epic'. (1986: 141-159). Musicals are the major omission in this list, and are an exception to the structural rules of action that Deleuze describes in relation to the action image. He does however explore the musicals of Vincente Minnelli in relation to the time-image in Deleuze (1989: 61-4).

15. Deleuze (1986: 141).

16. *ibid.* (141-2).

17. *ibid.*

18. The connection between belief and affect is vital for Deleuze in defining the ontological specificity of the cinema: 'It is clear from the outset that cinema had a special relationship with belief'. Deleuze (1989: 171).

19. Deleuze sets out the fragility of the relation between the milieu and the individual in the following passage:

    On the one hand, the 'milieu' is a false community, in fact a jungle where every alliance is precarious and reversible; on the other hand, the modes of behaviour, however studied they are, are not true habits, true responses to situations, but conceal a fault or cracks which cause them to disintegrate. ibid. (145).

    In contemporary studies of masculinity and *noir*, such as Krutnik (1991), the relation between the community and the authority of the individual is also at its most fragile in *noir* in because the individual frequently transgresses the established law of the milieu. Krutnik argues that many of the 'tough thrillers' of the Classic Hollywood era suggested a pre-contemporary feminist 'crisis of confidence' in the authority of masculine patriarchy, which foreshadows the crisis which is implicit in the Michael Douglas 'backlash' films mentioned above. The sub-genre to which *Falling Down* is most closely related is that which Krutnik calls the 'criminal-adventure thriller'. See (136-164) for an analysis of this type of *noir*.

20. Burch (1981: 124).

21. Deleuze (1986: 158).

22. *ibid.* (206).

23. *ibid.*

24. *ibid.*

25. *ibid.* (210).

26. *ibid.* (207).

27. *ibid.*

28. *ibid.*

29. *ibid.* (208).

30. This reading is most clearly enunciated by Stern (1995: 32-68). I shall be exploring her analysis in more detail in Chapter 3 in relation to *Menace II Society* (Hughes 1993).

31. Deleuze (1986: 211).

32. As Fredric Jameson famously notes:

    Pastiche is, like parody, the imitation of a...style, the wearing of a linguistic mask, speech in a dead language. But it is a neutral practice of such mimicry, without any of parody's ulterior motives, amputated of the satiric impulse, devoid of laughter and of any conviction that alongside the abnormal tongue you have momentarily borrowed, some healthy normality still exists. Jameson (1991: 17).

33. See Tasker (1993) for an account that engages with the gender politics of this new hyper-bodied protagonist.

34. Leo Charney notes this tendency in his essay 'The Violence of a Perfect Moment' in Slocum ed. (2001: 47-62). Charney quotes Joel Silver's (the producer of many contemporary action blockbusters) attitude towards action and spectacle. Silver states that 'The rule of thumb is that in every reel of a movie - that means basically every ten minutes - if you're making an action movie, every ten minutes you must have an action beat. Something dramatic and jolting must happen' (48).

35. Deleuze (1986: 215).

36. The journey of DFens through Los Angeles is also similar to Burt Lancaster's journey through various swimming pools and gardens in *The Swimmer* (Perry & Pollack 1968).

37. Schumacher interviewed by Salisbury, *Empire* 49 (1993: 77).

38. Douglas interviewed by Fuller, *Interview* 23 (1993: 113).

39. Clover, *Sight and Sound* 3 (1993: 18).

40. *ibid.*

41. Vernet in Copjec ed. (1993: 18-19).

42. *ibid.* (19).

43. *ibid.*

44. Hooks (1994: 44).

45. Diawara in Copjec ed. (1993: 261).

46. *ibid.* (264). Diawara mainly uses the literary example of Chester Himes' *Harlem* novels to illustrate his point. But the presence of black rage has been detectable in other literary examples - most notably Richard Wright's Bigger Thomas character in *Native Son*, (1940) and in the character of Bob Jones in Himes' novel *If He Hollers Let Him Go* (1945).

47. *ibid.* (266).

48. Schumacher interviewed by Fuller, *Empire* 49 (1993: 77).

49. Butler (1993: 18).

50. Davies (1990: 263).

51. Morrison (1993: 6).

52. See the next chapter for references.

53. See Prelinger (1992).

54. Given his Marxist approach, the deeper realities for Jameson are unsurprisingly economic. See Jameson (1991: 281).

55. *ibid.* (280).

56. Zizek (1991: 112).

57. Zizek in Zizek ed. (1992: 223).

58. *ibid.*

59. Darke, *Sight and Sound* 3 (1993: 27).

60. Such movies include *Rock, Rock, Rock* (Price 1960) and *Rally Round the Flag Boys* (McCarey 1958).

61. The term 'cynical reason' is originally coined in Sloterdijk (1983).

62. Zizek (1989: 29).

63. Hansen, *Screen* 34 (1993: 213).

64. Mailer (1968: 199).

Chapter Two

Gangsters and Gangstas:
Boyz N the Hood, and the Dangerous Black Body

If movies have the capacity for incarnation and disembodiment, the capacity to bring worlds into being, to engender bodies and transubstantiate matter, the question is...: what are the connections between those worlds willed into cinematic being, and other worlds, histories, social milieus?[1]

In the last chapter we looked at the way *Falling Down* attempted to break with the distanciated self-reflexivity of the postmodern blockbuster. One of the means through which it tried to achieve this shift was the appropriation of the affect which is provoked in the white cultural imagination by African-American culture and images of black masculinity in particular. I argued that the film is playing off the cinematic genre of New Black Realism, and the way that the reception of these films has been constructed in terms of their authenticity and immediacy.[2] But *Falling Down* also attempts to position the affective power of black cinema within a structure of knowing cynical realism. The film portends to 'show things as they really are' which means that it has to provide a global and encompassing vision which can account for the city of fragmented milieus and conflicts which form the locations of DFen's journey.[3] I described this vision as shaped by a kind of cynical reasoning, where the breakdown of the ideology of the American Dream and its cinema of the action-image was made apparent, but where the process of reproducing this ideology was allowed to continue without resistance. This continuation took the limited form of Prendergast's limited and contingent restoration of the (white male) individual's ability to act and modify the milieux he encounters. By the end of the film he has solved the 'mystery' of DFens' odyssey, reasserted his authority over his nagging wife, and subverted his boss's authority in front of the media, telling him 'Fuck you very much' on camera. The film uses cynical reason to reclaim for itself a greater degree of authenticity and cultural authority than that which New Black Realism has generated. But I also argued that this cynical realism is based on a misrecognition and denial of the impact of African-American cinema's reanimation of Hollywood action cinema and the sophisticated moves that it makes in assaulting the senses of the white cultural imagination.

This chapter will investigate the basis of New Black Realism's significance in the production of 1990s' action-cinema by analysing the complex processes of immediacy and distanciation bound up in the aesthetic structures and the critical reception that surrounded one film, *Boyz N the Hood* (Singleton 1992). There have been many films which could be said to fall under the label of New Black Realism, but *Boyz N the Hood* is generally recognized as being the first example of the West Coast-based wave of New Black Realism, both in its specific setting of the action in South Central Los Angeles, and in its financing.[4] In addition *Boyz N the Hood* provides the best starting point for a comparison with the very different New Black Realist film, *Menace II Society* (Hughes 1993), which will be explored in more detail in the next chapter. But *Boyz* also generated very specific fears and paranoia at the time of its release, and it is by investigating this affective response to the film that we can explore why New Black Realism, and the 'hood film in particular, has been constructed by the white cultural imagination as a Hollywood genre which is both immediate and authentic.[5] The ways in which *Falling Down* and the other new-brutality films of this book have attempted to imitate the immediacy of African-American film and culture is under question here. These films attempted to produce concrete and affective connections between their cinematic bodies and worlds, and 'other worlds, histories and social milieux', by appropriating or miming the responses provoked by the 'hood film in particular. Consequently we need to explore the basis of this affect in order to understand the different ways in which the white new-brutality film differentiates itself from the postmodern blockbuster.

Boyz N the Hood evoked at least three different responses in the white cultural imagination and a close look at these will go some way towards providing an analysis of the impact which new Black Realism had on the new-brutality. The first of these reactions is the initial shock provoked on the film's release, something which can be partially accounted in the immediate anxieties and paranoia historically produced in the white cultural imagination by images of 'dangerous' black bodies. The second response to the film is almost exactly the opposite of the first. *Boyz N the Hood* very quickly became a 'safe' film for white audiences in the sense that it became a kind of social document which white audiences felt gave them an insight into what black life was really like in the ghetto. But this second response of familiarity and comfort masks the way that *Boyz* invaded, 'contaminated and transformed what were previously predominantly white cinematic spaces. It is this cultural impact which had arguably the strongest influence on the white new-brutality film.[6]

'Look, a Negro' (and On Screen)

Boyz N the Hood tended to arouse sensations of immediacy before it was even released, and one of the predominant instant responses to the film centred on its marketing strategies, and specifically its trailer. Many commentators condemned the film on the basis of the trailer because they felt that it would provoke black audiences into acts of 'copycat' violence. Ed Guerrero notes this paranoia:

> *Some critics were quick to assert that Boyz raised the expectation of violence among*
> *its volatile youth audience, pointing out that the advertising trailer managed to*

include every instance of gunplay in the film, rather than emphasize its anti-violence message, or the father-son relationship at the film's moral centre.[7]

Gene Siskel's reaction was typical of this dualistic response. Within the same paragraph this influential mainstream critic attacked the trailer on the basis of its images of violence, and praised the film itself for its anti-violence message:

> *If you look at the trailer you would think that the movie was strictly about gang action. I had heard a lot about the film in Cannes and then saw the trailer, and thought 'this looks like trash'. But then I saw the movie and thought it superb and very clearly anti-violence and very pro taking responsibility for one's children and brothers and sisters. The people that perpetrated the violence are most responsible, but there must be a way to send a message that this is a different kind of picture than a rock'em, sock'em gangbanger picture.*[8]

Responding to the criticism of the trailer, John Singleton, the film's director, (and editor of the trailer) defended the promotional campaign on the grounds that *Boyz* was a Hollywood product, arguing that '(the trailer) got the motherfuckers into the theatre and that's the bottom line. If the trailer for *Terminator II* showed the part where he agreed not to kill anyone, nobody would have gone to see it'.[9] *The Hollywood Reporter* did report several cases of violence at the film's first showings around the US. Unsurprisingly, the fact that several cinema venues had taken out extra security measures, such as close circuit cameras and extra security staff (details that were reported in the same publication three days earlier), was not cited as a provocative factor contributing to this violence.[10] The question we need to ask is the one suggested by Singleton's defence of the trailer: Why was this trailer specifically targeted for criticism and why was this criticism marked by paranoia about the reaction of the film's potential black audience? The trailer for *Boyz* was comparable to the trailers for any other Hollywood action film in that it showed virtually all of the film's climactic scenes of dramatic intensity and violence. Yet, as Singleton implies, there were no similar documented security precautions taken at cinemas for the release of *Terminator II* (Cameron 1991).

In the first instance the answer to this question can be found by considering the way African-American people are constructed and experienced by the white cultural imagination in terms of an immediate paranoia about black violence. In a famous passage Franz Fanon notes the way that black male bodies in particular connote an immediate sense of danger for the white Western subject:

> *In the white world the man of colour encounters difficulties in the development of his bodily schema. Consciousness of the body is solely a negating activity. It is a third-consciousness. The body is surrounded by an atmosphere of certain uncertainty*

'Look a Negro!' It was an external stimulus that flicked over me as I passed by. I made a tight smile.

'Look a Negro!' It was true. It amused me.

I made no secret of my amusement.

'Mama, see the Negro! I'm frightened!' Frightened!

Frightened! Now they were beginning to be afraid of me. I made up my mind to laugh myself to tears, but laughter had become impossible.[11]

Fanon suggests that this perception of the black male as an entity to be scared of is produced by a historical-racial schema where the black body is sketched out by 'the other, the white man, who had woven me out of thousand details, anecdotes, stories'.[12] In other words, the history of the West has produced what Judith Butler calls a 'racial disposition of the visible'.[13]

The significant point, in terms of the question of cinematic affect, is that this historical, schematic racial organization of perception is experienced as something immediate and material by the white cultural imagination. Fanon engages with the way that the black body is 'othered' by white culture and how this in turn affects the psyche of the black male subject. But the construction of the black male body in terms of anarchic violence and authenticity is also interesting in terms of what it reveals about white American identity - or what it was to be American in the late twentieth century. As I noted in the introduction, Toni Morrison argues that there is an American Africanism present in white cultural identity, where not only are African-American people othered in terms of random violence and as a sign of urban modernity, but also these attributes both constitute, and are desired by, the white cultural imagination. This desire is paradoxically expressed in terms of an immediate fear and powerlessness. As Judith Butler notes:

In Fanon's recitation of racist interpellation, the black body is circumscribed as dangerous, prior to any gesture, any raising of the hand, and the infantilised white reader is positioned in the scene as one who is helpless in relation to that black body.[14]

When it comes to the relationship between American Africanism and American cinema of the 1990s, this anxiety, and the denial it reveals, is manifested in very particular ways.

More specifically the release of *Boyz N the Hood* and other examples of New Black realism provoked a fear of black audiences being provoked into 'copycat' violence by images of black violence on screen. Todd Boyd argues that this white anxiety dates in the US back to the 1911 motion picture footage of the African-American boxer fighting white champion Jim Jeffries. The interracial fight, and Johnson's victory in particular, was perceived by white audiences as a spark that would induce other, similar, interracial fight scenes in urban streets.[15] Jane Gaines argues that:

> *In this racialised image phobia we recognise a familiar old assumption about the public as dupes, unable to make a distinction between fiction and 'reality', which takes on a special racial tinge here with the implication that blacks cannot see the difference between motion picture image and events that 'happen' in real historical space and time.*[16]

A similar assumption was made about the potential black audiences of *Boyz N the Hood*, with the condemnation of the trailer and the extra security measures taken at cinemas where it was shown, suggesting that black audiences would be unable to distance themselves from the fictional events that the film portrayed. But, judging from Siskel's comments, the people who were unable to distanciate themselves from the immediacy of the trailer were the white critics who condemned it. They were unable to perceive the trailer in terms of the accepted knowledge between audiences and action film marketing practices, namely that trailers are closely related to a cinema of attractions and designed to assault the senses by bombarding the viewer with as many peaks of the action as possible in a very limited time span. One of the reasons for this is suggested by Jane Gaines when she argues that 'white-middle class talk about violence is smug and self righteous...this talk always fails to make a distinction between actual acts of brutality and representations of them.'[17] This misrecognition is exactly what the white critics of the trailer of *Boyz N the Hood* were accusing its potential black audience of being guilty of. But paradoxically, it was the failure of the critics to make a distinction between the represented violence of the trailer and the imagined violence of the potential audience of the film that was most noticeable in early reviews. This inability to distinguish between two types of violence - represented and 'real' - is partially due to the way that the white cultural imagination fabricates images of black bodies as immanently violent.

The trailer for *Boyz N the Hood* accentuated the immediate impact of the black male body on the white viewer. Trailers in general provide very little in the way of the narrative contextualisation to 'explain' violent images in terms of story, and the trailer for *Boyz* was experienced as dangerous because it filled the screen with all the images of black male violence in the film. This response was initially perpetuated when the film was released in its full form. Critics still discussed the film in terms of its power to assault the senses and body first. Almost all of the reviews stressed, in varying degrees, the 'gritty realism' of the film. *Sight and Sound* declared that '*Boyz N the Hood* is a tough, raw film'[18] while *The Hollywood Reporter* stated that:

> Boyz N the Hood *is a knock-down assault on the senses, a joltingly sad story told with power...No mere studio genre piece...Boyz is straight from the neighbourhood - Singleton grew up in South Central - and straight from the heart.*[19]

The striking aspect of these comments is the emotive and violent physicality of the language used. *Boyz N the Hood* is a film which attacks its spectator, a 'tough, raw' 'assault on the senses' which is stripped by these reviews of any mediating sophistication. Other reviews do speak of the director's skill, but in terms which themselves are always mediated by mentioning the fact that this is a feature from a first-time director, working with a low-budget.[20]

These comments are somewhat surprising because the narrative structure of the film is familiar to any viewer of Hollywood film, and cultural knowledge or habitual perception tends to distanciate any affective impact a narrative film might have. *Boyz N the Hood* is an Oedipal narrative *par excellence*. The story concerns three young African-American males Tre (Cuba Gooding Jr.), Ricki (Morris Chestnut) and Doughboy (Ice Cube) growing up in South Central Los Angeles, over a space of seven years in the 1980s. The narrative revolves around the place of the father in the lives of these three characters, and their fate is decided in terms of whether the father is absent or present. The story focuses particularly on Tre who is sent to live with his father after his mother decides that she cannot be the role model he needs to stay out of trouble. Tre must give up his mother as love object, and aspire to be like his father Furious Styles (Laurence Fishburne) in order to pass through the successful transition from boy to man. That Tre will never quite be like his father is also clear, especially in one particular scene where Furious lays down the law of Tre's new residence, telling him in true Oedipal style (but not without humour) that Tre is 'a prince' but he is 'the King'. In comparison, Ricki and Doughboy are brothers who have different fathers, both of whom have left their mother to bring them up on her own. While Tre does well at school and eventually escapes the ghetto by going to college in Atlanta, both Ricky and Doughboy have been shot dead by the end of the film. For Ricky there is some hope through a football scholarship, but this hope is only fuel for increasing the melodrama that follows when he is shot.[21] Doughboy is shown to make the only life possible for him to survive in the ghetto by dealing drugs and drinking, in between spells in prison. *Boyz N the Hood* is a 'rites of passage' movie which is overt in its Oedipal trajectory and in this sense it brings a world into being which is structurally reminiscent of the most orthodox of Classic Hollywood Realism films as they are defined by 1970s' theory, and also by Gilles Deleuze.[22]

As I noted in the last chapter, Deleuze argues that one of the symptoms of the crisis of the action-image was the inability of the viewer to believe in any one single milieu as a totality or unified world. Moreover, Deleuze argues that it is impossible to believe that any individual could act decisively to alter or modify the cinematic milieu in which he was situated.[23] Therefore the cinema of the crisis of the action-image is full of nomads unconnected to any concrete milieu, and dispersive fragmented situations. Fredric Jameson makes a similar point (from a quite different perspective) when he discusses what he calls 'the post-generic genre film'. He argues that these films are all allegories of each other, and of 'the impossible representation of the social totality itself'.[24] In other words, the point to note about postmodern films of the 1970s and 1980s is that they are difficult to situate in any one particular genre, because generic movies have become less about attempting to represent the extracinematic world, than referencing other movies and depending on what Umberto Eco calls the contemporary filmgoers instinctive semiotic knowledge of other film.[25] This is also true of many pre-postmodern films, but the important point that Jameson is making is that these post-generic films also mix and combine different milieux. There is no unified totalising space in which the characters are fixed as one could argue was the case with genres such as the Western. The post-generic film's space cannot be said to be a direct facsimile of set extra-cinematic spaces. In a film like *Blade Runner* (Scott 1982), we find the science-fiction film, the *film noir*, the conspiracy thriller, and the rites of passage movie all mixed in together. *Blade Runner* cannot be representative of a social totality because it is constantly referring to other genres and therefore other milieux. What this means is that there is very little direct affective or concrete connection between the cinematic world and the extra-cinematic world beyond the experience of fragmentation.

In this sense, *Boyz N the Hood* would seem to be almost anachronistic with its linear Oedipal narrative, and most of all in its story of an individual who is both tied to a single encompassing milieu, and has the power to alter or modify that milieu through individual actions. The 'hood mimes the unified milieu which formed an essential constituent of the action-image cinema. One of the most striking points about *Boyz N the Hood*, is that it creates a shock to the senses within the confines of what 1970s film theory called the Classical Hollywood narrative and the cinematic space that this structure produces. It could be argued that the film is in fact more of a 'genre piece' than the post-generic film which is now the dominant form of white Hollywood action film. *Boyz* creates the sense of creating a unified spatial totality which 1970s' theory argued was the case with Classical Hollywood genre film. The crisis and obstacles which beset Tre and the others do not need to be allegorized as in the majority of Classic Hollywood film - that fathers, action-taking and goals are necessary to a 'successful' conclusion and a state of harmonious balance is made explicit throughout.[26]

It may be because *Boyz N the Hood* has such a conventionally 'classic' narrative structure that the film eventually became 'safe' for white audiences and drew praise for its powerful 'sad' story. Many African-American commentators criticized the film because they felt that the film actually offered a voyeuristic position of authority, rather than assaulting the senses of white audiences and shocking them in a way that might provoke a reassessment of the boundaries of racial identity. The film enables white audiences to peer within the heavily demarcated borders of the 'hood without any fear of what they were seeing spilling over into the equally strongly drawn borders of white culture. Jacquie Jones describes the film as a 'contemporary inner city primer' for those who have had 'the luxury of learning about black-on-black violence or female headed households from the news or government studies'.[27] There are also doubts about the veracity of the representation of reality in the film among the makers of New Black Realism. According to Amy Taubin, the Hughes Brothers were 'outraged by the Hollywood-style sentimentality of *Boyz N the Hood* and made *Menace II Society* in order to 'report what really goes down in the ghetto'.[28] These criticisms of the film as conventionalized 'safe' Hollywood fodder seem to be borne out in Ed Guerrero's point that, during the height of the LA rebellion of 1992, 'responding to escalating tensions, California governor Pete Wilson came to appreciate the film's social import and felt compelled to recommend that all citizens see *Boyz N the Hood*'.[29] As I also noted above, Gene Siskel praises the film for its anti-violence message, after having seen the whole film. In this light it seems that the narrative of the film distanciated audiences because of the contextual meaning and cultural familiarity it provided, and this knowledge-based response was more dominant than any affective or immediate shock the film might have caused through it trailer or on its first release.

Having recognised the validity of some of these criticisms, I think such an assessment of the film underestimates the more subtle affective response that the film produced after the immediate shock evident in its marketing campaign and initial release. Analysing *Boyz N the Hood* in terms of the voyeuristic authority it grants to white viewers does not take into account the effect that these films had on action film of the 1990s. As we have seen in the case of *Falling Down*, New Black Realism became a major cultural influence in the new-brutality action film. It is precisely because *Boyz N the Hood* strategically mimed the spatial and narrative structures of what Deleuze calls the action-image that it and other 'hood films had such an affective impact on the white cultural imagination and 1990s' action cinema. But before investigating this claim the political objectives of the use of cinematic space and narrative in the 'hood film require analysis.

Cinematic Space as Social Politics

In the matter of its influence on white action film, New Black Realism is comparable to the only other black produced and black populated mainstream action film - the short-lived but very influential blaxploitation cinema of the 1970s. Films such as *Sweet Sweetback's Baadasssss Song* (Van Peebles 1971), *Shaft* (Parks Snr. 1971) and *Superfly* (Parks Jnr. 1972) were the first mainstream films to feature violently aggressive black males as action heroes within the context of a contemporary urban *mise en scène*, and the influence of this earlier form of black urban realism is significant in the aesthetics of the 'hood films of the 1990s. The influence of the blaxploitation film can also be detected in many 1970's white action films, such as Martin Scorsese's *Mean Streets* (1973), and even the James Bond film, *Live and Let Die* (Hamilton 1973). This influence proves that Blaxploitation has its own history of mimesis - both in terms of its own imitation of the white gangster film, and the way it was appropriated by white action film. Comparing blaxploitation films, like the *Shaft* series, and 'hood films, like *Boyz N the Hood,* provides some useful clues in detecting the particular influence of the 'hood film on the white cultural and cinematic imagination.

The 'hood films (as the term to describe them might suggest) emphasize the geographical location in which they are set. On a surface level the preoccupation of films like *Boyz N the Hood* and *Menace II Society* with the space of the urban ghetto would seem to point towards these films' drive towards an authenticity and realism. As we have seen, the rhetoric produced by some of the makers of the 'hood films also points towards a concern with the truth of the representation of these urban spaces within narrative film, with the Hughes' Brothers claiming a desire 'to report what really goes down in the ghetto'. Peter Brunette argues that this was also a major consideration behind *Boyz*:

> *What matters to him (Singleton), in the end, is that* Boyz N the Hood *is authentic 'to the brothers and sisters I made the film for. The people on the street. I got the supreme compliments from brothers in Inglewood, Compton, and South Central' (black ghettos in Los Angeles). Singleton says that* Boyz *allows them to see themselves on film and they can reflect upon it.*[30]

Some of this concern with presenting an authentic representation of life in the ghetto was also present in early blaxploitation films, and most notably in the first film to be placed within this genre, *Sweet Sweetback's Baadasssss Song* (Van Peebles 1971). Yet, as the genre moved on, the films focused more on the superhuman powers of their male and female protagonists and less on the realism of the representation of the ghetto. Examples of this shift include Richard Roundtree's James Bond-like performances as Shaft and the various characters played by iconic stars such as Pam Grier and Tamara Dobson in films like *Foxy Brown* (Hill 1974) and *Cleopatra Jones* (Starret 1973). The title of the last Shaft film, *Shaft in Africa* (Guillermin 1973), signals the genre's desire to move out of the ghetto and into more 'exotic' locales - though there is of course a political point being made here as well. New Black Realism on the other hand has resolutely placed the 'hood at the heart of its action throughout its short history.

One of the causes for this is that New Black Realism has remained much more overtly political and much more 'message-orientated' than the blaxploitation film.

This was partly because, as the name suggests, the blaxploitation film was characterized by the way it 'made a fast buck for their often white producers' as much as its cinematic realism, and as a mainstream space which gave black directors and actors a chance to work.[31] New Black Realism, although often financed by Hollywood studios as well as independent money, has openly and consistently engaged with social realities present in the specific locale of the urban ghetto.[32] Ed Guerrero argues that the genre has been allowed to remain at the level of the overtly political, and within the particular space of the 'hood, because films like *Boyz N the Hood* have 'fulfilled Hollywood's low-budget, high-profit black production formula'.[33] In other words, films like *Boyz* were permitted to stay in the 'hood because they sold.

On the other hand, this commercial success of *Boyz* conventional narrative allows the makers of New Black realism to utilize the 'hood as a space to express the political meanings at the heart of the films. As Guerrero suggests, the 'hood films have managed to articulate a 'black sensibility' through 'mastering the master's form'.[34] We can explore this mimesis in more detail by comparing the connections between space and narrative in the action-image. Classical Hollywood cinema, where linear narratives are most apparent, was seen by 1970s' film theory as limiting the spatial potential of film. Renaissance space was, according to Laura Mulvey among others, coded as male and therefore privileged. The narrative actions of male protagonists were inextricably linked to their command of the space of the film. This attempt at control, like the normalizing tendencies of the Oedipal trajectory, were naturalized and constituted Hollywood realism. Fredric Jameson notes the connection between narrative and cinematic space (in a different context) when he writes:

> a good deal of the film theory we classically associate with Screen magazine could be rewritten as the proposition that in the process of naturalizing narrative or the realistic story, Hollywood was very systematically obliged to organize, that is to say, to repress and to neutralize space, since space is what interrupts the naturality of the story-line.[35]

But *Boyz N the Hood* does not repress space to naturalize its narrative. The film uses the constraints of cinematic space common to the action-image in order to express the oppositional feelings of confinement and mobility which the narrative focuses on as the major political issue of the 'hood and its inhabitants.

From the outset, space (and its limitations) is a major protagonist in the film. As Manthia Diawara describes:

> The film opens with a shot in which the camera zooms in on a stop sign until it fills the screen. We see a plane fly over the roofs, and the next shot reveals Tre and three other

young kids walking to school. The subtitles say: 'South Central LA, 1984'. The chil-
dren walk by a one-way street sign. This sign, too, is depicted in close-up as the
camera travels above to establish the crossroad. Then the four kids take a direction
facing a wrong-way sign. They travel on that road and see a crime scene that is
circled by a plastic ribbon with the words: 'Police Line Do Not Cross'. Inside the
police line there are three posters of President Ronald Reagan with a sign saying:
'Reagan/Bush, Four More Years'. The kids cross the police line as one of them moves
closer to the Reagan posters. At that moment a rhythmic and violent editing reveals
each of the posters in close-up with the sound of a gunshot. There are bullet holes in
the poster.[36]

The various camera movements, barriers and signs of mobility (the plane flying overhead) signal that this is a film about space, and already encapsulated within these opening frames are many of the film's social messages. The police barriers suggest the feeling of confinement and entrapment within the ghetto as do the various filmed street signs (Stop, Wrong Way Street). The focus on the Reagan posters, the acousmatic sounds of gunfire, and the bloody crime scene all signal the themes of inner-city violence and political protest against Reaganite government policies that also lie at the heart of the film. The litter which almost covers the scene of crime signifies the motif of wasted black life in the 'hood which also dominates the film. These explicitly political points are prefigured by the credit sequence. In this sequence, we hear the sounds of a gang preparing to carry out a drive-by shooting, which is followed by the sounds of acousmatic gunfire, while on screen the message comes up that 'One out of twenty-one black Americans will be murdered in their lifetime'. In this context, the Stop sign that is zoomed in on is not only a barrier signifying the enclosed space of the 'hood, but also a call for those who live in this world to take action, to control the space of the world in which they live, to stop the waste of black lives in the community.

The Stop sign and the other barriers also represent choices of mobility for those living in the 'hood. The plane flying over the Stop sign is also an emblem of possible escape, as well as marking the limited opportunities there are for inhabitants of the 'hood to make that escape.[37] At the same time the film is didactic in its message that there are right ways and wrongs ways to achieve this mobility and agency. There are various 'wrong' kinds of mobility which Tre must avoid if he is to successfully pass through the various transitions in his life. These are allegorized in various sequences throughout the film. In one of the early scenes Furious asks Doughboy and one of the minor characters, Chris, (who is always on a skateboard in the early sequences) to pick up the leaves on his lawn for five dollars. Chris refuses, answering back that he could get more doing nothing, or 'working for his uncle'...which we infer from Furious' disapproval, means pushing drugs. In later scenes we discover that Chris has exchanged his skateboard for another set of wheels, a wheelchair, having been maimed in a 'drive-by' gang shooting. The customized cars that Doughboy and other gang members use are also shown as symbols of a limited mobility and agency. The cars in the film never seem to get anywhere. They are either symbols of death in the fact that they are the means of transport used to carry out most of the killings in the film, or fetishised commodity status symbols paraded at night on certain streets in the 'hood, or they get to where they want to go too late, as in Doughboy's vain attempts to save Ricky from a rival gang. In contrast to Doughboy's customized giant of a car, Tre's modest VW, paid for by his father's 'honest work', rather than drugs, is shown to carry Tre towards enlightenment. In an early scene Furious takes the young Tre out in the car on a fishing trip, and the wide open space of the sea is in stark contrast to the enclosed confines of the 'hood.

A more obvious metaphor of the choices of mobility is made when Furious takes Tre and Ricky to Compton, a black neighbourhood that the South Central based Tre and Ricky are scared to enter. Furious orates what Tom Doherty describes as a 'paranoiac jeremiad...on Asian-American gentrification and crack conspiracy' and promotes a philosophy of African-American self-help and self-determination.[38] Furious argues that the gang mentality and killings ('If some fool rolls up and tries to smoke me, I'm gonna kill the motherfucker, unless he kills me first') is playing into the hands of the 'they' that wants the race to kill itself off. He goes on to argue for a separatist Black Pantherite politics of self-help and Black property-ownership as the way to wrest control of the community. Furious' and the film's message is that to overcome the confines of the limited space of the 'hood, African-Americans must seize control of that space.

The Mimesis and Signifyin' of the Action-Image

The film works then as a political appeal and message to its African-American audience by using cinematic space as a series of metaphors to express the lack of African American control over the social, extracinematic space of the 'hood. However, while recognizing the importance of this reading, further investigation into the mimetic relations between white and black culture is required to explain the more lasting affect that the film, and New Black Realism in general, have had on the white cultural imagination and the new-brutality film. *Boyz N the Hood's* political message of black separatism and control over the very particular and localized space of the urban ghetto does not, on its own, demonstrate the threat to the stability and defined boundaries of white cultural identity which *Boyz* and other 'hood films have provoked. Such overt political meanings of the film can distance viewers rather than affect them as they operate on the level of knowledge and discourse, and do not cause the kind of body-first shock to thought which I have been arguing is one of the important responses to 'hood film.

In spite of this, the political 'message' of *Boyz N the Hood* resonates in its powerful affective qualities in the sense that critics tended to take the film 'seriously', and believe in the story as a kind of authentic social document of what life is like in the urban ghettos of the USA. This is despite the fact that the political discourse of the film is bound up in mimesis of the relations of decisive action between individual protagonist and milieu in action-image cinema which, as Gilles Deleuze notes, we can hardly believe in any more. Deleuze argues that belief in the sensory-motor connections between milieu and protagonist is no longer tenable as such ideas are constituents of an American Dream which has itself lost credibility since the end of the Second World War. Throughout the two *Cinema* books, Deleuze implies that cinematic affect and belief are intimately tied together and that 'it is clear from the outset that cinema always had a special relationship with belief'.[39] *Boyz N the 'Hood's* political use and reversal of the relations of action between individual and milieu reanimates anachronistic elements of the action-image.

Given the fact that the film's aesthetics are anachronistic, it would seem that the ability to take *Boyz* seriously is bound up in the immediacy which the white cultural imagination experiences when confronted with images of black bodies. In *Boyz N the Hood*, and New Black Realism in general, there would seem to be a link between the affective black body, the film's political discourse and authenticity. In *Boyz N the Hood*, the immediacy of the black body in its assault on the senses seems to outweigh the distancing affect of the film's familiar narrative structure and enable the film to be taken seriously. It is this affective power which *Falling Down* desires to achieve and supersede through its own cynical realism, and which ultimately positions New Black Realism as a kind of naïve, raw anger. As we have seen Joel Schumacher implies this in his assertion that 'there have been several movies in the US about anger in the street but they had all been by African-Americans'.[40]

But this reading of New Black Realism is itself naïve in the sense that these films are working on many different levels which undermine the ability of white cultural identity to define the boundaries of its own knowledge and cultural production as being 'white'. New Black Realism and *Boyz N the Hood* can be read as overtly political in terms of their narratives and representations of the ghetto. But the other important way we need to read *Boyz N the Hood* is in the way the film intentionally seeks to invade and alter cinema (such as the Classical Hollywood genre film) which has been perceived as predominantly white by the white cultural imagination. *Boyz N the Hood* effects this invasion through a strategic *mimesis* of these white cultural and cinematic spaces - and this is most marked in the film's imitation of the properties of the cinema of the action-image.

The narrative of *Boyz N the Hood* is striking because of the way that it reproduces the sensory-motor connections and relations of action between milieu and individual which characterised the cinema of the action-image. As I also noted, Ed Guerrero refers to *Boyz N the Hood's* mimesis of the structures of Hollywood realism and the action-image as 'the mastering of the master's form' and as an expedient commercial measure by which black filmmakers can tell their stories of the ghetto and present them on the big screen.[41] The implicit rationale underlying this reasoning is that, by representing the social realities of the urban ghetto within the constraints of the Hollywood narrative structure, African-American directors can operate in a limited way within the financial priorities of the big studios. But the mimesis of the structures of the action-image has another consequence. The authenticity and immediacy provoked by the 'hood film genre highlights the crisis of the white Hollywood action-image. If Deleuze is right and there are no longer what he calls sensory-motor links (or what I have been calling affect) between individual protagonists, situations and viewers in the Hollywood action-image, the white critical reception to *Boyz N the Hood* would seem to suggest that New Black Realism has not just 'mastered the master's form' but somehow reanimated Hollywood Realism. At the same time, the fact that these are films are populated by black bodies and made by black directors - and that their affective power is partially produced by this - signifies the impossibility of white Hollywood action film having the same impact.

We can explore this idea more thoroughly by restating the properties of the mimetic dynamic as it is through an understanding of this that the reanimation of the aesthetics of the Hollywood genre film can be explored. In her reading of Michael Taussig's work Jane Gaines argues that:

> *The awesome potency of the mimetic effect is based on a relationship between that which is represented and its representation in which the effigy or 'copy' comes to have the same powers of the original, and, in addition, power over the original....The copy may, in fact, be seen as more powerful than what it represents (its referent) because it derives its power from it without exactly being it.*[42]

The idea that the copy is more powerful than the original is somewhat problematic when considering mimesis within the cinema. As Walter Benjamin noted in 'The Work of Art as Mechanical Reproduction', film is so powerful precisely because its inherent mimeticism destroys the aura of 'the original' in the work of art, and in this sense, there are no 'originals' in cinema.[43] But the idea of the copy as being more powerful than that which it mimes *is* useful when comparing *Boyz N the Hood* to the general notion of a 'classical' action-image in Hollywood genre cinema.

If the copy is more powerful than that which it copies, there are several ways in which the strategic mimesis of New Black Realism highlights the crisis of the white action-image. The first of these is apparent in the tensions between an affective cinema and films which work on the level of discourse and meaning first which I detected in the different viewing positions of *Falling Down*. Throughout this book I have been using affect to describe those experiences which touch the body-first before conscious thought has time to 'make sense' of them or distanciate them by referring to cultural knowledge. These different responses are relatively autonomous and inform each other in the viewer's response to a film. For instance a violent image may cause the body to cringe or recoil before consciousness has a chance to position such images within the overall contextual meaning of the film, or extracinematic discourses such as the politics of racial identity. The 'hood films deliberately emphasise the tensions between these two responses by making the language and music of their films a site of unsymbolisable affect to an uninitiated white cultural imagination. A major characteristic of all the 'hood films, including *Boyz N the Hood*, is both a pumping rap soundtrack and almost exclusively African-American street vernacular which makes up the dialogue.

Rap is a medium which is concerned with invading white public space in an affective fashion - particularly at the level of cultural consumption. Robin D. G. Kelley argued, in 1995, that:

> *Music and expressive styles have literally become weapons in a battle over the right to occupy public space. Frequently employing high decibel car stereos and boom boxes, black youth not only 'pump up the volume' for their own listening pleasure, but also as part of an ad hoc war of position.*[44]

The fact that the lyrics and rhythms of rap were difficult for the uninitiated to understand means that it is often experienced as a bodily (aural) assault rather than as explicit meaning or signification. The meaning that was constructed around gangsta rap after this initial assault was again one of savage, often misogynistic, violence or cutting edge, urban cool, where the initial affect is transformed into a desire to copy - as in the so-called 'whigger' phenomenon.[45] The fact that the production and consumption of rap was, as Kelley notes, about invading public space is comparable to the way that *Boyz N the Hood* was about invading the white cinematic space of the Classic Hollywood action-image. The use of rap in the soundtrack of a film which predominantly utilises the formal attributes of Hollywood realism has a specific impact in terms of mainstream cinema as a traditionally and predominantly white public space. As Mark Winokur notes, there are three main ways that the rap soundtrack disrupts the cultural familiarity and smooth flow of the linear Hollywood narrative of cause and effect which *Boyz N the Hood* makes central to its action.

> *The rap and hip-hop music of* Boyz...*is filmically contrapuntal. First it is difficult for the uninitiated to understand. Second it is often violent and obscene. Third this violence interprets sequences not always immediately meant as violent, suggesting that violence is always immanent and imminent.*[46]

The white cultural imagination's propensity to distance the structures and cinematic spaces of the action-image as culturally anachronistic is constantly undermined by the constant, disruptive interruption of the rap soundtrack in *Boyz*. The fact that such music is often violent in tone, and is always promising some kind of imminent violence, suggests that its use in the film is a deliberate attempt to play on the fears and anxieties that are often constructed around images of the black body.

These points concerning the rap soundtrack of the film also apply to much of the dialogue of the film. Winokur also argues that there are moments in *Boyz N the Hood* and other New Black Realist films when the dialogue is almost incomprehensible to white audiences. He argues of African-American street slang that 'some black inflections are so difficult for white audiences to understand that...minutes can go by in *Boyz N the Hood*...that are difficult for the white audience to follow'.[47] The dialogue in films like *Boyz N the Hood* shares much in common with the lyrics of rap, especially in its use of poetic metre and stress. According to Richard Shusterman, 'verbal virtuosity is greatly appreciated in the black urban ghetto', and this factor is played upon in New Black Realism.[48] According to Winokur, this 'linguistic opacity' is a strategic assault on white audiences employed deliberately by African-American film-makers, and operates as a kind of Bakhtinian double-voicedness which subverts the traditional audience expectations of Hollywood film by signifyin' white desires. He argues of the subgenre that:

> The most linguistically challenging moments occur not when we suspect that only nonsense is being conveyed but at those moments during which we are supposed to be most titillated, most want to understand some meaning: they are moments of conversation about sex and violence. 'Jimmies' for condoms, 'flap some skin' for coitus, 'smoke' for kill. Our desire to be titillated is deployed against us. Instead of the safe, controlled arousal evoked by traditional Hollywood codes that activate and frustrate audience desire, we are instead forced in, trying to understand its language, to confront the desire of an Other.[49]

In terms of the white viewer's viewing of *Boyz N the Hood*, Winokur is describing a shock to the Symbolic reality of the white American milieu and a disruption of the cultural familiarity of Hollywood realism. The voyeuristic pleasure which 1970s' film theory has argued is a major constituent of the pleasure of Classical Hollywood film is challenged because, according to Winokur, the white audiences of the 'hood film understand that their 'own ignorance of black codes are being signified - our desire to be titillated is turned against us'.[50]

This shock acts in a fashion which is structurally analogous to some readings (and I am thinking of Slavoj Zizek here) of the Lacanian Real in the sense that the sounds heard on screen disrupt existing and familiar structures of meaning.[51] But the important point to note here is that this shock does not come from some primitivist, unknowable Real, but from an other, different Symbolic reality (of African-American filmmaking and culture) which is prepared to use violence against white Symbolic reality. In Lacanian/Zizekian terms we get a clash of Symbolics, a confrontation between two signifying structures. But this clash is experienced by the white viewer as immediate and affective cultural violence, and New Black Realism as a genre uses this power to make African-American culture central, whilst operating from a position of economic and social marginality - as what the white cultural imagination constructs as a primitivist Real. This tension is a major constituent of both the genre of New Black Realism and the white new-brutality film, and is one that I will continue to address in subsequent chapters. It is also a tension which needs thinking through in terms of the relationship between affect and signification, and the specific mimetic dynamic between *Boyz* and the classic gangster genre is fertile ground for this.

Gangsters and Gangstas

One of the points of comparison to note about both the classic gangster film and the gangsta film is in their reception. Like the 'hood genre, the classic gangster movies were constructed as a genre connoting immediacy and authenticity. The particular historical timing and the studio producers of gangster films encouraged audiences to think of the genre as a direct 'reflection' of society. The classic gangster film was chiefly associated with the Warner Bros studio, 'widely known for its 30s "social issues" movies, and with the development of sound by that studio...popularly understood as an instrument of realism'.[52] The gangster film was also received with a certain amount of fear and anxiety because of the genre's perceived potential to produce copycat behaviour amongst its audiences. As Pam Cook notes:

This supposed realism contributed, and still contributes, to recurring 'moral panics' about the effects of the films' violence, glorification of the criminal, and misogyny on young audiences, and consequently the history of the genre has been interlaced with censorship problems.[53]

The fears of copycat violence around the gangster film were inspired because many of these films featured vicious gangsters as their glamorous central protagonists, and many of the actors playing them became stars in their own right.[54] Produced at the time of the Great Depression when the American Dream appeared at its most fragile, there were establishment fears of social unrest, and films in which glamorous gangsters lived out the criminal underside of the Dream and its message of 'life, liberty and the pursuit of happiness' became subject to censure and censorship. As Thomas Schwartz argues:

because of their overt celebration of the gangster-hero and their less than flattering portrayal of contemporary urban life, these films were as controversial as they were popular, and threats of censorship, boycott and federal regulation forced the studios to restructure the gangster formula by the mid-30s.[55]

In fact the studios had made attempts to censure the seemingly glamorous lifestyle of the gangster before the official Hays Code of 1934 published its own instructions to the film industry. Most of the films ended in the demise of the gangster figure, with a tacked on 'moral message'. The subtitle of one of the early films of the genre, *Scarface - Shame of a Nation* (Hawks 1931), demonstrates the studio's desire not to upset the censors.[56] However, after 1934, the narratives of the gangster films were 'splintered into various derivative strains' with the rise of the 'G-Men movies' and gangster movies such as *Angels With Dirty Faces* (Curtiz 1938) where issues of social responsibility became major themes.[57]

But having recognized the similarities between the perceived immediacy and authenticity of the classic gangster film and the gangsta film it is also important to identify where *Boyz N the Hood* is different. The most obvious distinction is the fact that the classic gangster films were produced during the heyday of the action-image, and despite their contentious subject matter these films did very little to change the form of a cinema intimately entwined with the ideology of the American Dream. Belief in the aesthetics and philosophy of the action-image cinema was at its height in the 1930s and 1940s, and in structural terms, there is very little difference between the anti-hero gangster and the cowboy, romantic or historical hero of other genres. Tony Camonte's desire in *Scarface* to 'do it, do it again, and keep on doin' it' do not contradict the essential attributes of the action-image. In the gangster film the individual action-taker is still central and his relations with his world are still concrete in the sense that his actions are able to modify or change the milieu in which he is situated, and events that take place within that milieu are seen to have an effect on him. For the duration of the film the milieu of the underworld is also experienced as a kind of totality for the audience, with the one exception being that the milieu of the gangster is ultimately shown to be a false one, overtaken by the official and 'real' forces of law and order. But the neon sign that Tony Camonte sets so much store by provides an apt motto for the action-image and its viewers.[58] The fact that the underworld is presented as an ultimately precarious milieu does not undermine the American Dream as affective structure in any fundamental sense, nor does it threaten the action-image as the cinema of that Dream. As Gilles Deleuze notes, 'the American cinema had the means to save its dream by passing through nightmares'.[59] Rather like the *noir* films that came after it, the gangster film is part of the jeremiad which, as I noted in the last chapter, formed a constituent part of the American Dream. Such films tended to act as a warning as to what *could* happen should the American Dream become corrupted with individuals losing the ideology of responsibility to the community (one of the Dream's essential constituents) in their ruthless pursuit of wealth and happiness.

On the surface *Boyz N the Hood* seems also to function as a jeremiad. If we take the film's outward consciousness to be a combination of Furious' and Tre's, the film can be read as a warning against attempting to fulfil one's ambitions through violent criminal means. Furious' work in the community, and his speech concerning the dangers to the African-American community from both the violence within the 'hood and the white authorities outside, demonstrate a belief in the structures of the action-image structures in which the individual is capable of modifying and being affected by his milieu. The film's narrative consists of the choices faced by Tre - whether to face up to the responsibilities of the community by continuing his education, or risk being part of the destructive force within the community by becoming a gang member like Doughboy. But this African-American mimesis of the American Dream and the cinema of that dream is always aware of its own alterity. The philosophy espoused by Furious, and ultimately lived out by Tre, as he heads off for an Atlanta college at the end of the film never claims to be all-encompassing and universalist in the way that the American Dream did. As I noted above, Black separatism permeates Furious' polemical speech to Tre and Rikkii and Furious and Tre's particular 'dream' is always exclusive of white Americans. In this sense the strong relations between milieu and the individual, which the white cultural imagination is nostalgic for, resurface in the 'hood film as the result of the white economic and social oppression and segregation. The 'hood film is always about a local situation remaining local - rather than a local which aspires to be global as in the classic gangster film. On the other hand, Furious' message of social responsibility within the ghetto is also what makes the film a 'safe' one for white audiences. Although Furious is always emphasising the African-American right to defend oneself with violence, and to resist white oppression by building the African-American community from within, this separatism does not constitute a threat to the boundaries of white cultural and social identity. This is illustrated in Tre's ultimate escape to a black college, reminiscent of Booker T. Washington's philosophy of self-help within the black community, rather than an exposure of the white power structures which have created the ghetto in the first place.[60]

The character of Doughboy, played by Ice Cube, represents a much greater threat to white viewers and also has a much more profound affective impact on the white cultural imagination. bell hooks makes some suggestive comments in relation to this in interview with Ice Cube:

> *Tre just came off like a wimp, a crybaby. He was just so weak. He came off weak in the movie...I feel like if I was a kid lookin' at that movie, I wouldn't wanna be him, I'd wanna be you, because your character had the jazz. I mean your character was cool...*[61]

The fact that Doughboy is played by a rap star adds to the character's desirable coolness. Other reviewers have also spoken about Doughboy and Ice Cube in terms of the authenticity and immediacy which I suggested were predominant in the film's initial reception. Tom Doherty for instance argues that 'Ice Cube is Singleton's ace in the hood, the authentic human presence without whom the melodrama would play as travelogue'.[62] He goes on to assert that:

> *Ice Cube has the pent-up intensity of a caged panther. Where actors Gooding (Tre) and Chestnut (Ricky) look and sound as if they've been bussed in from the 'burbs, Ice Cube is to the manner born. Playing a role so close to home, he has the stance, the style, the slang, and the gaze that means business and the girth to back it up.*[63]

These comments again emphasise an animal-like violence and suggest that Ice Cube is not performing but reproducing a version of himself living in the ghetto before celebrity and success.

I have already discussed the reasons for this apparent immediacy in relation to white fears and desires around the dangerous black body. But what is striking about Ice Cube's performance, and what many critics omit to mention, is its stylized nature which deliberately invites comparison with the white gangster of the thirties. In the gangsta style there is a self-reflexive intertextuality at work in the sense that figures like Doughboy are directly related to the violent anarchic actions of classic gangster played by Jimmy Cagney and Edward G. Robinson in the 1930s. As Winokur notes 'the new ethnic gangster is a completely self-conscious gloss on previous entries in the genre'.[64] This book has discussed intertextuality and self-referentiality in terms of Fredric Jameson's argument that such aesthetic techniques have led to a waning of affect within the postmodern age. As I noted above, Jameson's analysis is produced through his association of affect with bodily, emotional depth, and intertextuality with an ahistorical, random referencing of the surface of previous popular culture. The two are mutually incompatible. While he might have a point with the apolitical self-referentiality of the postmodern blockbuster, the intertextuality of the 'hood film and the gangsta figure operates as a strategic assault on the collective white cultural memory. And it is actually the stylized self-consciousness of the gangsta which might be said to produce the greatest affective impact of *Boyz N the Hood*, particulalry in the way the film threatens to disrupt the boundaries between white and African-American cultural identity.

Mark Winokur provides a clue as to why this should be so when he notes that the gangsta 'reflects a desire for the ethnic other to be both itself and other - the signifier of white culture'.[65] This point is reminiscent of Toni Morrison's account of American Africanism in the sense that, as we have seen, she argues that African Americans are constructed as both a site of anarchic, savage violence and desirable hipness and cool. Cinematic gangsta figures such as Doughboy and extracinematic rap stars like Ice Cube evoke both these of these reactions in the white cultural imagination. But as Winokur points out the 'ethnic other' is also a signifier for white culture. Those attributes which form the basis of the white cultural imagination's signification of black culture are actually a constituent of white cultural identity itself. The gangsta figure is a mime of vicious, grapefruit-squashing, refinery-burning proto-capitalist gangster created by a white Hollywood in the 1930s.[66]

In other words the gangsta's strategic mimesis works as a reminder of the violence that lies at the heart of white American national identity and the cultural imagination associated with this. It is possible to read this evocation of white cultural memories in the 'hood film in terms of a cinematic shock. One way of elucidating this point is to read the relationship between the gangster and the gangsta through Lesley Stern's definition of the involuntary memories provoked by the cinematic experience. Involuntary memory is the process where 'some sensation in the present, and the most familiar example is Proust's account of the taste of madelines, summons an experience of the past'.[67] She argues that cinema is particularly good at evoking involuntary memories and 'even in the middle of the most mundane film the viewer can be suddenly and unexpectedly seized by an overwhelming sensation of sensuous reminiscence'.[68] Images and structures of different films automatically trigger off memories of other films, and the time between those films contracts. This acting on the memory can be more than just playful postmodern referentiality or intertextuality, if the immediacy of the cinematic image means that the connection between images is less a matter of conscious thought on the part of the viewer than a kind of involuntary jolt.

The figure of the gangsta achieves this immediacy both because of the affective power of the dangerous black body on the white cultural imagination, while at the same time evoking memories of those violent white gangsters who formed a key part of the cinema of the action-image and its accompanying ideology. A temporary confusion is provoked because those characteristics of savage, random violence associated with black culture are temporarily merged with memories of the gangster figure - and with a cinema which was indistinguishable from the affective structure of the American Dream, and memories of a time when it was still taken seriously. The white American cultural imagination is temporarily forced to confront the fact that the myths which sustain the nostalgic memories of the white American Dream were themselves constituted of the kind of anarchic, criminal violence which is projected onto African-American culture.

However before celebrating the transformative and transgressive power of the processes of affect and involuntary memory produced by *Boyz N the Hood* and the gangsta figure, it is important to remember the fact that the white reception of the film did not acknowledge the violence at the core of white American identity, or that the white culture's fear of the other, violent, black body is actually a fear and denial of itself. I noted above that in the first instance of the film's reception the white cultural imagination constructed fears and paranoia around black audiences naively miming - what for these knowing audiences is - the heavily stylized and ironic mimesis of white culture performed by the figure of the gangsta. In the second instance the critical reception generated by the film focused on what was constructed as the film's 'anti-violence message' and the safe containment of black violence produced by Furious' message of black separatism and Tre's utopian escape.

But I would argue that these responses should be read as a kind of denial of the most powerful affect of the film - the miming of the anarchic violence which lies at the heart of white cultural identity. But the white denial of the affective shock to cultural memory provoked by Boyz and New Black Realism is itself undermined by the white mimesis of the 'hood film and African American culture which, as I will be arguing in following chapters, is the defining aesthetic constituent of the films of Quentin Tarantino. The threat to the stability of the boundaries between white and African-American cultural identity, provoked by the 'hood film, is realised in the ways that the white new-brutality film mimics and expresses a desire for the aesthetics of 1990s' black culture and cinema.

But before engaging with that question, I want to explore another film that emerged from the 'hood genre, *Menace II Society* (Hughes 1993). Much less commercially popular than *Boyz N the Hood*, this film does not offer the same options for the white cultural imagination to contain and distance the challenge to the authority of white identity. Much more than *Boyz* this film brings into question the violence that lies behind the history of the formation of white American cultural and cinematic identity, and it achieves this through a much more extensive and furious assault on collective white cultural and cinematic memories. The film engages with the questions and history of belief in and the affect of white cinema to a much greater extent than *Boyz N the Hood* in the sense that the film evokes involuntary memories of history of both the action-image cinema and the cinema that came after. It is through an investigation of the way that *Menace II Society* achieves this assault that will prove the most productive position from which to begin an analysis of the significance of the films of Tarantino.

Notes

1. Stern (1995:8).

2 Diawara includes the films of Spike Lee, *Juice* (Dickerson 1992), *Boyz N the Hood* (Singleton 1991), and *Straight out of Brooklyn* (Rich 1991) as key films in the development of New Black Realism in Diawara ed. (1993: 3-25).

3. Joel Schumacher, director of *Falling Down,* interviewed in Fuller, *Interview* 23 (1993: 112).

4. One could argue that New Black Realism was initially based in New York on the East Coast with

the films of Spike Lee, including *She's Gotta Have It* (1986) and *Do the Right Thing* (1989).

5. Academic writers like Diawara also put *Boyz* at the centre of their analysis, as does another important source: Guerrero (1993: 180-208).

6. Some of the arguments in the next two chapters also appear in my article 'The Affective City: Urban Black Bodies and Milieu in *Menace II Society* and *Pulp Fiction*' in Shiel and Fitzmaurice eds. (2003: 180-199).

7. *ibid.* (183).

8. Gene Siskel quoted in King, *The Hollywood Reporter* (15 July 1991: 122).

9. Quoted in Brunette, *Sight and Sound* 2 (1992: 13).

10. King, *The Hollywood Reporter* 318 (16 July 1991: 1, 6) and *The Hollywood Reporter* 318 (12 July 1991: 9,16).

11. Fanon (1967: 110-113).

12. *ibid.*

13. Butler in Gooding-Williams ed. (1993: 18).

14. *ibid.*

15. Boyd in Carson and Friedman.

16. Gaines, Jane 'Films That Make You Want to Fight Back (And Why White People Fear Them)'. (unpublished at the time of writing.)

17. *ibid.*

18. Brunette, *Sight and Sound* 2 (1992: 13).

19. *The Hollywood Reporter* 318 (12 July 1991: 16).

20. Peter Brunette for instance calls *Boyz N the Hood* a 'sophisticated if somewhat preachy account of three young boy's violent coming of age in the black ghetto of South Central Los Angeles...twenty-three year old John Singleton is clearly enjoying the attention'. *Sight and Sound* 3 (1991: 13).

21. Sport has traditionally been one of the few ways that white America allows individual African-Americans to 'escape' the ghetto. The tenuous nature of this route is displayed brilliantly in the documentary *Hoop Dreams* (James 1994).

22. This oedipal narrative is also symptomatic of the way films like *Boyz* and other 'hood films focus almost exclusively on black men and masculinity. There have been many critiques of this concentration on the 'crisis' of black masculinity in films like *Boyz* and gangsta rap in general. See McDowell in Stecopolous and Uebel eds. (1997: 361-86).

23. 'We can hardly believe any longer that a global situation can give rise to an action which is capable of modifying it - no more than we can believe that an action can force itself to disclose itself, even partially'. (Deleuze 1986: 206).

24. Jameson (1992: 5).

25. Eco in Lodge ed. (1988: 454).

26. As Ed Guerrero notes 'For Singleton, all these young men's futures turn on the absence or presence of their fathers'. (1993: 185).

27. Jones & Doherty, *Cineaste* 18 (1991: 17).

28. Taubin, *Sight & Sound* 3 (1993: 17).

29. Guerrero (1993: 186).

30. Brunette, *Sight and Sound* August (1991: 13).

31. Bogle & Goldstein, *National Film Theatre Programme Guide* (1996: 5).

32. *Boyz N the Hood* was financed and marketed by Columbia.

33. Guerrero (1993: 182).

34. *ibid.*

35. Jameson (1992: 74-5).

36. Diawara ed. (1993: 21).

37. As Guerrero notes, the plane metaphor 'goes back to a revealing opening moment in Richard Wright's classic novel *Native Son* (1940), when Bigger Thomas looks up from the confines of Chicago's South Side ghetto at a sky-writing airplane overhead to the bitter realization that anything to do with flight - mechanical, imaginative, or otherwise - is for 'white boys' and far beyond his reach'. (1993: 184).

38. Doherty & Jones, *Cineaste* 18 (1991: 18).

39. Deleuze (1989: 171).

40. Schumacher interviewed by Fuller, *Empire* 49 (1993: 77).

41. Guerrero (1993: 184).

42. Gaines (1994).

43. Benjamin in Mast, Cohen & Braudy eds. (1992: 665-81).

44. Kelley in Perkins (1995: 89).

45. It has been well documented how white US youth has mimicked black popular culture, adopting black hip-hop fashion and black street vernacular. See the 'Whigger' edition of *Oprah* (1993).

46. Winokur, *The Velvet Light Trap* 35 (1995: 27).

47. *ibid.* (26).

48. Shusterman *New Literary History* 22 (1991: 615). See also Brennan, *Critical Inquiry* 20 (1994: 663-693), and Shusterman, *Critical Inquiry* 22 (1995: 151-8) for a debate on the viability of rap as an art worthy of academic attention.

49. Winokur, *The Velvet Light Trap* 35 (1995: 26).

50. *ibid.*

51. See Zizek, Slavoj (1989: 168-172) for his clearest definition of the way that the Real works to disrupt Symbolic reality. See also Zizek (1991: 3-21).

52. Cook (1985: 85-6).

53. *ibid.*

54. Jimmy Cagney and Edward G. Robinson are two of the most famous examples.

55. Schwarz (1981: 82). See also McArthur (1972), and Warshow (1970), for early but more definitive accounts of the gangster genre.

56. The supplementary nature of these moral messages is demonstrated in the case of *Scarface*, where the final scenes showing the trial and hanging of Tony Camonte were added on after the main shoot, and when Paul Muni was unavailable for filming. The desire to keep the censors on side is also apparent in the fact that the producers of *The Public Enemy* (Wellman 1931) issued a postscript which stated that they wanted to 'depict honestly an environment that exists in certain strata of American life, rather than glorify the hoodlum or criminal'. Walker ed. (1997: 604).

57. Schwarz (1981: 82). The G-Men genre included the MGM-produced *Public Hero Number One* (Ruben 1935) - an obvious spin on the earlier *The Public Enemy*.

58. Tony is fascinated by a travel agent's sign which reads 'The World is Yours' and in a sense this is also how the Hollywood action-image operates as a global situation.

59. Deleuze (1986: 145).

60. A great critique of this philosophy can be found in Ralph Ellison's *Invisible Man* (1947), where the Invisible Man's experiences at a black college in the South represent a thinly veiled attack on the white-funded all-black colleges existing in the first half of the twentieth century.

61. hooks (1994: 132).

62. Doherty & Jones *Cineaste* 18 (1991: 16-19).

63. *ibid.* (16).

64. Winokur, *The Velvet Light Trap* 35 (1995: 24).

65. *ibid.* (24).

66. I am referring here to two famous scenes in two James Cagney films - *The Public Enemy* and *White Heat* (Walsh 1949).

67. Stern (1995: 39).

68. *ibid.*

Chapter Three

Gangsters and Gangstas Part Two:
Menace II Society and the Cinema of Rage[1]

'O'Dog was America's worst nightmare...young, black and didn't give a fuck'.[2]

In the last chapter, I argued that *Boyz N the Hood* provoked three different kinds of responses in the white cultural imagination. In the first instance the film, and particularly its trailer, caused an immediate reaction based on white fears around the 'dangerous black body' - which, as Judith Butler argues, is part of a historically formed, 'racial disposition of the visible'.[3] The trailer provoked these fears further by showing a string of images of violence explicitly connected with the bodies of young black males. I suggested that, because of the lack of narrative contextualisation of these images, white audiences were unable to distanciate them from the extracinematic paranoid anxieties produced around the dangerous black body. One result of this reaction was the white establishment's inability to tell the difference between the violence of cinematic images, and the imagined fears of young black audiences mimicking the images of violence seen on screen.

I then suggested that the second response to *Boyz N the Hood* from white audiences and critics was one of ultimate acceptance and praise for the film's overtly political message of education, black self-help and the destructiveness of black on black violence. The film was interpreted as an African-American version of the American Dream because of the central narrative of Tre's self-improvement and escape from the ghetto. White reviewers also tended to read the film as authentic despite the fact the film is an example of what Gilles Deleuze refers to as the cinema of the action-image. Belief in a cinema of concrete relations of action and affect between an individual protagonist and unified milieu is no longer possible, according to Deleuze.

However *Boyz N the Hood* is not a nostalgic simulation for this kind of cinema but it performs a mimesis of the structures between individuals, actions and situations which were predominant in the action-image cinema - a cinema where 'where everything is individuated'.[4] *Boyz* is a film where individuals are able to take action and both modify and be affected by their milieu. In stark contrast to the images of fragmentation and meltdown of ties between community and individual displayed in *Falling Down*, the 'hood functions in *Boyz N the Hood* as a milieu where sensory-motor relations between the individual protagonist and the filmic world are intact. This mimesis is affective because of the overriding affective power of the dangerous black body on the white cultural imagination. The film uses this power to create a strong structure of belief between its white viewers and the world it presents on screen, while using a style of Hollywood realism which, when reproduced in contemporary white cinema, is regarded as familiar, and almost anachronistic. *Boyz* is able to do this because of its emphasis on the local situation remaining local rather than aspiring to be global.

I also argued that a more lasting affect produced by *Boyz N the Hood* and New Black Realism could be found in the gangsta, and the way that this figure evokes involuntary memories of the violence which lies at the heart of white culture and cinema. In terms of the critical reception of the film, the power of the gangsta to affect cultural memories was repressed in the discourse produced around Ice Cube's performance as Doughboy. While his performance received a great deal of critical attention, most of this focussed again on the authenticity and immediacy of the primitive, dangerous African-American male body. This emphasis is symptomatic of a denial of the involuntary shock to white cultural and cinematic memories evoked by the gangsta's mimesis of the figure of the gangster. The gangsta shocks white audiences because he is both the same and other to the classic gangster, evoking the violence that is at the heart of the affective structure of the American Dream and adding the immediate danger that is provoked in the white cultural imagination by the dangerous black body. At the same time the ideology of black self-help that permeates *Boyz N the Hood* does allow the white cultural imagination to deny the threat to white cultural identity, immanent in the character of Doughboy. *Boyz N the Hood* ultimately became a 'safe' film partly because it reproduces too closely the anachronistic pleasures of the action-image. In spite of this, it is the cinematic figure of the gangsta and the aesthetics of rap which have had most influence on Quentin Tarantino's new-brutality films, *Reservoir Dogs* and *Pulp Fiction*, which are not anachronistic. But before turning to these examples of the mimesis of African-American culture, I want to look first at another example of New Black Realism, *Menace II Society,* to draw out in more detail the ways in which an African-American film can assault the senses and confuse notions of cultural identity, through both the mimesis of iconic white American culture *and* the evocation of involuntary memories which cause a shock to thought.

Menace II Society, like *Boyz N the Hood*, performs a mimesis of the structures of Hollywood action film, but it produces a much more thorough attack on the cultural memories which sustain nostalgic conceptions of what it is to be American. The film is much more aggressive in producing an affective and distracted response in the sense that it is almost impossible for white viewers to contextualise the film within the familiar structures of meaning provided by the relatively orthodox narrative of *Boyz N the Hood*. *Menace II Society* deliberately plays upon the affective responses provoked by images of dangerous black bodies by focussing on the random and unpredictable violence of the gangsta figure, and the confined milieu of the 'hood. This is particularly marked in the gangsta, O'Dog, who performs a series of casual, violent crimes which appear to fulfil white constructions of young black men as anarchic and primitive.

However the film also constantly undermines this immediate response by deconstructing this character as a representation of black reality. Even more than the figure of Doughboy in *Boyz N the Hood*, the film draws explicit parallels between O'Dog and the classical white gangster figure, and through this mimesis it reveals something of the violence which lies at the heart of white American cinematic and extracinematic culture. *Menace II Society* is also more extensive than *Boyz* in its mimesis of American cinema, and goes beyond imitating the cinema of the action-image. The film constantly references and mimes the aesthetic styles and structures of American film from classic genres like the gangster film, through to *film noir*, up to the period of cinema that Deleuze categorises as the crisis of the action-image (particularly the films of Martin Scorsese), and through to TV genres like the so-called 'True Crime' programmes which dominate American schedules. The common link between the styles of images which *Menace* cites is that, at one time or another, all of them have been categorised in terms of their authenticity and affective power.

On one level, this intertextuality is very postmodern in spirit. By 'quoting' different styles of cinema *Menace II Society* calls into question the nature of cinematic realism as a whole. The film constantly draws attention to the fact that different kinds of realism are cinematic styles and subject to conventions as much as any other kind of aesthetic practice. More specifically the film also suggests that African-American cinema is a sophisticated aesthetic practice just like any other form of cinematic realism - despite the tendency of critics to view such films as documents of 'social truth', and subject them to the 'burden of representation'. This citation of other images is particularly prominent in the scenes of violence in the film, where the affective power of images of dangerous black bodies is at its most potent. The film's violent episodes are shot in a multitude of both cinematic and non-cinematic styles, and one possible reading of this is again that such stylisation lessens the authenticity which the white cultural imagination tends to ascribe to images of African-American violence.

But the sheer amount and pace of the film's allusions to different kinds of cinematic violence also produces another kind of distracted response in the viewer. The furious speed at which the citations unfold on screen is affective in the sense that the viewer does not have time to categorise or think about the history of these images in a way which could distanciate them. There is not enough time to reference collective cinematic knowledge and think about the origins of the references that the film presents with any degree of authoritative knowledge. There is also no room for the kind of nostalgic response that commentators, such as Fredric Jameson, have described as the central experience of postmodern intertextuality.[5] The connecting thread of films like *Body Heat* and *Blade Runner* is that they evoke memories of, and a desire for, the kind of belief and ability to 'take it seriously' that viewers of the action-image cinema were assumed to have. For instance, Steven Shaviro notes that *Blade Runner* 'presents simulation as loss of the real'.[6] Even though the nature of the real is precisely what is under question in *Blade Runner's* world of artificial life, and in its ambiguity about what is human, it is precisely the absence of truth about the real which produces a nostalgic view of a time and cinematic culture when it was imagined that such certainties existed. As Shaviro goes on to suggest:

> Blade Runner*'s science fiction world is oddly permeated by nostalgia. The film composes its broken-down future, not out of elements of the past, but out of their absence. The desire for outmoded scenes and situations, for the easy legibility of conventions of genre and gender is validated - rather than frustrated - by the irrelevance and unattainability of such scenes and by the ostentatious artificiality of their postmodern reproduction.[7]

Menace II Society, on the other hand, presents simulation as an intensification of the real, in the sense that the distracted response to the pace and number of allusions in the film produces a much more intense evocation of involuntary memories than that experienced when watching *Boyz N the Hood*. When a number of cinematic memories are involuntarily evoked in a short space of time the response is bodily and immediate rather than conscious.

The vast array of cultural and cinematic memories that are evoked by *Menace II Society* are not randomly made. The film draws together a number of moments in American cinema which are connected through the underlying presence of, what I want to term, a white racial rage. The film juxtaposes this racial rage with what the white cultural imagination experiences as a violent, anarchic and unpredictably savage black rage which is embodied in O'Dog in *Menace II Society*. The film does not deny that black rage exists, but it suggests that random, meaningless and unpredictable savage violence emanates from white culture, while black rage is strongly connected to and motivated by the frustrations and confinement produced by the social milieu of the ghetto. The gangsta is ambiguous in this context, in that the film indicates that these figures are imitating the unpredictable and anarchic violence of white culture, while at the same time, characters like O'Dog are shown to be a product of the political and social conditions of the urban black ghetto.

This ambivalence towards the origins of the gangsta is a result of mimesis in the sense that the copy is both the same and other to the white gangster figures which precede him. The extra power of the gangsta is that he forces the white cultural imagination to confront the real of violence which lies at the heart of white American cultural identity. What I mean by this is that the often unspoken violence, which is an integral part of the affect of the American Dream, is revealed by the gangsta's mimesis of that Dream. This idea ties in with Toni Morrison's suggestions that the violent attributes which are fabricated as African-American are those which form the basis of white American cultural identity.[8] Clearly these are assertions that need unpacking, and we can begin this process by exploring the way that *Menace II Society* engages with questions of cinematic authenticity and affect much more thoroughly than *Boyz N the Hood*.

Two Readings

Menace II Society is the story of fatherless young African-American men growing up in 1980s' and 1990s' Los Angeles. The story is centred around Caine, and follows a 'rites of passage' structure similar to that of *Boyz N the Hood*. Unlike Tre, Caine has no father or mother by the time of his late teens, and lives with his out of touch, bible-quoting grandparents. His father, a drug-dealer, has been shot dead, and his mother has died from a heroin overdose. Most of the film's running time follows the course of Caine and his friend's lives over the summer following his graduation from high school. Through a series of vignettes, we see Caine involved in a number of criminal activities (drug-dealing and car-stealing) and random violent encounters, and this action is punctuated through the narrative presence of Caine's acousmatic voice-over. As the film progresses, Caine is presented with several options to escape the ghetto. The first of these is a potential move to Kansas, with his friends, Sharif ('an ex-knucklehead turned Muslim'), and Stacy, who has won a football scholarship at a Kansas college.[9] Sharif's father, Mr Butler - who also acts as one of number of surrogate father figures to Caine - advises him to leave LA or end up dying in the 'hood. The second avenue of escape for Caine is to depart the 'hood for Atlanta, with Ronnie and her son, Antony, who has been fathered by the imprisoned Pernell - one of Caine's father's friends, and another surrogate father figure who 'showed him what being a hustler was all about'. Caine decides to take this course of action, when he is violently gunned down in a drive-by shooting, carried out by the cousin of a woman who claims she is pregnant by Caine from a casual sexual encounter.

As this brief summary of *Menace II Society* suggests, the film's narrative content and *mise en scène* are very similar to *Boyz N the Hood*. Both are set in the urban ghettos of Los Angeles, and both focus their attention on young African-American men over the course of a summer in their lives. Looking at these factors alone, both films could be said to belong to the 'social realism' school of filmmaking, and much of the mainstream reception of *Menace II Society* has taken this approach. As Paula Massood writes, '*Menace II Society* concerns itself with similar topics (to *Boyz N the Hood*), in a similar milieu, but attempts to take its story one stage further'.[10] The Hughes brothers, who wrote, produced and directed the film, have encouraged this concentration on the film's powers of representation. They have also promoted the idea that they were taking narrative realism further than *Boyz N the Hood*. Amy Taubin notes that, 'As legend already has it, the Hughes brothers...were outraged by the Hollywood-style sentimentality of *Boyz N the Hood*. They convinced New Line Cinema to give them $2.5 million to report what really goes down in the ghetto'.[11] Albert Hughes himself has said of the film that 'it is based on true, day to day life in Watts'.[12]

On the basis of the ending alone, one could argue that *Menace II Society* does seem, in commonsense terms, to take its narrative realism further than *Boyz*. The death of Caine, the main protagonist, comes after he has decided to pursue one of the utopian escapes on offer, and it is no coincidence that Atlanta is his planned destination - this is also the place that Tre and Brandi escape to in the off-screen space of *Boyz N the Hood's* 'sentimental' ending.[13] Tragic endings are as much of a cinematic convention as happy ones, as often seen in classic gangster films like *Scarface*. But Caine's death was perceived as 'realistic' because it bears out the real-life statistics which begin the credits to *Boyz*: 'One out of every twenty-one black Americans will be murdered in their lifetime.'

Indeed many commentaries focussed on the film in terms of its relevance to social debates around the 'black on black' violence in the urban ghetto. Amy Taubin argues that the narrative acts as realism because it lays bare 'the self-destructive cycle of black on black violence, the pathological internalisation of the values of a racist society so that black men grow up believing their lives are worth nothing'.[14] Bell hooks argues that the film is problematic because of this bleak picture it paints of life in the urban 'hood. She asserts that the film is 'really just a reactionary film on so many levels' because of its representation of the stylised violence of African-American masculinity.[15] She suggests that the film passes itself off as:

> ...being about blackness, as being a statement about black young people and where they are, but it is in truth a film about how white supremacy has shaped and per-verted the imagination of young black people. What the film says is that these people have difficulty in imagining any way out of their lives, and the film doesn't really subvert that.[16]

hooks comes to this conclusion because the characters in *Menace II Society* sit around watching classic gangster films. The film is saying that, 'these black boys learned to do this shit, not from black culture, but from watching white movies'.[17] She goes on to note that 'the film points out that the whole myth of the gangsta - as it is played out in rap and movies - is not some Afrocentric or black-defined myth, it's the public of that's in all our imaginations from movies and television'.[18]

In one sense this thinking echoes the mimetic connection between the gangsta and the gangster that I made in the previous chapter. But for hooks, *Menace II Society* is reactionary because it does not offer a way out from the vice-like grip of the white myth of the gangster, and merely replicates rather than disrupts white structures of violence. The most brutal character, O'Dog, (and therefore in hooksian logic the character who has swallowed the white myth, hook, line and sinker) survives at the end of the film.[19] In contrast, the character who imagines a way out of the ghetto, Caine, is brutally gunned down. This means that *Menace II Society*

> ...*says to you: When you finally decide to imagine a way out, that's when you get blown away. The deeper message of the film is: Don't imagine a way out, because the person who's still standing at the end of the film has been the most brutal...*Menace II Society *suggests - mythically almost - that the genocide we are being entertained by is not going to be complete, that there will be the unique and special individuals who will survive the genocide, but they're not the individuals who were dreaming of a way out.*[20]

In other words, the argument is that *Menace II Society* (as a product of, as well as a representation of, gangsta culture) has bought into the debased flip-side of the American Dream. The film has taken on board a poor 'black-faced' version of white American myths and dominant fictions without question.[21] Like Taubin's focus on 'the pathological internalisation of racist discourse', hooks also reads the film in terms of the insularity of the film's depiction of the urban ghetto, without taking into account the affect such images have on viewers outside of the 'hood.

This reading of the film has much in common with Cornel West's analysis of gangsta culture in general. *Menace II Society* seems to confirm his polemic concerning the spiritual and emotional well-being of young African-American men, with its pattern of cyclical violence, and the ambiguity of Caine's attitude towards survival (he tells his grandfather that he doesn't know whether he wants to live or die). West argues that an 'epidemic of nihilism' was rife in the African-American community of the 1990s, and particularly virulent in young male African-Americans, where 'psychological depression, as well as a lack of economic and political well-being culminates in the meaningless of black existence'.[22] He goes on to argue that one way in which black men expressed this nihilism was through the self-commodification of their own bodies as violent and dangerous:

> *For black men, power is acquired by stylising their bodies over space and time in such a way that their bodies reflect their uniqueness and provoke fear in others. To be bad is to be good, not simply because it subverts the language of dominant white culture, but also because it imposes a unique kind of order for young men on their distinctive chaos, and solicits an attention that makes others pull back with some trepidation...This young black male style is a form of self-identification and resistance in a hostile culture; it is also an instance of machismo identity ready for violent encounters. Yet in patriarchal culture, machismo identity is expected and even exalted - as with Rambo and Reagan.*[23]

According to this logic the 'limited stylistic options of self-image' pushed gangsta culture into a trap set by oppressive white male and capitalist power structures, which encourage the fetishisation of the violent black male as an image to be exploited. This is an image which did little to solve the problems of the meaningless of black existence in the ghetto. Instant (drug-financed) wealth, fast cars, guns and flashy clothes (which West identifies as important icons of 1980's and 1990s' black culture) merely mirrored the dominant ideology of white capitalism. In other words, gangsta culture acted as a kind of poor copy of the American Dream. Writing from the late 1980s, West states that, 'in this sense, George Bush, David Duke, and many gangster rap artists speak the same language from different social locations'.[24]

The major omission of both hooks' and West's analysis is the way that they underestimate the power of the mimetic image to shock thought. In this respect both of these commentators apply a simplistic dynamic to the relation between the images of dominant white culture and gangsta culture. They imply that gangsta culture fetishised the images of white cultural myths, and did little more than repeat them. hooks and West correctly identify the fact that images of white myths formed a fundamental part of gangsta culture but it is their reading of the fetish which underestimates the power of these images to assault the white cultural imagination. Or more precisely, their reading of fetishisation is one that constructs the fetish as a static process where images operate as a kind of false consciousness which blinds African-Americans to the reality of their situation. This is what West refers to as the 'limited stylistic images of self-image' in the sense that gangsta culture's concentration on the trappings of white American capitalism (fast cars, wealth and machismo violence) produced young black males who were oblivious to the fact that it was white culture which created the poverty of the urban ghetto. hooks also assumes that the African-American imitation of white cultural myths results in poor, naïve and inferior copies. However the underlying argument of this book has been that mimesis (or the act of copying) adds an extra dimension to the object which is being imitated, and this needs some unpacking within this politically important topic.

Michael Taussig argues that one of the most powerful instances of mimesis in Western modernity centres around what he calls the 'particulate sensuality' revealed in the fetishism around commodities.[25] In an argument which is very pertinent to the violent, macho images and the imitation of the American Dream which hooks and West identify as the biggest political difficulty of gangsta culture, Taussig pushes Marx and Benjamin's conceptualisation of the commodity fetish to the point where it acquires a tactile, material sensuousness, capable of changing the way that the world is perceived and thought. Taussig argues that the basis of Karl Marx's theory of commodity fetishism is the loss of contact between producers and the objects they create. The market creates a world where commodities acquire value in relation to other commodities, and not according to the labour that the workers put into producing it:

> *The relation of producers to the sum total of their own labour is presented to them as a social relation, existing not between themselves, but between the products of their labour...simply because in it the social character of men's labour appears to them as an objective character stamped upon the product of that labour.*[26]

Like Marx, Taussig goes on to argue that it is this loss of contact between the producer and the object produced which produces the illusory status of the commodity. This separation and lack of 'real' contact between the worker and the fetishised object is analogous to the criticisms that hooks and West make of gangsta culture's fetishisation of the iconic images of white America. Their argument is that such fetishisation is illusory because it ignores the real relationship of economic and social difference, and the distance which exists between the ghetto and the economic and political power of white America.

But Taussig goes on to argue that it is the fetish quality, or the 'animism and spiritual glow of the commodity' which enables modern mimetic machines such as the advertising-image to 'play with and even restore this erased sense of contact-sensuous particularity animating the fetish'.[27] He compares the commodity fetish with what Benjamin calls the aura in the sense that, like the work of art, the commodity is perceived as having its own unique properties and mystique. But modern mimetic machines, like the advertising image, have the capacity to transform the aura because of the way that they can alter the perception of the commodity or work of art. Objects or works of art become transformed into different things once they are copied in mechanical reproductions such as advertising and cinema:

> *By holding still the frame where previously the eye was disposed to skid, by focusing down into, by enlargement, by slowing down the motion of reality, scientific knowledge is obtained through mimetic reproduction in many ways. We see and comprehend hidden details of familiar objects. We become aware of patterns that had hitherto invisibly ruled our lives.*[28]

For Taussig and Benjamin, the important aspect of the capacity of mimetic machines to alter the way that the world is thought or perceived is the affective impact of such transformations. Both theorists insist upon the tactility, and the assaultive qualities of the mechanically reproduced image, arguing that new thought and knowledge is borne out of this body-first reaction. Taussig argues that 'the unremitting emphasis' of Benjamin's analysis of film and advertising 'is on the unstoppable merging of the object of perception with the body of the perceiver and not just with the mind's eye'. Both habitual and conscious thought are replaced by the bodily impact of the moving-image, and the various ways in which the camera can transform familiar objects changes the way we see and think about those objects:

This capacity of mimetic machines to pump out contact-sensuousity encased within the spectrality of a commoditised world is nothing less than the discovery of an optical unconscious, opening up new possibilities for exploring reality and providing means for changing culture and society along with those possibilities.[29]

Both Benjamin and Taussig argue that mimetic machines such as the cinema have the power to change the habitual perception which informs our view of the world, by miming that world in unfamiliar and new ways.

Taussig's reading of Benjamin is problematic in the sense that it is an analysis which is still based in the historical moment of modernity where mechanical mimetic machinery was still in its relative infancy. This results in a reading of the affective powers of the mimetic image which assumes that the bodily shock to thought which mimetic apparatus like the cinema provoke is immanent and ahistorical. Since Benjamin's writings on film, cinema itself has become constituted as a body of knowledge by critics and theorists where certain films (which have acquired the label 'classic') have gained an aura in much the same way as the non-mechanical art described by Benjamin in his seminal essay.[30] In the chapters above we have already discussed the way in which genres of film such as *noir* and the classic gangster film have become objects of postmodern nostalgia rather than images which excite some kind of immediate, bodily affect. I argued that part of the nostalgia for *film noir* was due to the fact that contemporary audiences yearning for the same kind of affect that they imagine was produced in the original viewers of the genre. This does not mean that Taussig's notion of mimesis is irrelevant in the study of contemporary film but it does mean that 'the optical unconscious' like the Freudian or Lacanian unconscious is shaped by historical process and is racialised within the American context.

The notion that images have an immanent capacity to reshape thought and the way we see the world by shocking the body has implications for the way that *Menace II Society* juxtaposes images of the dangerous black body and iconic, fetishised images of white culture. One of the significant points concerning *Menace II Society's* mimesis of other images is that the film is very aware of the way that previous cinema has become fetishised rather than immediate and affective.[31] And it is this awareness which also makes the concept of mimesis a useful one from which to problematise hooks' and West's respective political critiques of the film and gangsta culture in general. The film performs a mimesis of images which have gained an auratic presence within the white cultural and cinematic imagination, and this imitation reveals a genealogy of the racial organisation of the white

American optical unconscious, because it reanimates those objects with the affective presence of the black body.

Although *Menace II Society* refers to a dazzling array of different styles of image-making, I want to focus on the film's mimesis of three different types. *Film noir*, the Scorsesean cinema of the 1970s, and the 'True Crime' TV genre of the 1990s have all achieved an affective impact in their contemporary historical moment. They have also been subsequently discussed by critics in terms of their stylistic properties after this initial impact. These images signify transitional moments in the historical development of the optical unconscious of the white cultural imagination. Crucially it has been the visibility or (invisibility) of blackness that has played a defining role in this development, and the mimesis of these images by *Menace II Society* reveals this genealogy. The rest of this chapter will be concerned with these three different stages of the optical unconscious as they are charted by the film.

All of this is not to deny that West and hooks are right to point out that there is a certain kind of nihilism present in the violence of gangsta culture and that *Menace II Society* reflects this. The bleak unremitting picture of urban black violence confirms the fears of genocide and black male self-hate feared by hooks and West. But this nihilism cannot be thought outside of the constant mimetic allusions that gangsta and hip-hop culture make towards iconic images in white American culture. *Menace II Society* celebrates its own capability to provide cinematic immediacy and affect, while suggesting that white cinematic genres struggle to move beyond the knowledge-based and distanciated nostalgia of the postmodern blockbuster - as we saw in the first chapter of this book with *Falling Down*. The way that *Menace II Society* encourages both of these readings of the film makes it difficult to produce a clear-cut analysis which is not politically ambivalent, but this ambiguity in itself means that it is difficult to approach the film with authoritative knowledge.

The Mimesis of Noir

One of the key places where it is possible to read the film as a portrait of black nihilism and as an affective challenge to the white cultural imagination is in its relationship to *film noir*. *Menace II Society's* mimesis of *film noir* highlights the repression and marginalisation of images of African American peoples and culture in Hollywood cinema. The post-war moment of *noir* is also the period when Gilles Deleuze argues that the affective structures of the action-image were at their most fragile.[32] Cracks were appearing in the concrete sensory motor-relations between the individual protagonist and the milieu in which they were situated. Chance and coincidence were more prevalent in the world of *noir*, and the certainty of the individual being able to overcome obstacles and modify the milieu he inhabited were less secure than in previous Hollywood genres of the action-image. As I noted in Chapter 1 orthodox readings of *film noir* have discussed this fragility in terms of both its stylistic properties (particularly European influences such as German Expressionism) and as an uncovering of the violent, pessimistic reality which lies behind the false optimism and confidence of the American Dream. In contrast to this, Marc Vernet and Deleuze read these cracks in the structures of the action-image as a kind of buttress against any fundamental damage to the ideology of the American Dream. As Deleuze puts it, 'the American cinema had the means to save its dream by passing through nightmares'.[33]

But one of the reasons why it is difficult for contemporary audiences to be affected by *film noir* is the almost total exclusion and marginalisation of any African American presence. In post-war years one of the major threats to the American Dream, and its ideology of individualism with a responsibility towards a well-defined and stable community, has been the growth of African-American political and social protest and the urban ghettos. These are not purely post-war phenomenon, but the politics of race has gained a much greater visibility in the media. Consequently it is almost impossible to 'take seriously' a predominantly urban genre like *noir*, where African-Americans are almost completely absent. *Menace II Society*, like other films in the New Black Realism genre, reanimates the affective power of the *noir* genre by juxtaposing its familiar theme of the corruption of the American Dream with the affective power of the black body.

Manthia Diawara argues that New Black Realism imitates *film noir* and these films 'orient the *noir* style towards a description of a black public sphere and a black way of life'.[34] He traces this development by comparing the aesthetic properties of *noir* to the African-American crime writer Chester Himes, who was producing novels such as *A Rage in Harlem* and *Cotton Comes to Harlem* contemporaneously with white *noir*. Diawara argues that the most famous reading of *noir*, provided by Borde and Chaumeton, describes '*noir* as purely a style which uses the tropes of blackness as metaphors for the white characters' moral transgressions and falls from grace'.[35] Himes, on the other hand, uses conventional *noirish* tropes of violence and pessimism 'to subvert its (the *noir* genre's) main tenet: that blackness is a fall from whiteness'.[36] According to Diawara, the main point of Himes' novel, *A Rage in Harlem*, is social protest at the way that 'black people are trapped in the darkness of white captivity, and the light shed on them is meant to render them visible not white':[37]

In a paradoxical sense, the redeployment of the noir style by black film-makers redeems blackness from its genre definition by recasting the relation between light and dark on the screen as a metaphor for making black people and their cultures visible.[38]

According to Diawara, the violence and pessimism in Himes' novels are utilised to express the 'black rage at white America' for creating the confined poverty-stricken conditions of the urban ghettos.[39] New Black Realism's display of the violence of the 1990s' urban ghetto is in the tradition of Himes, and the figure of the gangsta is a descendant of Bigger Thomas in Richard Wright's seminal novel of black rage, *Native Son*. Unlike the readings of gangsta culture produced by bell hooks and Cornel West, Diawara argues that 'It is misleading...to see black femme fatales, neurotic detectives and grotesque bad guys as poor imitations of their white counterparts'.[40] Both Himes' novels and the films of New Black Realism contain such representations to self-reflexively show the way that black rage manifests itself within the urban ghettos of the US. At the same time these cultural productions are themselves infused with this rage and these representations reflect this.

Diawara goes on to note that:

> ...this rage often takes the form of an eroticised violence by men against women and homosexuals, a savage explosion on the part of some characters against others whom they seek to control, and a perverse mimicry of the status quo through recourse to disfigurement, mutilation and a grotesque positioning of weaker characters to stronger ones.[41]

These comments are suggestive, but in his focus on the representational content of '*noir* by noirs', Diawara does not explore the distinct aesthetic and affective properties of the literature of Richard Wright, Chester Himes and the films of New Black Realism - beyond the assertion that 'there is something in the narrative of films like *Boyz N the Hood* that links them to existent reality in Black communities'.[42] This book is arguing that New Black Realism and gangsta culture's 'perverse mimicry of the status quo' is as much about the aesthetics of black cinema and the affect that this cinema has on the white cultural imagination. The mimesis of the *noir* style in *Menace II Society* reveals the aesthetic crisis in white cinema, where it is only black action films which can be taken seriously, and provoke an affective or immediate impact. The film celebrates and uses this power to assault white audiences. But the film is also constantly distinguishing between its power to affect and the tendency for the white cultural imagination to associate blackness with the authenticity or the 'reality' of its representations.

We can explore this by looking in detail at a typical stylistic device of *noir* also used by *Menace II Society*; the retrospective narrative voice-over of a central protagonist who is revealed to be dead by the end of the film. Caine's 'dead voice-over' links the film directly to *noir* 'classics' such as *Sunset Boulevard* (Wilder 1955), *Laura* (Preminger 1944) and (virtually) *Double Indemnity* (Wilder 1944). On one level we can read the use of this device as a deconstruction of the white cultural imagination's tendency to over-invest in blackness as a sign of authenticity and truth. The cinematic voice-over has often been read by theorists and critics as a device used by filmmakers to evoke authority and truth, and to provide a reliable focal point for the viewer's attention. As Paula Massood notes, *Menace II Society* disrupts this tendency:

> *Although this technique is most closely associated with traditional narrative styles in which identification with the protagonist is unified and absolute,* Menace II Society *subverts this technique by simultaneously giving truth and primacy to Caine's version of events, while underscoring Caine's unreliability as a narrator (and the unreliability of all narrators). In voice-over, Caine repeatedly questions his actions and seemingly makes a decision, only to oppose that decision without offering any explanation.*[43]

There are several key instances of this ambiguity between what Caine says and what the action of the film shows. Two of the most notable examples are first, when Mr Butler attempts to persuade Caine to leave for Kansas, and second, when Ronnie asks him to accompany her and her son to Atlanta. Caine's narration implies that both of these attempts to make him leave the ghetto have been successful. But the following action shows Caine to be firmly ensconced in the nightmarish violence of the ghetto and seemingly unable to act on his decisions. He is stopped either because unforeseen obstacles (such as random beatings from the police), or events which occur as consequences of his own actions (such as the revenge attack of the cousin of the woman who is pregnant by Caine), prevent any flight from the 'hood.

Caine occupies the focal point for the viewer's sympathies in much the same way that Tre does in *Boyz N the Hood*. It is through Tre's eyes that the audience is encouraged to both view and believe that what they are seeing is the reality of life in the 'hood. But as I noted in the last chapter, this 'truth' is relayed to the viewer within the comparatively anachronistic structures of the action-image where the individual protagonist's relationship to the milieu of the film is primary. In the action-image, it is possible for the viewer to believe that the individual protagonist has a degree of power by controlling the terms of that relationship through action. Therefore at the end of *Boyz*, Tre is seen to be taking the 'right' action by rejecting the continuation of violence offered by Doughboy in his revenge shooting of Rikki's killers. It is these anachronistic structures of the individual's power over the milieu which makes *Boyz* a safe film for white audiences to watch, because the ideology of the American Dream is preserved - and indeed strengthened because it is a black character who is seen to uphold its ideological reality. In *Menace II Society*, the ambivalent narrative of Caine prevents a similar security in the viewing pleasures of white audiences, because the safe structures of the action-image are revealed as unstable. Caine's authenticity as a narrator (granted to him by the tendency of white culture to invest in blackness as a signifier of 'truth', as well as the conventions of *noir*) is undermined because of his unreliability.

This is not to say that *Menace II Society* denies the affective power that images of black masculinity have on the white cultural imagination, but the film is attempting to prevent images of blackness becoming a site of voyeuristic pleasure. The viewer is not granted a position where they know and control the reality of black life in the urban ghetto through identification with a reliable black narrator. In fact, the film attempts to leave the viewer in a position of powerlessness, in terms of knowledge of the 'hood, and in terms of the solidity of the cultural memories of cinematic genres such as *noir*.

Joan Copjec offers a Lacanian reading of the dead voice-over device in classic *noir* which is useful in placing *Menace II Society's* mimesis of the genre and its capacity to affect a contemporary audience within a specific historical moment. She argues that the division between the past tense dead voice-over and the 'present' visible body of the narrator in the film's real time action signified the emergence of the Lacanian Real in *film noir*. The voice-over is not a method to make seamless the gap between the knowledge of the narrator as actor in the diegesis and as an omniscient, unseen presence - which has been the orthodox theoretical position. Rather, this technique signals 'the positivisation of the narrator's absence from the very diegetic reality his speech inscribes'.[44] In Lacanian terms the Real only surfaces fully during the subject's death. Before that, the subject is bound up in the breaches and lacks that provoke desire once she or he enters and functions in the world of language or Symbolic reality. This is not to say that even in death the 'impenetrable kernel' of the Real is ever fully exposed. It is rather that the drive has finally won out over desire because desire no longer exists in the dead subject. In terms of the dead voice-over, Copjec argues that the inconsistencies between the action and the narration of the voice-over suggest the emergence of the Real or the drive over desire. The Real is not exposed in these inconsistencies in a Symbolic description but the position of the nonsensical void of the Real is.[45]

Copjec argues that there are historical and cultural reasons for the emergence of the Real in post-war film, and these echo the suggestions of Deleuze that *noir* is where the relations between individual protagonist and his milieu are at their most fragile in the cinema of the action-image. Copjec argues that post-war America was a time when there was an emphasis on the 'choice of private enjoyment over community'.[46] The displacement of population during the war, the growth of consumerism, suburban expansion, ethnic and racial segregation and existentialism are symptomatic of this change.[47] This fear of the shift away from the public importance of stable communities can also be detected in *It's a Wonderful Life* (Capra 1946). The brilliant *noir*-like sequence I discussed in Chapter 1 where George Bailey is shown what Bedford Falls would be like if he had chosen private individual enjoyment instead of maintaining his concrete links and responsibilities to the community, indicates anxieties around the breakdown of the small-town American community upon which the American Dream was dependent.[48] Copjec goes on to note that *noir* is symptomatic of the breakdown of distinctions between public and private and illustrates that 'one's privacy ceases to be something one savours when sheltered from private eyes, and becomes instead something one visibly endures'.[49] The shocking aspect of *noir* for contemporary audiences was that its narratives exposed dark, sinister and private secrets which were previously unspoken and belonged to the realm of the Real. The Real, as the most impenetrable aspect of that private domain, necessarily starts to emerge as public and consequently it results in the death of the existing Symbolic structures of the community - because it changes the rules of what previously constituted the public. The private becomes public which 'changes the very character of privacy and, indeed, of 'society' in general' - because the new 'public' private causes the old public community 'to shatter into incommensurable fragments'.[50] In other words, the concentration on the individual and the private as estranged from the familiar and well-grounded milieu of 'community as undivided world' results in the further fragmentation of that community. The inconsistencies between the 'private' narrative voice-over and the public actions of the protagonist are symptomatic of the fact that the Symbolic rules of the community are being disrupted and threatened by the private and individual drive - which has now become public because of post-war social changes. This shocking aspect of *noir* is no longer present in today's audiences, because the dead voice-over device is seen to be simply that, a clichéd stylistic device which becomes a pastiche or parody when utilised in films such as *Blade Runner* (Scott 1982) or *Goodfellas* (Scorsese 1990).

Menace II Society both reanimates and reverses the affective power of dead voice-over. From the perspective of Copjec's argument, the inconsistencies between Caine's private narrative and his public actions echo that of the protagonist in classic *noir*, as the Real of Caine's private drive of survival through an escape from the 'hood cannot be fully expressed as a desire in his narrative. The elisions and gaps in his public/private voice-over suggest this conflict. Caine has public Symbolic functions which keep him embedded in the ghetto, and O'Dog, who is the figure most ensconced in the 'hood, is quick to remind him of this, calling him a 'sell-out motherfucker' when he finally decides to leave with Ronnie. In another sense though, Caine is in a position which is the reverse of a *noir* hero, because the public space of the 'hood has already become the embodiment of the Real. Classic *noir* displays a world where the Symbolic codes between individual and milieu still retain a residual presence. Even if the police are corrupt and the heroes ambiguous, there still remains a structure of what is acceptable in the everyday functioning of the *noir* world. In other words, there still remains a division between the Symbolic codes which govern society and the unspoken anarchic and violent Real which erupts with increasing regularity. In *Menace II Society*, it is the private Caine expressed through the elliptical, misleading voice-over, who desires a sense of Symbolic order, and the public space of the 'hood which acts like the Real, in the sense that violent meaningless events happen without warning.

The opening scene marks the instability of the Symbolic network of the 'hood, and the unpredictable appearance of the Real. Caine and O'Dog walk into a Korean store to buy beer, and after a comment made by the storekeeper about feeling sorry for their mothers, O'Dog shoots the storekeeper and his wife, takes the CCTV video and the takings, while Caine watches on in horror and disbelief. All Caine's voice-over can say to this horrifying scene is, 'went into the store to get a beer - came out an accessory to murder and armed robbery. It was funny like that in the 'hood sometimes...you never knew what was gonna happen and when'. The 'hood is a world where the police kidnap you and dump you in a hostile neighbourhood, and where 'meaningless' violence is an everyday occurrence. Caine's situation is a mimesis of that of George Bailey's in the sense that both protagonists desire to leave their respective milieu. As with all examples of mimesis there is both similarity and alterity, and the difference between George and Caine's situation is that the 'hood which Caine wants to leave is the same as the imaginary Bedford Falls which George is shown by the angel in the nightmare sequence. Both milieux appear to be governed by the anarchic and savage Real where unpredictable violence is likely to occur at any given moment. What had previously been the private nightmare of the individual has become the public horror of a whole community.

Yet, reading this screen representation of the 'hood as the embodiment of the Real raises several questions concerning the affect of *Menace II Society* on the white cultural imagination. Such an interpretation suggests the possibility that the white viewer is able to categorise black rage and the urban ghetto as a meaningless and anarchic void, and watch the film as an ethnographic voyeur, untouched by this violence. There is a key scene in the film which encapsulates this position. One of the film's few white characters comes to the black gang's house in Watts to employ them as car thieves for an insurance scam. When this white-collar criminal is asked to come back to the ghetto at night, he becomes visibly afraid, inviting a tirade of abuse from a gang-member who criticises him for not being too scared to get a black man to steal for him. As long as the white character is able to stay out of the physical confines of the 'hood, he is able to use its violence for his own advantage, without having to face the dangers it contains. There is an analogy here with the position of the white cinema-goer. The black-character in the scene is well aware of the paranoia and anxiety that the white cultural imagination has when confronted with the 'hood, and he is also aware that this is a world that the urban African-American has to achieve some kind of meaningful existence within. In other words, what the character and the scene suggest is that there is a clash of two Symbolic cultural discourses.

In the last chapter I argued that the cinematic use of the language and music of gangsta and rap culture worked to both titillate the white viewer and obstruct meaning at crucial moments when the voyeuristic instinct was most provoked. The gap between the intentions of Caine's voice-over, and his actions is another example of this conflict between different Symbolic structures of signification. His 'inner conflict' is an attempt to negotiate both Symbolic structures as he voices the desire to fulfil the American Dream of life with his surrogate family, while engaging with and being subject to, the reality of gang life in the 'hood. The dream of escape is something which the white cultural imagination can understand, and causes the white viewer to identify with Caine, while the sudden outbreaks of violence and Caine's participation in that violence constantly rupture this empathy.

The film does more than disrupt the identification processes of the white cultural identification with the lead character. The incomprehension and powerlessness of the white viewer in the face of the violence also highlights the way that the urban ghetto functions as a space of the Real for white Symbolic structures of meaning. Moreover, it also points towards the reasons why the white cultural imagination has constructed urban black communities as a space where the violence is meaningless, primitive and savage. The other reaction of the white character of the scene I have been discussing is one of guilt, as he pathetically apologises to the gangsta character for his fear and ignorance of the codes of the ghetto. Similarly, the film as a whole makes it clear that the conditions of the ghetto are caused by white racial rage towards the black community. At the outset, the viewer is presented with a potted history of white oppression during the civil rights movement, and the white responsibility for the flow of drugs into the ghetto. For the white cultural imagination to admit responsibility and guilt for the conditions of the 'hood is to entertain the irrational violence of racial rage towards black communities. Such an acknowledgement would also undermine the central tenets of individual freedom and responsibility towards an undivided community which are at the heart of the American Dream. The 'hood then becomes a place of senseless violence for the white cultural imagination, because to ascribe meaning to the violence of black rage would be to destabilise the authority of white American cultural identity while accepting that this identity has been built on white racial rage. The film plays on this repressed sense of guilt by its constant allusions to the violence which constitutes the cinema and culture of white America.

Racial Rage and the Crisis of the Action-Image

In relation to the question of cinematic affect, and the history of American cinema, *Menace II Society* also points towards the moments where white racial rage and the clash of two Symbolic structures of signification destabilise the cinema of the

American Dream - the cinema of the action-image. Despite the best efforts of Hollywood cinema to repress white racial rage through the marginalisation of African-American bodies and cultures within action-image genres such as noir, it has manifested itself in ways which has produced the downfall of this kind of cinema. This decline has been marked in terms of the action-image's ability to affect and be 'taken seriously', rather than its commercial success. Or as Deleuze puts it, 'the greatest commercial successes always take that route, but the soul of cinema no longer does'.[51]

In chapter one I suggested (after Deleuze) that Martin Scorsese's films are exemplary examples of the cinema of the crisis of the action-image. Films such as *Taxi-Driver* and *Mean Streets* self-reflexively display situations where the bonds between individual, situation and milieu have become dispersed and fragmented to the point where it is no longer possible for the protagonist to modify the world he inhabits through action and for the milieu to affect him. The cinema of the crisis of the action-image is filled with 'white events, events which never truly concern the person who provokes or is subject to them, even when they strike him in the flesh'.[51] Both Travis Bickle (Robert de Niro) in Taxi Driver and Charlie (Harvey Keitel) in Mean Streets have this weakened relationship with the cinematic world they exist in. Scorsese's films are filled with, what Lesley Stern calls, moments of 'dramatic intensity' rather than a central narrative which is structured and defined by the protagonist's relationship of action with the cinematic milieu. These are dispersed throughout the text 'so that individual scenes, moments, gestures, are invested with sensate significance'.[52] The dominant affective images of Scorsesean cinema are not necessarily central to the narrative of the film, but the distinct moments of sweeping camera movements, use of slow motion, still shots, and repetition of scenes provide its affective power.

Menace II Society alludes to Scorsese's cinema on many occasions and does so from the outset. The narrative structure is circular rather than linear, and the film's most trenchant moments are marked by their visceral intensity. In the first scene we get long slow tracking shots following O'Dog and Caine through the liquor store, intercut with orthodox shot-reverse shots of the Korean woman watching over them, and speeded up pan-shots between them and the shopkeeper. The unsettling fluidity of the camera movements, along with the sometimes barely audible dialogue between O'Dog and Caine (whose identity we are unaware of at this stage), is directly reminiscent of the cinema of Scorsese. The u uuuuuu npredictability and extreme movements of the camera work against the banal 'everydayness' of the setting to produce similar points of 'dramatic intensity'. The Scorsesian image is also utilised at the actual moment of narrative violence when O'Dog shoots the shopkeeper. The camera fixes on Caine's face as the argument between O'Dog and the shopkeeper ensues, and just before the shooting starts we get a fast-moving zoom-in on Caine as he drinks his beer, and drops the bottle as the shooting starts. In a way which also evokes the narrative violence of Classical Hollywood, we do not get to see the actual shooting but just a flash image of the dead Korean.

Paula Masood argues that this kind of mimesis is no more than the masterful execution of a 'stylistics of violence, standardised since its introduction in *Bonnie and Clyde*'.[53] But I would suggest again that the mimesis of this 'non-Hollywood Hollywood cinema' provokes a rethinking and reanimation of that cinema.[54] Scorsese's cinema of the seventies marks a particular moment when the symptoms of white racial rage could no longer be contained and repressed within the cinema of the action-image. Many of the moments of dramatic intensity that replace the linear narrative and well-defined relations between protagonist and milieu in Scorsese's cinema of the crisis of the action-image are caused by the self-reflexive unfolding of scenes where there is conflict between two racially organised Symbolic structures of meaning.

The fear and desire which is evoked in white American culture by black bodies is played out in *Mean Streets* with Charlie's fascination with a black dancer in the club where much of the film's action takes place. He sits in the bar gazing at her on the stage, while his voice-over questions his attraction to her in terms of race:

She is really good looking.

I gotta say that again...She is really good looking

But she's black.

You can see that real plain, right?

Well, look there's not much of difference anyway, is there.

Well, is there?

It is race which remains the unanswered example of the many questions which Charlie is confronted with throughout the film. He sticks by what he believes to be his Catholic duty in his loyalty to Johnny-Boy and Theresa. But the prevarications and ambiguity, that accompany his drive to go beyond the Symbolic boundaries of his own ethnic structure, remain intact - and without a sense of closure for him or the viewer. He arranges to meet the black dancer for a date and drives straight past the place they are supposed to meet. Unresolved racial tension is signalled again at the end of the film when an image of the dancer flashes up on screen as Charlie crawls out of the near-fatal car wreck.

This scene suggests that the threat to the Symbolic structures of white cultural identity come from the anxiety around, and desire for, ethnic difference which constitutes the unspoken Real of the white cultural imagination. More precisely it is the paranoia and racial rage, provoked by this Real, which destabilises a clear sense of white cultural identity. The power to act within a milieu is disrupted by the dread of the unknown, and the desire to preserve the authority and stability of ethnic identity is the greatest risk to that identity. In *Goodfellas* (1990), the only 'made man' or true member of the gangster family is someone with 'one hundred per cent Italian blood' which is why Tommy (Joe Pesci) is eligible, and Henry (Ray Liotta) and Jimmy Conway (Robert de Niro) are not. Yet it is Tommy who poses the greatest threat to the community of gangsters as the embodiment of the violent excess which underpins their whole Symbolic structure. The fact that racial rage lies behind this excess is marked by the repetition of a particular scene in *Goodfellas*. We see two scenes of Tommy shooting Stax Edwards (the only black figure involved in the Lufthansa heist) twice - once for no obvious narrative reason, and then again to the accompaniment of Henry's voice-over. In terms of the conflict between the action-image and the crisis of the action-image, Tommy must die because he acts as a kind of Real for the milieu of the Mafia in his complete disregard for the etiquette and rules governing the status of the 'made man'. Scorsese's films are about the disintegration of clearly defined milieux which destroy themselves through their own surplus of the Real. Johnny-Boy in *Mean Streets* and Tommy in *Goodfellas* are the excess embodiment of the violence which underpins and supports the community of gangsters and 'wise guys'. They act as the buttress to, as well as destroyer of, the gangster milieu in the same way as psychoanalysts describe the function of the Real and the Symbolic in more universal terms. This is one of the reasons why Tommy appears in the scene at the end, firing directly at the camera and resurrected from his narrative death. The Symbolic structure of the narrative cannot contain his Real presence.

Taxi Driver demonstrates most clearly the way that racial rage and fear of racial difference prevent the protagonist being able to take effective action to modify the milieu, and the fact that the events produced in the world he inhabits no longer matter to him. And it is *Taxi Driver* that provides a clear example of the difference between the cinema of the action-image and that of the crisis. This is largely because, as Lesley Stern points out, '*Taxi Driver* remakes *The Searchers* (Ford 1956) in part through resurrecting the character of Ethan Edwards in Travis Bickle, but also through its filmic exploration of the pathological narrative.'[55] She goes on to note that this remaking is not 'in the sense of producing a simulation of the original...but rather by recasting or acting out a scenario that simmers within the classical constraints of the Fordian text'. She argues that what is recast in *Taxi Driver*, through the symmetrical relationship between the restless wandering of Travis Bickle and the goal-orientated travel of Ethan, is the question of 'what troubles a man?'[56] I would suggest further that the question which is reanimated is 'what troubles a white man?'

Stern suggests that the reason why this question burns within the filmic text, for both the characters and the viewer, is the way in which 'an oscillation between "home" and "away" is modulated'.[57] The concept of home for both Ethan and Travis has been altered in a way in which home is no longer home. Ethan's home has been destroyed by the massacre of the Edwards family and the abduction of Debbie by the Indian Chief, Scar. Travis is totally out of joint with the world he lives in, and home for him is reduced to the mobile and unstable shell of his taxi-cab, through which passes a variety of people he is unable to interact with in any meaningful way. As Stern notes, both Ethan and Travis attempt to resolve their homelessness through 'an impulse to rescue - to "return home" a woman who does not want to be saved'.[58] For Ethan, the woman is his niece, Debbie (Natalie Wood), and for Travis, she is Iris (Jody Foster), a twelve-year old prostitute, held under the influence and force of her pimp, Sport (Harvey Keitel). In both films, we are talking about the destabilising of a well-defined relationship between milieu and protagonist, but in *The Searchers*, the consequences of this are repressed within the centrality of the orthodox revenge narrative, while *Taxi Driver* refutes the importance of narrative in favour of the moments of dramatic intensity discussed above. Yet, in both films there is the presence of an obsessional drive to both restore a sense of home and find someone to blame for its loss, and this is racial rage. In *The Searchers* the 'other race' as threat is what motivates the narrative, and Ethan's drive to rescue and restore. Ethan is consumed by fear and anger at the thought of Scar 'polluting' Debbie with his sexual touch, to the point at which it is unclear whether Ethan will save or kill his niece. As Stern notes, 'for Ethan the Indian "other" becomes the locus of pollution, and the white girl is seen to be contaminated by his touch'.[59]

As Stern notes, 'In *Taxi Driver* the racial issue is more dispersed, but no less germane'.[60] Unlike *The Searchers* the fear of the other race as a contagious pollutant is not the obvious central motivating factor behind the film's narrative and the central protagonist's actions. Indeed Travis' narrative of rescue and restoration has no easily definable linearity to it at all. Iris, the object of his unwanted salvation, is not even seen until some way into the film, and it is about two thirds of the way through before she and Travis have any kind of a conversation. But throughout the film there is the suggestion that racial rage is one of the key motivating factors behind Travis' actions. There are several key moments which suggest that Travis views African-Americans as the 'animals' which come out at night and who are responsible for the decay of the city. In one diner scene, a slow and low, off-centre tracking shot distracts the viewer's attention away from the other taxi-driver's conversation to Travis' view of the black pimps sitting opposite, with one of them languidly and menacingly tapping a match on the table. The static medium shot of Travis and the other taxi-drivers marks a vivid contrast to the slow movement of the medium close-ups of the pimps. The perspective of the frame, the movement of the camera and the shades, suits and wide-brimmed hats of the pimps give the impression that the diner and the city is full of these characters, even though there are only two of them in shot. The idea of racial anger underpinning Travis' actions is even stronger when taking into account some of the factors behind the film's production. Lesley Stern notes that:

In the commentary on the film on laserdisc Scorsese reveals that Sport was originally conceived of as black, and it is worth remembering that the Motion Picture Production Code of 1930 stated that 'miscegenation (sex relationships between the white and black races) is forbidden'.[61]

The nihilistic, random, psychotic violence which the white imagination projects onto the black rage in films like *Menace II Society* and images of the real black community, are visible as white phenomena in both of these films. In *The Searchers* the classical narrative attempts to conceal this through its structures of narrative and secondary identification. The viewer is encouraged to see the film through the eyes of Ethan, and it is he who carries the action and narrative drive of the film. Having said this, the tensions and ambiguities in the underlying Real of racial rage do surface at key moments to disrupt the classical form. The film does not produce the ending that its classical structure requires in the sense that Ethan's actions do not signal closure. As Stern argues:

Ethan neither finds Debbie nor kills Scar. His actions consist of not-shooting Debbie and of scalping Scar. Although these two actions might seem to strain in different directions they are intricately bound up together and can be thought of as a single act, one that is inscribed as an obsessive repetition rather than a resolution (thus signalling further re-enactment).[62]

Racial rage is not resolved in the film even if Debbie has been saved. Ethan's inability to act (except for the scalping) signals a crisis in the certainties of action in the Western milieu, and also a crisis in the viewer's willingness to maintain an untroubled belief in that cinematic world. Ethan can no longer affect the milieu he inhabits because that milieu has become fragmented, and it is no longer possible for the audience to believe in the certainties of the Fordian homestead, and Debbie's place within that milieu when the central protagonist is consumed with an irrational rage, and unable to act. More questions than answers are raised by the film's conclusion. What will Ethan *not* be able to do next? *The Searchers*, like *It's a Wonderful Life*, signals a point of crisis for the sensory motor connections between protagonist and milieu in the action-image cinema.

The debilitating effects of racial rage are more pronounced in the actions of Travis Bickle. In terms of the actions of the central protagonist, '*Taxi Driver* presents a hero who definitively acts, perpetrating single-handedly an extremely bloody massacre'. But, as Stern again notes, the scene where Travis 'rescues' Iris is:

> not presented narratively as a resolution; rather it too is inscribed as an obsessive repetition, in a narrative that is profoundly disturbed in its frequent veering into aimlessly compulsive trajectories. Doubling the misrecognition over and over again, Travis Bickle, the hero as psychotic, has risen like a double-headed King-Kong from the ashes of The Searchers.[63]

Discussing *Taxi Driver* in terms of a narrative closure misses the point because of the film's own obsessive drive to disrupt and break away from the conventions and codes of the action-image. Travis' story is not one which comes to an end when the film ends - a fact signified by the continuing images of the city from the taxi's rear-view mirror as the final credits roll. The film releases the psychotic racial rage which is straining within the classical structure of *The Searchers*, so that it reverberates throughout the whole film in a series of almost disparate images, rather than as an element in a narrative build-up to a final climax - or non-climax in the case of *The Searchers*.

Scorsese's cinema is symptomatic of the moment when it became impossible to believe in the cinema of the action-image. But this too is a cinema which has become less one of affect and more one where knowledge is a key aspect of the viewing experience. The stylistic flourishes of the Scorsesean camera and the circular, disjointed narratives of the films have become as clichéd as the action-image cinema they helped to supplant. It is also a cinema which expresses a nostalgic return for the certainties of the cinema of the action-image, with its nomadic protagonists mourning the loss of the well-defined structures of situation and action between themselves and a milieu. The racial rage that drives the excesses of a character like Travis Bickle are reanimated in *Menace II Society* by the presence of a politically-charged contemporary black rage. This mimesis can be explored by returning once again to the opening scene of *Menace II Society*.

The grocery store hold-up is a scene which has occurred in dozens of films where white outlaws or gangsters are on the run or just looking for some easy money. In *Taxi Driver* this stereotypical scene is permeated with racial rage. Shortly after acquiring his arsenal, Travis shoots a black man demanding cash from the till and threatening a white storekeeper with a gun. After the would-be robber has been shot dead, the white storekeeper repeatedly and savagely smashes the dead black body with an iron bar. *Menace II Society* replays this scene using the unpredictability of the Scorsesian image to reinforce the seemingly psychotic violence of O'Dog, who has no obvious intention to rob the store. But underlying the apparently random motiveless violence of O'Dog is the political racial relations between the Korean and African-American community.

Mike Davis notes the 'catastrophic collapse of relations between LA's black and Korean communities' which was sparked off by the shooting of fifteen-year-old Latasha Harlins in the back of the head by a Korean grocer, Soon Ja Du, over a $1.79 bottle of orange juice, in 1991. 'A white judge, Joyce Karlin let Du off with a $500 fine and some community service'. Davis argues that the LA riots of 1992, far from being 'blind, systematic destruction', were 'ruthlessly systematic' in their targeting of 'the myriad Korean-owned liquor stores' in the areas from Compton to Koreatown itself.[64] In this light the Korean store-keepers comments about feeling sorry for O'Dog's mother takes on a new, politically and racially charged meaning for the Symbolic codes of the gangsta, as opposed to the 'meaningless' affect such violence has for the white cultural imagination.[65]

Authenticity and Affect in the Video Image

In the first chapter I suggested that one manifestation of the use of black bodies to provide an affective charge in the 1990s was the 'True Crime' TV genre. Programmes such as *Cops* and *Tales of the Highway Patrol* produce image after image of African Americans suspected of and being arrested for criminal activity. Most of these programmes also use 'live' video footage from 'fly on the fender' cameras to signify the authenticity of the action. But the belief that what is happening in these programmes is real is provided chiefly by the predominantly black suspects, and the instant reaction which young black males provoke in white viewers. The genre serves as another example of the way in which the white cultural imagination of the 1990s harnessed the racially organised disposition of the visible to confuse the affective response provoked by African-American bodies with the authenticity of its own cultural productions. *Menace II Society* mimics this process in several key scenes to deconstruct the association between the affect of blackness and authenticity.

The scene which immediately follows the opening credits is a news report of the Watts Riots of 1965. The sequence begins with an overhead black and white shot of the Watts district which evokes memories of a similar shot of New York in *The Naked City* (Dassin 1948) - a film noted for its documentary-like realism. The film then presents a series of images showing the white police and National Guard violently suppressing the black rioters with batons, rifles and machine guns, accompanied by a soundtrack featuring fragments of reports of the riots which are joined together with no discernible continuity. The interesting point about the images of violence in this sequence is that even though we get the impression we are watching and hearing the original footage of the riots, the pixels on the images are enlarged so we cannot see the faces of the police and the rioters. This is a video technique used regularly on 'Reality TV' to 'protect' the identity of the predominantly black suspects. Simulating this type this kind of image in the context of 'historical' footage of the 1965 Watts Riots has two affects. First, the video effect of the large pixels gives the footage a kind of contemporary immediacy which plays on associations of blackness, violence and authenticity. The scenes achieve this by contracting the time and distance between footage which has the authority of 'historical reality', and the kind of immediate reality which fly on the fender techniques give to Reality TV shows.

But second, and paradoxically, the 'pixilation' of these images also raises uncertainties about the authority of the immediacy of the 'real-life' video television *and* historical footage. If the historical film-image can be manipulated to seem contemporary, then the question is raised as to the unreliability of the fetish that the visual imagination places on such footage. Black and white news footage gains an authority based in realism because of its distanced status as 'history' - a standing which is reinforced by the fact that such footage was regarded as the 'truth' at the time it was shot. Contracting the time between 'then and now' by manipulating such images through video destroys the fetish constructed around TV news history. The authority of all images is open to question - not just in the sense of its narrative accuracy - but also in the way the image itself can be created to produce certain meanings. The fact that there is a discontinuous soundtrack of fragments of different new reports adds to this uncertainty, giving the impression that narrative wholes and ways of making sense and reality are produced from fragments.

The questioning of video as method of immediacy and authenticity is also raised in the constant resurfacing in the film's narrative of the CCTV videotape of opening killing. The film uses the videotape to evoke and question several assumptions that the white cultural imagination makes about different types of cinematic and narrative realism. The tape is first mentioned at a party scene early on in the film where we are introduced to Caine's homeboys or fellow gang members, with the film moving into slow motion when a new character is introduced by Caine's voiceover. (This scene is again reminiscent of Scorsese, and particularly the bar scene in *Goodfellas* where various 'wiseguys' are introduced by Henry's voiceover). Caine voices his concern over rumours that O'Dog has been showing the incriminating tape to other gang members and we get to see the former doing this for ourselves in a scene set in one of the gang member's houses. O'Dog shows the video to other gangstas, as Caine looks on in discomfort. For the first time we also get to see the shooting of the Korean shopkeeper in full, as O'Dog and the other gangstas add their remorseless and morbidly humorous commentary. O'Dog threateningly jokes that he is going to start selling copies of the tape for $59.99, literally turning the images of reality into a commodity which can be viewed again and again for the gang's entertainment. Seeing the actual moment of violence for the first time on video and in this setting increases the shock of the killing. The videotape again evokes a sense of reality and immediacy because of the cultural associations which underlie this type of image. But the shock is increased with the montage of shots of the gang members giving a kind of film criticism of the action, as they remark on Caine's shocked reaction to the killing. Their distanced reaction to the tape adds to its sense of shocking immediacy for the viewer.

Just as important as this use of tape is the way it acts as a kind of object-token throughout the film's narrative, constantly threatening to resurface and incriminate Caine. In the scenes where Caine gets arrested for car theft, he constantly reiterates his fears that the tape will fall into the hands of the police, especially after they have found his fingerprints at the store. Then finally at the end of the film the tape reappears again, as a gang member seals it in an envelope addressed to the police in revenge for being beaten up by Caine at Ronnie's leaving party. The significant point of these reappearances is that they have no direct consequences in the film's narrative - Caine is shot dead and the film ends just after the tape is sent to the police, making irrelevant as a narrative device. As Paula Massood notes, 'While it builds tension and a false sense of foreboding, nothing comes of it - the video never connects directly to the film's later events...the video becomes nothing more than a red herring'.[66] In a classical narrative, the viewer might expect the tape to be of causal significance, and the film confounds this. Thinking of the tape as an object which means nothing also evokes *film noir* like *The Maltese Falcon* (Huston 1941) and *Kiss Me Deadly* (Aldrich 1955) where the object is ultimately everything in terms of narrative, as well as the Hitchcockian McGuffin. The fact that video becomes a 'false' hook into the narrative once again raises questions concerning the authenticity and immediacy of the video image.

Conclusion

Menace II Society's mimesis of these three types of image, the action-image, the crisis of the action-image, and video can be read as revealing an aesthetic crisis in the white cultural imagination's ability to produce images which cause an affective, body-first reaction. Moreover the film charts a history of 'white' images which have produced immediacy through racial rage. This rage has been expressed by repressing the visibility of blackness in the action-image genres of *noir* and the western, and by displaying the explosion of this rage in the cinema of the crisis of the action-image. *Menace II Society*'s mimesis of the 'True Crime' TV genre suggests that the desire to use the affective reaction caused by black bodies has shifted into mediums other than the cinema.

But in the end, the most significant consequence of the film, and New Black Realism as a whole, is the expression of black rage in a manner which reanimates the possibility of an action cinema that can produce a bodily affect. The strictly enforced confines of the cinematic milieu of the 'hood evoke the violent structures of the cinematic experience itself or what Noel Burch's calls the cinema's 'structures of aggression'.[67] The physical and psychic constraints of the images of the 'hood echo the temporary imprisonment the film viewer experiences in terms of physicality and consciousness - assaulted by the rays of light flickering on the screen in the darkened auditorium of the cinema. For the two hours of the film the viewer is like Caine, stuck within the confines of a world where violence may occur at any time. There is, in other words, a particularly strong mimetic link between the affective black body, urban milieu and the cinema viewer. The 'hood (as embodiment of the Real for the white cultural imagination) is strongly connected to the Real of the cinematic experience.

What I have been suggesting in these last two chapters is that *Boyz n the Hood* and, in particular, *Menace II Society* construct, and think through, a history of American cinema which is conceived in terms of affect, racial rage, fabrications of blackness, and a mimesis of black culture and cinema. This history also evokes and emphasises a state of aesthetic crisis in 1990s action cinema, by foregrounding the power of contemporary black cinema. New Black Realism and the gangsta film reconstituted the potential of Hollywood cinema to assault the senses and evoke thought and memory through shock. *Boyz N the Hood* and *Menace II Society* imitated, referenced and recycled the cinematic forms and structures of white Hollywood film in order to strategically attack the US white cultural imagination. On the surface, New Black Realism appears to play on white fears and anxieties surrounding 'real-life' African-American men and random criminal violence. The films can be read as cinematic social realism, 'reflecting' and reporting on 'what really goes down in the ghetto', underlining mainstream America's construction of African-American life in the ghettos of Los Angeles.[68] The representation of worlds and milieux where random violence, drugs, and general 'criminal' activities pervade every aspect of everyday life would seem to affirm fears generated by 'reality media' products, such as the 'True-Crime' fly on the wall television programmes like *Cops*. New Black Realism and the gangsta film are also full of scenes which show black bodies as dangerous bodies, reinforcing white fears of being the victims of black violence.[69] This has left the gangsta film open to charges of doing no more than fleshing out these mainstream media images with a cinematic narrative, and providing white audiences with an almost ethnographic and documentary-like voyeuristic insight into the violent life of the ghetto.

But any comfortable knowledge of the real-life conditions in the 'hood, imparted by New Black Realism (and the implicit mastery that accompanies such a voyeuristic viewing position), is prevented and reversed by the gangsta film's display and strategic employment of a sophisticated 'cine-literacy'. As I also noted, *Boyz N the Hood* and *Menace II Society* mimic white Hollywood genre characters, situations and visual styles in ways which unsettle preconceived conceptions and knowledge of cinematic realism. In *Menace II Society* especially, this recycling is particularly marked in scenes and episodes of cinematic violence. From the classic gangster film, to *film noir*, to the western, to Peckinpah, to Scorsese, to the 1980s' postmodern action film, memories of just about every Hollywood aesthetic style of visual violence are evoked in the film. But this mimesis of previous forms and images is more than what Paula Massood calls the 'masterful, pleasurable and *familiar* cinematography of violence'.[70] There is an absence of nostalgia for the frequently assumed realism and immediacy of the Classical Hollywood film in the 'hood film which makes it distinct from postmodern film's obsession with intertextuality. The gangsta film is not about yearning for the familiar pleasures and imagined imaginary participation of previous cinemas. Instead, a film like *Menace II Society* employs past stylistics of violence in order to make the familiar unfamiliar - especially for the white cultural imagination.

There are two major ways in which the mimetic appropriation of New Black Realism and the gangsta film assaulted and transformed habitual cinematic perceptions. Firstly, a racial rage underlies many of the classic and more recent white genre films, and films like *Menace II Society* draw attention to this through imitation and reference. Secondly, the dazzling speed at which the vast number of allusions hit the viewer's sense of cultural knowledge in a film like *Menace II Society*, produces a distraction in the viewer which discourages a perception of these films as familiar reworkings of other genres.

As I noted one of the chief symptoms of racial rage in past Hollywood genre film is manifested in the excessively demarcated worlds of gangsters, cowboys and alienated individuals depicted in films like *White Heat* (Walsh 1949), *The Searchers*, *Goodfellas* and *Taxi Driver*. Boundaries and borders abound in the cinematic worlds of these films, and it is often ethnicity which is the cause of this - even if in the action-image it is unspoken. An action-image film like *White Heat* is driven by the classic gangster narrative structure of the division between the worlds of law and order, where every character is firmly embedded in, and can act within, the specific milieu in which they exist - whether it be the world of the gangster or of the policeman. The downfall of gangster world is determined within the logic of the individualised narrative. Cody Jarrett's demise is prefigured by his psychopathic breakdown, with references to discourses of American 'vulgarised' psychoanalysis, particularly marked in his 'mother fixation'. It is not a case of outside forces breaking down the gangster milieu but the internalised torments of an individual throwing that world in crisis.[71] One of the reasons for the aesthetic certainties of the classic gangster films is that, like many other Classical Hollywood-style films, there is a complete absence of reference to African-Americans, a factor which is most obvious in the lack of black characters on screen. Ethnicity is a narrative factor but only in the fact that many of the gangsters of the Warner Brothers cycle are of immigrant descent - usually Italian or Irish-American. The films may suggest that ethnicity is one of the social reasons for the emergence of gangsters, but as a reason, it does not tend to interfere with, or confuse, the clearly defined milieu of the gangster. In fact, the immigrant ethnicity of the gangsters is frequently used as a means to strengthen the borders between the world of the gangster and that of the law.[72]

In *The Searchers*, a film which marks the emergence of the crisis of the action-image, the clearly and excessively defined milieux of 'Cowboy and Indian' show signs of breaking down, as does the classic narrative structure the quest. Ethan's paranoid fear of racial contagion and pollution drives the narrative, but it pushes it to a point where he is unable to act decisively at the film's closure. His inability to decide how to act towards Debbie (after the whole film has been spent building up to their encounter), and his alienation from his 'home' milieu of the Edwards family, (caught perfectly in the famous final silhouette shot of the film) signify the stresses and strains that racial rage has placed on Ethan as classical hero - and consequently, the film as an example of action-image cinema.

The racial rage that threatens to rupture the contained milieu of the cowboy in *The Searchers* is much more openly expressed on the formal structures and urban worlds of the seventies cinema of Martin Scorsese. In *Mean Streets* the clearly-defined loyalties and actions of the protagonist *and* relations of action with the classic gangster milieu become dispersed into a series of scenes of 'dramatic intensity'. This fragmentation is also evident in *Taxi Driver*, and Travis Bickle, the modern-day cowboy, is disassociated and alienated from the urban milieu in which he lives. As we have seen, racial confusion, paranoia and rage underlies the breakdown of the concrete relations between the protagonists and their milieux in both films. And because the central connection between the individual and milieu is in crisis, then so is the fundamental formal element of much Hollywood film - the protagonist driven cause and effect narrative structure. This is not to say that there is a simple cause and effect relationship between racial rage and Scorsese's innovative visual style and structure. But the old relations between protagonist and milieu were no longer able to function as believable, and if US cinema was to engage with contemporary social reality, it had to develop new reflexive ways to do it. Characters like Travis Bickle or Johnny-Boy could no longer be contained within classical structures and unified cinematic milieux - as demonstrated by the excessive strains apparent in *The Searchers*.

Boyz N the Hood and *Menace II Society* reconstitute the racial paranoia and rage of all these different types and eras of genre film, through a vast array of direct and indirect references. The enclosed milieu of the 'hood provides a setting for the gangsta film, which paradoxically mirrors the aesthetic form of the action-image's relations between protagonist and milieu - elements which were crucial in giving the films of the forties and fifties their assumed immediacy and 'believability'. *Boyz N the Hood*, in particular, uses the contained milieu of the 'hood as a stage on which to play out a cinematic narrative, which is directly reminiscent of many 'Classic Hollywood' films. In *Boyz N the Hood*, the narrative is relatively orthodox in its linearity, with the central figure of Tre seeking to escape the confines and obstacles of the ghetto through the utopian and Hollywood-style means of an escape through honest endeavour and resistance to the 'easy' way out of drug-selling and violence. *Menace II Society* also uses the 'hood as confining and self-contained *mise en scène* and milieu, although its narrative rejects the possibility of utopian escape.

The important difference between both films and action-image cinema is that the borders which enclose and demarcate the ghetto as *mise en scène* and milieu are obviously organised directly on the lines of 'race'. It is because the protagonists of these films are young African-American men that they belong to, and know how to act in, the milieu of the gangsta. But if the 'race' of the protagonists enables them to function within this milieu, then it also prevents them from breaking out of it, again because of obstacles and cause and effects constructed through 'race' - both outside and within the 'hood. In contrast to the clearly defined worlds of Classical Hollywood genre film, where the concrete relations between the protagonist and his milieu grant him an authority to act decisively in overcoming the barriers between him and his goal, at the heart of the relations between the gangsta and his milieu, there is a powerlessness, and an inability to act in any goal-orientated and decisive fashion. In my discussion of *Falling Down*, I argued that even in the convoluted and confusing world of classic *film noir*, the protagonist still recognises, and is at home in, the milieu of the gangster and the criminal, and also that of the policeman and the politician. Ultimately the Marlowe of *Farewell My Lovely* (Dymtryk 1944) is able to achieve his quest - even if the hunt for Moose's Velma ends in the death of both.[73] In the gangsta film this power to act is denied to the main protagonist. As we saw in *Menace II Society*, every time Caine makes a decision, he is prevented from acting on it. Even Tre in *Boyz N the Hood*, although defined in terms which make him a more classically orthodox hero than Caine, is a figure who is unable to act decisively. Tre's most profound action is the non-action of *not* accompanying Doughboy in avenging the death of Ricki.

In both of these films the characters who act most decisively within the milieu of the gangsta are the *homo marginalis* figures of Doughboy and O'Dog.[74] These characters are able to act far more convincingly within the violent world of the ghetto than the central protagonists. But the fact that these figures are narratively marginal, and that their violent actions threaten to tear apart the fabric of the 'hood, places a question mark over the notion of the action in cinema as a whole. In terms of their structural function as action-takers, the *homo marginalis* figures are strongly connected to, and evoke cinematic memories of the central protagonist of the Classic Hollywood genre film. This connection combined with the destructively nihilistic and narratively marginal depiction of *homo marginalis* puts into doubt the validity of the centrality and authority granted the protagonist in action-image cinema. The power of these individuals to control and alter their world in any fundamental sense, and also provide the impetus for a linear narrative structure, is thrown into doubt for the viewer by the memories evoked by the gangsta film, and their positioning of action-takers as narratively marginal. The reality which underlies the basis of the white Hollywood fantasy of the action-man protagonist is recast as a powerlessness because of the connection with the impotency of the 'hood film's central protagonists, such as Tre and Caine.

If this condensed connection between the powerlessness of the 'hood protagonist and the action-image hero seems too stretched, it is worth reflecting again on a scene from *Menace II Society*. After Caine has returned from hospital, having recovered from the gunshot wounds received during the theft of his cousin's car, there is a sequence where he and his grandparents are sitting in their living-room watching *It's A Wonderful Life* (Capra 1946) on television. The sequence of this film that we are briefly shown is the close-up shot of George Bailey (James Stewart) embracing his family, having returned from a suicide attempt, after the angel Clarence has pointed out his vital importance to the community of Bedford Falls. On one level, this clip is used in *Menace II Society* to show the gap between this fantasy and the 'reality' of life in the ghetto, as well as the 'generation gap' between Caine and the grandparents he lives with. Caine reacts with barely concealed disgust to the sentimentality of the white middle class family in restored harmony, while his grandparents smile approvingly. However the memories evoked by this particular film reference are more complex and subtle than this diegetic reason for its use.

It's A Wonderful Life is the epitome of the Classical Hollywood style, with its extraordinarily tight narrative structure of a central individual protagonist, motivated by crises and obstacles to reach a state of resolution and closure by the film's end. But, like the central protagonists of the 'hood movies, *It's A Wonderful Life* is also the story of a protagonist whose sole conscious desire is to leave the milieu which he is so strongly connected to. The transgressive desires and attempted actions of George to leave Bedford Falls are denied again and again - even to the point where a temporary departure in the form of a honeymoon is prevented. But the relations between protagonist and milieu are so concrete in *It's a Wonderful Life,* and the film effects closure with such an oppressive force - denying its protagonist any kind of transgressive desire - that the film's form almost bursts. The film displays the implicit contradiction of the cinema of the action-image by playing out to an extreme the ambiguous situation where the narrative emphasis is on the individual as agent of the film's action, (the one who makes the story 'happen') but the same time where the individual is almost erased as a figure with any kind of agency or free-will. The contradictions which this crisis of the action-taking situation reveal can only be resolved by what Kaja Silverman calls the 'celestial suture' where the return of George Bailey to his milieu and culture can only be guaranteed or made tenable by the meta-narration of the Christian God.[75]

The ultimate contradiction that is displayed in *It's a Wonderful Life* is the powerlessness of the individual that underlies the myth of the American dream - especially in its Populist form. On the one hand, the dream promises 'life, liberty and the pursuit of happiness for all', and on the other, the individual seeking to achieve this is always held back by the paternal responsibility to those members of the community who are unable to achieve the dream in any form. This contradiction is even more pronounced in the aftermath of the Second World War with the gap between the small-town capitalism that could facilitate the role of paternalistic individual and the growth of depersonalised monopoly and corporate capitalism. *It's a Wonderful Life* allegorises these contradictions through the figures of George and the evil Potter (Lionel Barrymore), and the consequences of the victory of the latter are played out in the sequence where George sees Bedford Falls as it would exist without his existence.[76] Again, it only the 'celestial suture' that enables the film to contain these contradictions and effect a Populist closure.[77]

The underlying powerlessness of George Bailey is echoed in the 'hood film. Caine and Tre are both incapable of extracting themselves from the milieu to which they are connected. With Caine the attempt to do so leads to death, and with Tre the only escape comes via a strained, utopian, off-screen Hollywood-style closure. But the concept of powerlessness runs through the gangsta film at a deeper level than that of similarities in the representation of the hero of the action-image cinema. Lack of mastery and authority also permeates the relationship of immediacy between the white viewer and the gangsta film in its images of black violence, and on a more formal level in the speed and enormous variety of allusions to film, popular music and television. The combined impact of the rapidity of this visual shifting and the referencing of white Hollywood genre film and other media leads to doubt surrounding the basic cultural assumptions that underlie, for example, the individual protagonist of the action-image cinema.

The importance of New Black Realism's assault on the white American cultural imagination is at least twofold. Firstly the gangsta film highlighted the impossibility of white Hollywood cinema representing a world on screen as a totality. In other words, New Black Realism drew attention to and emphasised the inability of white Hollywood to recapture the modes of realism, immediacy and action within the concrete relations between individual and milieu which had previously sustained it both politically and aesthetically. Secondly the gangsta film's assault on social and cinematic memory and knowledge enabled it to capture and augment the contemporary sense of powerlessness of the white cultural imagination. As we have seen, this powerlessness is evident in white fears and paranoia towards black violence and images of violent black bodies, but it is also evident in the aesthetic crisis of postmodern Hollywood, where what Deleuze would call an 'inflation of the represented' attempts to regain the imagined immediacy of the action-image.[78] Inflated male bodies, *mise en scène*, and grandiose special effects are common features of the postmodern blockbuster, and it is this excess which potentially symptomises a desire for a return to an imagined cinematic moment where the Hollywood film could distract the viewer from conscious and habitual thought.

A sense of powerlessness paradoxically provides the immediate power of New Black Realism and it is this affect which the new-brutality film sought to imitate. After the impossibility of 'taking seriously' the cinema of the action-image, the crisis of the action-image, and the empty mimesis of the postmodern blockbuster, there is a marked tendency in the new-brutality film to recover and restore the viscerality of the image and the distraction of the viewer in the action film of the 1990s. This has been partially explored in Chapter 1 with the case of *Falling Down*. This is a film which wants to have it both ways. It appropriates the way that blackness operates as a manifestation of the Real in the white cultural imagination - as embodied by the figure of DFens. But at the same time, the film distances itself from the consequences of that response by providing a focal point in Prendergast which allows the viewer to understand black culture as naïve, savage and anarchic. In the next two chapters, I will be exploring films which also demonstrated a desire to appropriate the affective properties of African American bodies and culture, including Quentin Tarantino's *Reservoir Dogs* (1991) and *Pulp Fiction* (1994). But I shall be arguing that the mimesis of black culture in these films is not an attempt to categorise and 'know' black culture - as was the case in *Falling Down* - but to produce the kind of bodily affect which provokes an ambivalence of thought, and which reveals the instability of white cultural identity.

Notes

1. Some of the arguments of this chapter can also be found in Gormley in Shiel and Fitzmaurice (2003: 180-200).

2. *Menace II Society* (Hughes 1993).

3. Butler in Gooding-Williams ed. (1993: 18).

4. Deleuze (1986: 142).

5. Jameson (1992: 279-97).

6. Shaviro (1993: 5).

7. *ibid.* (3).

8. Morrison (1993: 6).

9. The improbability of this escape is perhaps suggested in the allusion to *The Wizard of Oz* (Fleming/Vidor 1939). Dorothy's refrain in the film, 'There's no place like home' refers to Kansas, and the fact that this place is chosen to be a possible escape for Caine reflects the way the film shows escape from the ghetto to be fantastical.

10. Massood, *Cineaste* 20 (1993: 44).

11. Taubin, *Sight and Sound* 3 (1993: 17).

12. T.R.U.T.H., *Artrage* February/March (1994: 13).

13. Atlanta also has the reputation of being one of the most successful black-run cities in the US, both culturally and economically.

14. Taubin, *Sight and Sound* 3 (1993: 17).

15. hooks (1994: 45).

16. *ibid.* (46).

17. *ibid.*

18. *ibid.*

19. *ibid.* (45-7).

20. *ibid.*

21. The term 'dominant fiction' is from Kaja Silverman's concept of the governing 'reality' of a society which, through hegemonic means, encapsulates the individual in a kind of neo-Althusserian interpellation. See Chapter 1 in Silverman (1992).

22. West (1993: 12).

23. *ibid.* (89).

24. *ibid.* (31).

25. Taussig (1994: 23).

26. *ibid.* (22).

27. *ibid.* (23).

28. *ibid.* (25).

29. *ibid.*

30. I am referring to the 'The Work Of Art in the Age of Mechanical Reproduction' in Benjamin (1970).

31. Like Taussig, I am reading the commodity fetish and the artistic aura as analogous.

32. Deleuze (1986: 145).

33. *ibid.*

34. Diawara in Copjec ed. (1993: 263).

35. *ibid.*

36. *ibid.* This reading of *noir* is the American Africanism, defined by Toni Morrison, where tropes of blackness are used to signify anarchy and primitive violence, which constitute, but are denied by white cultural identity. (Morrison 1993).

37. Diawara in Copjec ed. (1993: 263).

38. *ibid.*

39. *ibid.*

40. *ibid.*

41. *ibid.* (266).

42. Diawara ed. (1993: 24).

43. Massood, *Cineaste* 20 (1993: 44).

44. Copjec in Copjec ed. (1993: 188).

45. Zizek describes the Real as being the 'starting point, the basis of symbolisation', but after the subject has acquired the ability to symbolise (engage with language), the Real also remains as a

space which is 'the product, remainder, leftover, scraps of this process of symbolization, the excess which escapes symbolisation, and is produced by the symbolization itself'. (Zizek 1989: 169). In other words, the Real is a place which stores all those irrational events and emotions which cannot be explained by the conscious awareness and coordination that the subject experiences as Symbolic reality. Consequently, because it is a place outside signification, it can never be explained or described by language. As soon as these experiences are they no longer belong in the realm of the Real.

46. Copjec in Copjec ed. (1993: 188).

47. *ibid*. (185-6).

48. For good reading of this sequence and its relationship to noir see Krutnik in Clarke (2001).

49. *ibid*. (183).

50. *Ibid*.

51. Deleuze (1986: 206).

52. *ibid*.

53. Stern (1995: 5).

54. Massood, Cineaste 20 (1993: 44).

55. Tallack (1991: 64).

56. Stern (1995: 33).

57. *ibid*.

58. *ibid*.

59. *ibid*.

60. *ibid*. (58).

61. *ibid*.

62. *ibid*.

63. *ibid*. (42).

64. *ibid*.

65. Davis (1992: 5).

66. In *Falling Down*, there is an attempt to appropriate the affective power of racial rage in a similar scene set in a Korean store. The beginning of DFens' rampage involves him smashing the store to pieces in another thinly-veiled attempt to signify his association with African-Americans.

67. Massood *Cineaste* 20 (1993: 44).

68. Burch (1981: 124).

69. Taubin, *Sight and Sound* 3 (1993: 17).

70. Most New Black Realism films feature very few white characters at all, and very rarely show white victims of black crime. But it could be argued that the absence of white characters serves to demarcate the lines between white and black culture, highlighting the white cultural construction of blackness and the ghetto as a dangerous no-go area, beyond white control and understanding. As I noted in the previous chapter, these fears are nicely played out in a scene in *Menace II Society*, where a white middle-class criminal employs black gangstas to carry out the physical crime of a car theft, so he can commit a white-collar insurance fraud. The white criminal is happy to employ black gang members, but is shown up to be visibly scared at entering the ghetto after dark, in case he becomes the victim of 'random' black violence himself.

71. Massood, *Cineaste* 20 (1993: 44).

72. White Heat is of course a relatively late entry into the classic gangster film genre (It was James Cagney's comeback as a gangster after nearly a decade of other roles), and like the low-budget *Dillinger* (Nosseck 1945), which portrayed the gangster (Lawrence Tierney - who plays 'the big boss' in *Reservoir Dogs*) emerging as a result of weak parenthood (particularly fatherhood) these

late entries tended to 'blame' the rise of the gangster on individual psychopathology. Previous examples of the Warner Brother's cycles such as *The Public Enemy* and *Scarface*, tended to place the rise and fall of the gangster film in a more social context - which also meant that early criticism of the genre tended to view the films in terms of 'reflecting' contemporary urban decline and reality. As Pam Cook notes, 'For early criticism the apparently close relation between generic change and contemporary reality encouraged notions of 'reflection'. This was made all the easier by the association of the classic gangster film with the Warner Bros studio, widely known for its 30s 'social issues' movies...' (Cook ed.1985: 87). It should also be noted that, even though there was a inclination towards exploring some of the social background to the rise of the gangster in the early 'classic' examples of the genre, the focus was still very much on narrative action driven by individualised and psychologised protagonists, connected to clearly defined milieux.

73. Films like *Scarface* and *Angels With Dirty Faces* (Curtiz 1936) illustrate the use of ethnicity as a narrative device to strengthen the self-contained milieu of the gangster. This is taken to its logical conclusion in *The Godfather* (Coppola 1972) and *The Godfather Part Two* (Coppola 1974), where the Italian family becomes the foundation of an autonomous and clearly defined milieu which exists with mainstream capitalist America in an almost parodic relationship. As Gilles Deleuze notes these two films are late examples of the gangster and crime film where an organisation is 'related to a distinctive milieu, to assignable actions by which the criminals would be distinguishable'. As we have seen, Deleuze argues that the cinema of the crisis of the action-image tended to confuse the heroes and criminals, the law and crime. See Deleuze (1986: 209). However, the question of ethnicity in the gangster film also complicates the division between the gangster and the policeman. In *Angels With Dirty Faces* for instance it is the Irish Catholic priest (Pat O'Brien) who persuades the gangster (Jimmy Cagney) to turn cry-baby at his execution, in order to dissuade the Dead End Kids from following his path. In many classic gangster films it is also Irish-Americans who are portrayed as policemen. These ethnic divisions are also a key element of The Coen brothers' contemporary period gangster film, *Miller's Crossing* (1990).

74. The 1975 remake of *Farewell My Lovely* (Richards) is very interesting in the context of the way that 'race' tends to blur the milieux of the Classical genre film. A particularly pertinent scene is where Moose (Anthony Zerbe) and Marlowe (Robert Mitchum) enter the bar where Velma used to work, only to discover that it has become a black club. The surprise which registers on both men's faces indicates their discomfort at crossing into a different racial milieu. Of course the film tends to foreclose any possible ramifications of this awkwardness, by showing the development of a surrogate father-son relationship between Marlowe and the mixed-race son of the dead trumpet player. However the film does at least engage on a basic level with the idea that borders and boundaries based on race were fundamental to the organisation of cinematic milieux - despite, indeed because of, the absence of representations of African-Americans on screen.

75. Winokur, *The Velvet Light Trap* 35 (1995: 22-32).

76. Silverman (1992: 93-102). Incidentally, the interesting point about the sequences where the references to God are explicitly made is that they are also the points where the formal tendencies of Hollywood realism also break down. Think for instance of the freeze frame of George Bailey where we and Clarence are introduced to him as an adult as a first time. This stopping of the action is almost Scorsesian. As I noted above in Chapters 1 and 3, the sequence where George is shown the consequences of his absence also breaks with many of the conventions of Hollywood realism, and introduces a *noir*-like quality to the film. Silverman argues from a position which attempts to synthesise Althusserian theories of ideology and Lacanian psychoanalysis, that the setbacks that George suffers symbolise a series of castrations 'upon which his subjectivity depends' (102), and which threaten the power of the Oedipal Complex to bind the white male to the 'dominant fiction' of mainstream American culture. She goes on to argue that in the end, George:

not only accepts these 'wounds' as the necessary condition of cultural identity but takes pleasure in the pain they induce in him...So open a display of wounds would normally be totally incompatible with an affirmation of the dominant fiction and its phallic representations. It is only by giving Christianity an authoritative position that It's a Wonderful Life *is able to accommodate the spectacle of George's castration and masochism within an ideological system predicated upon the equation of the penis and the phallus, since that discourse (Christianity) not only acknowledges the distance separating the actual from the symbolic father, but make renunciation and suffering the necessary path leading from the former to the latter.* (102-3)

I would argue that the fairly unusual step the film takes in incorporating the discourse of

Christianity so directly (in the screen presence of God and the angel Clarence) demonstrates the crisis of the formal aesthetic systems of the action-image. For Silverman, this crisis comes about because of the collective trauma of the Second World War, and Deleuze also cites the war as one of the major reasons for the crisis of action-image. See Deleuze (1986: 206).

77. See Williams in Nichols ed. (1976: 65-78) for a fuller account of Frank Capra's ideological engagement with American Populism.

78. The fact that the Populist sentiments of the film were outdated is perhaps indicated by the film's poor performance at the box-office. See Rose, *The Journal of Popular Film* and *Television 6* (1977: 65-78).

79. Deleuze (1989: 164).

Chapter Four

Miming Blackness:
Reservoir Dogs and 'American Africanism'

The aesthetic shifts of the new-brutality film only begin to make sense in the context of both the affective power that New Black Realism has on the white cultural imagination, and the aesthetic (rather than commercial) crisis of the postmodern blockbuster. This chapter will focus on *Reservoir Dogs,* as this film, along with *Pulp Fiction,* was the catalyst for the way that the new-brutality film moved away from both the distanciated and spectacular pleasures of the set-piece action scenes of postmodern blockbusters and towards a direct mimetic engagement with the cultural 'hipness', authority, and perceived immediacy of rap culture and the 'hood films. *Reservoir Dogs* (along with Tarantino's later film *Jackie Brown*) could be described as a 'wannabe' black film and the chapter will explore the way that the film both knowingly and unconsciously imitates the aesthetics of rap and the gangsta film in the following pages.

Denying the postmodernity of *Reservoir Dogs* would seem to contradict the evidence of the film's self-reflexive intertextual references to other cinematic genres and popular culture as a whole. There is no doubting that this 'knowingness' is a key feature of this film. But there is a key distinction between genres like the blockbuster of the 1970s and 80s which perform an 'empty' mimesis of past Hollywood, and those like the 'hood film which recast the cultural memories of these films, reanimating the affective potential of the cinematic experience. Many postmodern blockbusters play on, and use, the white cultural imagination's nostalgic desire for Hollywood's power to affect and distract, while paradoxically depending on a 'concentrated knowledge' of cinema. In other words the blockbuster seeks to produce an aesthetic affect while playing on the viewer's knowledge of past cinema. *Reservoir Dogs* incessantly refers to both past cinema and other forms of popular culture. However intertextuality reveals nostalgia to be a white cultural phenomenon which signifies a kind of cultural powerlessness. White culture is constructed as being incapable of producing contemporary cinematic affect and 'hipness'. In contrast African-American culture is fabricated as a space where intertextuality is a means to provide a cinematic affect constructed in terms of contemporary authenticity and cultural authority. *Reservoir Dogs* mimes New Black Realism's ability to reanimate past cinematic genres with the affective power of the black body.

White Jazz

Reservoir Dogs tells the story of a 'heist gone wrong' and much of the film's running time is spent in a disused warehouse, as surviving gang members, filmed in predominantly 'real-time' sequences, try to discover what went wrong, and who 'ratted' them out. Interspersed between these sequences are a series of complex flashbacks telling the story of the planning of the heist, fleshing out the backgrounds of various characters, and revealing to the viewer the identity of the undercover cop who betrayed their plans. The gangsters are all white and there is barely a sequence of the much-celebrated dialogue of the film which is not racist in its content.[1]

The gangsters constantly refer to African-Americans in a derogative sense with the intent on stating their own superiority on the grounds of race, and nearly all of these racist comments construct African-Americans as randomly violent and sexually primitive. For instance, in the scene where Mr Pink (Steve Buscemi) attempts to prevent a violent showdown between Mr White (Harvey Keitel) and Mr Blonde (Michael Madsen), the gangsta figure is used as example of a primitive, violent 'other':

> *Am I the only professional...Fucking guys...you're acting like a bunch of fucking niggers. Man! You ever worked with niggers, huh? Just like you two. Always saying they're gonna kill each other.*

In another scene between Joe Cabot (Lawrence Tierney) and Mr Blonde, Joe again uses the racist notion of the African-American as the excessively violent criminal without the strict codes of conduct expected of the white gangster. When Vic complains of the strict rulings of his parole office, Joe rants,

> *You know it never ceases to amaze me...Fucking jungle bunny goes out there and slits some old woman's throat for twenty-five cents gets Doris Day for a parole officer. Goodfella like you winds up with a ball-busting prick.*

Later on this same scene, Nice Guy Eddie playfully mocks Vic for using gangsta vernacular by constructing the African-American as sexually licentious, with particular reference to the stereotype of the black prisoner as homosexual rapist:

> *Ain't that a sad sight Daddy? Man walks into a prison a white man and comes out talking like a fucking nigger. You know what? I think its all that semen been pumped up your ass so far, now its backed in your fucking brain...it's coming out of your mouth.*

This quote and the others self-reflexively draw attention to the fact that, throughout the film, the gangsters themselves have been rapping like gangstas. The dialogue of the gangsta character (frequently played by rap stars such as Ice Cube, Ice T and Tupac Shakur) often uses the same kind of rhythmic patterns and intertextual allusion as the hip-hop song.[2] The white gangsters in *Reservoir Dogs* mime the same snappy and quick-witted mode of speech, utilising a whole range of references to popular culture from the opening thesis on Madonna's 'Like a Virgin', to mocking references to Lee Marvin, and back seat discussions of Pam Grier and the blaxploitation film.[3]

Amy Taubin argues that '*Reservoir Dogs* is an extremely insular film' because the screen space is dominated by images of racist homophobic white masculinity, while 'women get no more than thirty seconds of screen time, people of colour get zero'.[4] As we shall see the observation about 'people of colour' is inaccurate, but her point about the domination of the screen by white male gangsters is convincing - from the fetishistic slow-motion strut of the gang in the opening credits to the bloody chaos of the film's finale. More interestingly, Taubin also goes on to contradict her point concerning the film' insularity by suggesting that the constant references 'to coons and jungle bunnies, to jailhouse rape' signifies that 'the unconscious of the film is locked in competition with rap culture'.[5] Taubin oversimplifies here and (in common with many other 'representational' approaches to film) equates the characters' language with the unconscious of the film. Such analyses imply that the film is completely oblivious to the effects of the racist rantings *and* the copycat rap which come out of the characters' mouths. There is a connection between the characters' unconscious mimesis of 'street' African-American idioms and the film's own appropriation of black aesthetics but they are not the same thing.

It is possible to argue that the gangsters assume their own identity through their desire for racist constructions of African-Americans at the level of diegetic representation. Like the gangsters in *Goodfellas* and *Mean Streets*, the 'Reservoir Dogs' build their identity by drawing strong Symbolic lines between themselves and what they construct as the meaningless, chaotic and threatening Real of the African-American. The conduct of the gangsters in *Reservoir Dogs* is similar to the Scorsesean 'goodfella' and based on a racial rage, as they attempt to define themselves in terms of codes such as professionalism and loyalty - codes which are the very opposite of their construction of the petty, meaningless and uncontrolled violence of the gangsta. But at the heart of *this* racial rage there is an uncertainty and instability to the Symbolic network of the white gangster which is expressed both through the fear of slipping into the racial Real they have constructed, *and* the desire to be that which they fear. Moreover the gangsters also attempt to define their identity and difference to the racial Real they assemble by constantly referring to the ephemeral and equally unstable world of a (mostly white) popular culture.

The instability of the certainties and clear demarcations of white identity is played out in one of the most memorably comic scenes of the film. In one the film's multiple flashbacks Joe Cabot debriefs the gang members and gives them their false identities. None of the gang members are meant to know each other's identity and are given colour-coded aliases. Throughout the scene the gang members constantly question the names that Joe Cabot has assigned to them. Mr Pink wants to change his name, arguing that 'Mr Pink sound like Mr Pussy', and makes the suggestion that the gangsters should pick their own names. In a revealing moment Joe Cabot dismisses this request: 'No way, no way! Tried it once and it doesn't work. You get four guys fighting over who's going to be Mr Black. They don't know each other and nobody wants to back down'.

Joe's choice of 'neutral' names is doomed to failure because of the immanently unstable and mimetic nature of naming by a father figure. Judith Butler notes that the act of the father in attempting to fix or construct identity through naming is always a 'citation of original fixing, a reiteration of the divine process of naming, whereby naming the son inaugurates his existence within the divinely sanctioned community of man'.[6] She goes on to suggest that the baptism or naming of any person or object is constantly prone to 'catachresis', an 'improper' use of a proper name, because the initial naming of a person is already mimetic. All baptisms are a reiteration and copy of the originating act of God naming Adam. To take the most obvious example, the second person to ever call a child Adam immediately positioned the original Adam into relationship of similarity and difference with the second Adam. To reiterate a name or even the process of naming is to change its original 'proper' meaning.[7]

Butler is explicitly referring to the Christian ritual of baptism as part of Western culture's Symbolic practices in her analysis, but the notion of catachresis is suggestive in the context of the naming scene in *Reservoir Dogs* and the genre of the white gangster film as a whole. The organisation of the criminal gang in the Hollywood film is often portrayed as a kind of microcosmic parody of the western patriarchal family and big business corporate structure. The gang or 'family' is always headed by the big boss father figure who rules in authoritarian manner, through the imposition and continuation of a series of rituals. For instance, as we saw with Tommy in *Goodfellas*, being 'made' is one such ritual which grants full membership and privileges to the aspiring gangster. These codes and conventions are necessary to repress the violence which underpins the structure of the gang and this process is apparent in the Joe's attempt to head off violent confrontation through the 'baptism' of the gangsters with false aliases and identities. But the choice of apparently 'meaningless' and neutral colours immediately produces catachresis, because colours have a myriad of different meanings in the culture of the white gangster - and in the US cultural imagination as a whole. Mr Pink is no longer Mr Pink but Mr Pussy, and as Joe already knows, the choice of the colour black will lead to violence. The scene suggests that it is the desire to impose Symbolic order and the immanent violence beneath that order which has lead to a crisis in white cultural identity, and we have already seen the way that the American Dream and its cinema were based on similar foundations.

The desire to be Mr Black, and the fact that such a desire could lead to violence, is indicative of both sides of an 'American Africanism' where the white cultural imagination imagines blackness as both anarchic and as a signifier of 'cool'. Toni Morrison notes that African American culture is used in white culture to 'signal modernity' and is appropriated for the 'associative value (it) lends to modernism - to being hip, sophisticated, ultra urbane'.[8] The characters of *Reservoir Dogs* reveal a desire to be this cool, and simultaneously Joe's comments about 'five guys fighting' over who wants to be Mr Black suggest that there is always an immanent, unpredictable violence within this desire.

In many ways the gangsters of *Reservoir Dogs* (and DFens in *Falling Down*) are related to Norman Mailer's 'White Negro'. The hipster is drawn by Mailer as the epitome of white fifties counter-cultural chic and cool. This figure mimes the urban Black man in terms of language, music, style and criminality. According to Mailer the hipster is 'a philosophical psychopath' who had absorbed the existential synopses of the Negro and for practical purposes could be considered a White Negro'.[9] This absorption is based on Mailer's own construction of the urban African-American as a product of white oppression, and again as a source of indiscriminate violence. According to Mailer, the effects of white racism on the African-American identity are manifested in terms of a constant readiness for violence, strategic mimicry of white cultural codes and language, and most of all movement and fluidity of identity and cultural practices.[10] The 'White Negro's' mimicry of black idiom is perhaps his key defining feature. Expressions like 'groovy' or 'getting into the groove' connote never-ending movement because of the allusions to the circular motion of a record, and contrast with the rigidity and fixed connotations of 'the square' - the opposite of a hipster.[11] The hipster uses black idiom as a tool of modernistic estrangement and distance from white mainstream American language and culture. Such an argument cannot be applied to the white gangsters of *Reservoir Dogs*. The gangsters - except for Mr Orange - are completely unaware of their mimicry of the gangsta and his language, and all their references to popular culture are nostalgic allusions to a popular cultural past and signify a different kind of estrangement. Their alienation is one of a longing for the authority they imagined they once had rather than one of never having had. The gangsters are postmodern and regressive hipsters - from their old-style gangster black and white suits to their fond remembrances of seventies 'pop bubble-gum tunes'.[12] But the film itself displays an awareness of its own mimicry of rap, and uses it to self-reflexively display the instability of white identity as represented by the gangsters.

This is not to argue that *Reservoir Dogs* is some kind of politically progressive text which consciously engages with the implications of race in 1990s America. Indeed the film is not self-reflexively aware of a different kind of American Africanism that is visible in its images. If the gangsters constitute African-Americans as both meaninglessly violent ('always saying they are going to kill each other') and 'hip' (they all 'wanna be Mr Black') then the film itself constructs the African-American as a locus of cinematic authenticity and knowing authority, as well as 'cool'. This can also be partially explored through the film's characters, and especially by contrasting the only on-screen black character with the gangsters. The appropriately named Holdsway Randy Brooks) is the central causal agent of the film's narrative and is able to play masterfully with changing and constructed identities of the underworld - while the white gangsters are flailing around in their attempts to both find the identity of 'the rat in the house', struggling to keep control of both their own identities and those imposed upon them by Joe Cabot. Holdsway operates as kind of surrogate father figure and mentor to Mr Orange/Freddy (Tim Roth) the undercover cop. It is Holdsway who has to reprimand Freddy by telling him who his 'amigos' are, and most importantly it is Holdsway who acts as Freddy's acting teacher, preparing him for his role as Mr Orange. He tells Freddy that he's 'gotta be Marlon Brando...to do this job you gotta be a great actor, you gotta be naturalistic...you gotta be naturalistic as hell'. The reference to the Actor's Studio style of performance is revealing in that it associates Holdsway with a celebrated form of cinematic and theatrical realism. The allusion also reveals that he is conscious of the fact that such a style of realism belongs to the past, and he is able to refer to it reflexively as just one mode of reality.

Unlike the gangsters, Holdsway is also shown to belong to a world of contemporary realism. There is a stark contrast between the settings in which the gangsters are predominantly filmed and the scenes featuring Holdsway. The gangsters are mainly filmed in the enclosed spaces of the post-heist warehouse and Joe's office, and both these settings could belong to any Hollywood gangster movie from any era, and are geographically non-specific. The majority of the scenes featuring Holdsway open up a world that is instantly recognisable as 1990s' Los Angeles - from the diner where he is seen for the first time to the hip-hop graffiti scrawled walls of Freddy's 'stage' for the final rehearsal of the story he has to convince Joe and the other gangsters of his authenticity as a criminal.[13] The positioning of Holdsway in spaces, which could easily be taken from films like *Menace II Society*, indicates the desire of the film to associate itself with the immediacy provoked by New Black Realism.

The linkage of the only black character in the film with a knowledge which understands the artifice of postmodernity (as expressed in Holdsway's grasp of once-fashionable conventions of realism) is in stark contrast to the powerless artifice of the white characters in controlling and knowing their own identities and situations. This ambivalent opposition runs throughout the film. All of Tarantino's films equate black culture with a contemporary and immediate reality, and white culture as a place of empty, nostalgic artifice. Holdsway symbolises the contemporary authenticity and 'believability' which is missing from the stock genre gangsters. His reference to the Actor's Studio style of method acting is as much a self-reflexive comment on the clichéd and anachronistic realism of performances given by Harvey Keitel and the other white characters as it is a sign of his own ability to distinguish between the reality and artifice of postmodernity.

Holdsway's connection to the 'here and now' is apparent in the fact that, out of all of the characters, he is the least cinematically familiar. The white gangsters are constituted as genre throwbacks, from the *Mean Streets*-style slow-motion credit sequence to the self-consciously anachronistic black suits which hark back to almost every gangster film ever made.[14] The citation of past genre characters extends beyond costume into the roles the gangsters play within the structure of the gang: there is the undercover cop, Mr Orange, the violent psychopath, Mr Blonde, the 'Goodfella' Mr White, the diminutive whiner, Mr Pink (Steve Buscemi), and the loyal, infantile boss's son, Nice Guy Eddie (Chris Penn). In terms of the gangster genre Holdsway is an unconventional character. His status as authoritative cop and father figure to Freddy is rare in a genre which either, tends to cast African-Americans on the margins as randomly violent criminals some way down the gangster pecking order (as is the case with Stax Edwards in *Goodfellas*) or omits their presence altogether.

Holdsway is an allusion to the contemporary genre of New Black Realism rather than the genre pictures of Hollywood's past, and his position as father figure to Freddy can be usefully compared to Joe's attempt to be father to the gang. As we have seen the figure of the father is crucial to the narrative structure of the 'hood films. Manthia Diawara notes of *Boyz N the Hood* that 'Tre's father...is the central figure of judgement in the film', and Holdsway's authority over Freddy, and the way that Randy Brooks plays the character, is strongly reminiscent of Laurence Fishburne's Furious Styles.[15] The fact that the character is taken from a genre which holds a believability and affective power lacking in white Hollywood, highlights the difference between his character and the big gangster boss figure of Joe who is drawn from a white action-image genre which has lost its affective power. Joe is a comic-book character lifted from a popular cultural past. This is emphasised by the fact that Joe is played by Lawrence Tierney, most famous for his role in the low-budget, 'late' classic gangster film, *Dillinger* (Nosseck 1945). But the most apparent signifier of Joe's status as a simulation of the past comes in Mr Orange's description of him as 'The Thing'. This is a direct allusion to the 1950s D.C. comic, *The Silver Surfer*, and foregrounds the status of Joe as a fantastical genre character. The characterisation of Joe as 'The Thing' also brings to mind the Lacanian 'Thing of the Real', the material embodiment of the chaotic and lethal violence of the Real - which is what Joe fails to control through the imposition of the conventional codes of reality of the gangster. Joe is the embodiment of the pure artifice of white postmodern culture, the violence which lies beneath that culture, and the way that the size and ephemeral nature of popular culture acts as a kind of Lacanian Real in the white cultural imagination.

Reservoir Dogs and the Crisis of White Culture

The construction of white culture as lacking authority is evident in the way popular culture is used in *Reservoir Dogs*. Popular culture is assembled as a kind of inchoate mass which randomly surfaces at any time during the action - either during conversations between characters, or through the film's visual and formal allusions. In *Reservoir Dogs*, popular culture becomes trash culture in the sense that it is everywhere and means nothing. Tarantino also sees his own work in terms of disposable culture:

> *My stuff so far has definitely fallen into what I consider pulp fiction...the whole idea of pulp, what it really means, is a paperback you don't really care about. You read it, put it in your back pocket, sit on it, on a bus, and the pages start coming out, and who gives a fuck? When you're finished with it you hand it over to someone else to read, or you throw it away. You don't put it in your library. Pulp sneaked in through the cracks, it was made for a certain brand of reader.*[16]

Tarantino's definition of pulp as 'slipping through the cracks' is analogous to one manifestation of Real which Zizek finds in Robert Heinlein's science fiction novel, *The Unpleasant Profession of Jonathan Hoag*. The novel features a 'grey formless mist, pulsing slowly with inchoate life', which the two central protagonists inadvertently allow to take over the Symbolic reality of their world. Zizek argues that this mist is a representation of the Real - 'the pulsing of presymbolic existence in its abhorrent vitality'.[17] Constant references to an obscure, half-forgotten, popular cultural past dominate and swamp the diegetic reality of *Reservoir Dogs* in a similar fashion to the fog in Jonathan Hoag's world as almost every other sentence in the film's dialogue is an allusion. Zizek describes the Real as a 'hard, impenetrable kernel resisting symbolisation *and* a pure chimerical entity which has itself no ontological consistency'.[18] The analogy between this definition and the construction of trash culture in *Reservoir Dogs* is striking. The intertextuality of *Reservoir Dogs* refuses interpretations which would give the citations an ontological depth or meaning. In spite of this, both the characters of the film and film critics seek to assign meaning to the various products of popular culture which *Reservoir Dogs* cites.[18]

To read popular culture as the Real of *Reservoir Dogs* raises some problematic questions. How can representations from past popular culture be construed as outside of the Symbolic in the Lacanian sense of the Real, when all representations are Symbolic and produced by discourse and language? The film's construction of the Real in this sense echoes Fredric Jameson's argument that the unconscious has been colonised by postmodern media and its images, to the point where there is no space beyond simulation.[20] Popular culture is treated by the film as multi-surfaced but without depth in terms of meaning. But unlike Jameson's argument that the bombardment of intertextuality and pastiche in postmodernity has led to a waning of affect, the recycling of popular culture in *Reservoir Dogs* is one of the chief sources of a body-first reaction in the viewer.

This contradiction suggests that we need to rethink the relations between affect and meaning. One of the problems with Jameson's argument is that affect and postmodern culture are construed as being in a dialectical relationship of opposition, and this is equally the case with Slavoj Zizek's Lacanian model of the Real and the Symbolic. In Jameson's case affect is equated with meaning and emotional depth, while postmodern culture consists almost entirely of surface discursive, intertextual play. In other words, like Zizek's conceptualisation of the Real, affect for Jameson is that substance which cannot be put into language. But the allusions to popular culture in Reservoir Dogs demonstrate that both intertextual allusions to the past can produce affect, and that affect can also produce new meanings in culture. While there may be no deep emotional or intellectual meaning to the various allusions to popular culture in Tarantino's films, there is no doubting that moments such as the torture scene in *Reservoir Dogs* with its ironic, catchy soundtrack, the opening credits to *Pulp Fiction*, with its surfing music accompaniment, and the opening tracking shot of *Jackie Brown*, with its homage to the iconic images of blaxploitation and *The Graduate* (Nichols 1967), are capable of making the skin crawl and tingle in equal measure. All these scenes are capable of producing a body-first reaction - which this book has been equating with affect.

All of Tarantino's films accentuate the random unpredictability of popular culture by producing, what appear to be, anarchic and pointless citations which have no significance beyond the various cultural memories they evoke. The scattergun affect of citing a multitude of different sources in a seemingly random manner would not necessarily move Tarantino's films beyond the knowing artifice of postmodernity. If we go along with Fredric Jameson's analysis, intertextuality and pastiche are a constitutive aesthetic feature of postmodern cinema.[21] The evocation of popular culture from the past depends on nostalgia for that past to gain its emotional power. Consequently this kind of affect has no lasting power because the viewer realises that 'realness' of the reaction evoked by memories of the past does not exist in the present - except as the emotion of nostalgia.[22]

But, as I have partially explored, Tarantino's films attempt to head off these feelings of nostalgia by miming the aesthetic structures of a contemporary popular culture which still provokes a different kind of affect in the white cultural imagination based in belief and immediacy - the culture of rap and hip-hop. 1990's African-American culture is used by the film to produce a different kind of affect to that produced by allusions to obscure white popular culture. In *Reservoir Dogs* blackness becomes an authenticity, depth and meaning beyond the endless surface play of postmodernity. In Blackness also comes to signify an immediate, bodily, substantiality, which is in contrast to the random nostalgia of postmodernity. The films draw on the affective power that the black American body has on the white cultural imagination, but also produce African-American culture as an authoritative space where the 'reality' of postmodernity is understood. Moreover the film associates the empty nostalgia and simulacra of postmodernity with white American culture. Whiteness in these films comes to be artifice and a lack of depth. To use Richard Dyer's words whiteness 'is often revealed as emptiness, absence, denial, or even a kind of death'.[23]

In other words, both *Reservoir Dogs* and *Pulp Fiction* contain examples of American Africanisms. Indeed the films' construction of whiteness as depthless simulation and blackness as a contradictory space of affect and meaning links them to a long tradition of American cultural production. In her survey of the American literary canon, Toni Morrison argues that where writers such as Melville and Twain encounter an Africanist presence, they have always produced a construction of black culture as a space of depth, affect and contradictory meaning. This is in contrast to images of whiteness which are presented as meaningless, simulated and undefined:

> If we follow through on the self-reflexive nature of these encounters with Africanism, it falls clear: images of blackness can be evil and protective, rebellious and forgiving, fearful and desirable - all of the self-contradictory features of the self. Whiteness, alone, is mute, meaningless, unfathomable, pointless, frozen, veiled, curtained, dreaded, senseless, implacable. Or so our writers seem to say.[24]

And like *Menace II Society*, Tarantino's films - and *Reservoir Dogs* in particular - present a white cultural imagination in crisis, where attempts are made to impose a Symbolic order on situations which appear to be anarchic and random. Like the films of New Black Realism, *Reservoir Dogs* and *Pulp Fiction* can be read as unveiling an anarchic racial rage at the heart of the white cultural identity, and which disrupts attempts to impose its authority.

But it is in the attempt to produce a specifically cinematic affect and the cinema as a privileged space that the mimesis of New Black Realism and rap culture is most marked in Tarantino's films. *Reservoir Dogs* and *Pulp Fiction* imitate the affective power of African-American culture in order to reanimate the potential of the cinema to produce a particular kind of bodily shock. I noted in the introduction that Noel Burch suggests that there are structures of aggression built into the cinematic experience which come into effect in the 'very special, almost hypnotic, relationship that is established between screen and viewer as soon as the lights go down in a theatre'.[25] According to Burch, the immediacy of the assault of the images of the cinema screen on the viewer are potent enough to diminish 'critical awareness' and temporarily override the cultural knowledge which enables the viewer to makes sense or meaning of the world. The question that needs to be confronted, is how potent this particular kind of cinematic affect is in the era of postmodernity, when images are constantly assaulting us from a number of different media sources? This question also needs to be asked in the context of the waning of belief in the old-action image structures of cinema which still permeate the contemporary action film - albeit in an exaggerated and ironic form.

I have suggested that the postmodern blockbuster is no longer able to achieve affect because of its reliance on cultural knowledge in the form of knowing intertextuality, and nostalgia for a time when it was imagined that viewers were caught up in the world of the film. The blockbuster *does* attempt to make the cinema a privileged space by providing affective thrills through its dependence on the special effect. The underlying marketing ploy of these films - like the historical epics of the 1950s - is that you must see these films on the big screen to fully appreciate them. But the spectacularity of the blockbuster's action set-pieces has now also become a object of familiarity, with viewers prepared for the next leap in technology from, say, George Lucas' Industrial Light and Magic or the producers of *The Matrix Reloaded* (Wachowski 2003), rather than being subject to the unexpected. Tarantino's films attempt to 'reload' the belief and affective power of the cinematic experience by drawing on images and structures of black culture which still retain a powerful intensity and authenticity in the white cultural imagination. The reanimation of the cinematic experience through the mimesis of the affective belief evoked by black culture, and the construction of whiteness as empty space of simulation is apparent in at least three distinct elements of *Reservoir Dogs*. In addition to the diegetic reality and dialogue of the characters, other important areas of the mimesis of blackness and the cultural powerlessness of whiteness are also the much-discussed scenes of violence and the cinematic body, and the film's contradictory use of space.

Miming Black Bodies

Reservoir Dogs harks back to Scorsesean cinema of the 1970s in several key ways. Scorsese's cinema exposed the underlying racial rage of white genre cinema through its material embodiment in characters such as Johnny Boy and Travis Bickle. As we shall see below in more detail, Mr Blonde in particular is a direct descendant of these figures. In its contemporary moment, Scorsesean cinema also had to produce a new immediacy and distraction. This was because it needed to both engage with seventies urban reality - because of the impossibility of doing so with the old cinematic forms - and also compete with the startling and short-lived emergence of the blaxploitation film - which in terms of representation had a greater cultural authority and immediacy because of its on and behind-screen

African-American presence, and its own strategic signifyin' of white genre film. *Reservoir Dogs* also mimetically engages with African-American culture in the form of the 'hood film and hip-hop to make its audience 'take it seriously'. Holdsway's fatherly knowledge of 'what is really going down' echoes the favourable white liberal reception of *Boyz N the Hood* as a straightforward documentation or reflection of reality. But if Holdsway represents the self-conscious and deliberate mimesis of the perceived social realism of the 'hood film, then the complex combination of the Real and artifice of the white gangsters points towards the more complex processes of mimesis, distraction, immediacy and black rage we saw in *Menace II Society*.

The way that *Reservoir Dogs* positions white genre cinema within a mode of nostalgia (as opposed to the cultural immediacy and contemporary authority it grants to New Black Realism) is very significant in the films' display of cinematic bodies. *Reservoir Dogs*, like the gangsta film, belongs to a cinema which plays with the immediacy and material excess of the body to shock audiences from their preconceived habitual knowledge of cinematic histories and cultural constructions of 'race'. In the last chapter I noted Cornel West's criticisms of the gangsta's tendency to stylise their body over space and time - to exaggerate everyday gestures (such as the hand movements which Doughboy uses to indicate the aggressive 'dissing' of enemies) and dress (such as the excessive commodity fetishism of jewellery and brand names). I also noted that this fetishisation of the black body is apparent in the cinematic image of the gangsta, and especially in the images of violence and gunplay, with its multiple imitations of past aesthetics of cinematic violence. However the very excessiveness of these fetishising images prevents the viewer from dwelling on them in a static celebratory manner - which West argues reinforces the machismo identity expected and exalted in white patriarchal culture.[26] This is because the stylisation of the black body both evokes similar fetishistic moments in white genre cinema and distances itself from nostalgia for such images by exposing the racial rage that was behind many of these iconic images.

The white gangster bodies in *Reservoir Dogs* are fetishised in a way that imitates the gangsta film. This is particularly evident in the self-consciously artificial, generic construction of the gangsters and their anachronistic costume, and Tarantino makes some revealing comments when he discusses their suits:

> *When Jean-Pierre Melville was making his crime films, he talked about how it was very important that his characters have a suit of armour...I've always said that the mark of any good action film is that when you get through seeing it, you want to dress like the character...The black suits...that's my suit of armour. Guys look cool in black suits.*[27]

The desirability of 'blackness as chic' is again apparent here, and it is combined with Tarantino's desire to make the viewer imitate his screen creations - to make films which, in Linda William's words, 'make the body do things'.[28] This wish to make the viewer's body act through an involuntary impulse evokes both the early aspirations of filmmakers (such as Eisenstein) to shock thought through the image, and Walter Benjamin's theories of the mimetic potential of the cinema. In many of Tarantino's comments there is the voicing of a desire to achieve the power of the imagined distraction and loss of self of past cinema, most notable in his admiration of various auteurs.[29] This desire has been harnessed in Hollywood commercial strategies by attempting to make Tarantino an auteur of the nineties.[30] But while *Reservoir Dogs* attempts to replicate those past glories through homage to various auteurs, it also undercuts them with images of the body which depend on their affect through a mimesis of African-American film.

Like the figure of the gangsta, Tarantino fetishises the bodies of the gangsters throughout the film. The referencing of previous iconic images which have focused on the materiality and mimetic power of the cinematic body is evidence of this - from the slow-motion strutting of the gangsters in the early sequences (which resembles John Travolta's 'strut' in *Saturday Night Fever* (Badham 1977) and *Staying Alive* (Stallone 1983)), to Mr. Blonde's torture dance, and to the numerous instances of gunplay throughout the film.[31] But Tarantino's use of the word armour to describe the predominant fetishistic element of the suits also suggests that what lies beneath this most iconic object of white genre film is a body that needs protecting. The images of cool gangsters that pervade *Reservoir Dogs* are undermined by images of *white* bodies that bleed and bleed, suggesting the vulnerability of white generic bodies and cultural identity.

Tarantino uses these images of vulnerable white bodies in conjunction with the temporal structure of the film to provoke an affective impact. The film's running time is structured around the real time it takes for one of the characters, Orange, to bleed to death, and Manhola Dargis argues that this:

> ...*spins familiar male pain into different contexts and conditions. Unlike the slow-motion waltzes into death in Peckinpah's The Wild Bunch or John Woo's The Killer, the torment in Reservoir Dogs is measured out drop by anguished elemental drop. From the first scene to the last, Tarantino decelerates pain.*[32]

One consequence of this drawn-out violence is the strong mimetic connection between the cinematic body of Orange and the body of the viewer. The temporal structure in which Orange is imprisoned with no escape except death is the same as that of the viewer. Deleuze has argued that this affective connection through time is what gives the cinema its particular ontology. As John Beasley-Murray notes, 'the cinema viewer is maintained as part of an immanent functional (and corporeal) effect of the film's unfolding through time...the specificity of the cinema remains in its unfolding of the image in the real time that becomes the lived time of thought and the body.'[33] This slowing down of pain so it fits the real time of the movie is also in stark contrast to the rapid cartoon-style violence of the postmodern blockbuster of the 1980s. As Dargis again notes:

> *In Hollywood action pictures such as Die Hard and Lethal Weapon, the hero is bruised but never beaten: like an inflatable rubber clown he bounces back with an idiot grin for more (do it again). In movie after movie, he takes punches, kicks even bullets to prove the inviolability of...his body.*[34]

The invulnerability of a Gibson, Willis or Stallone is symptomatic of the postmodern action film's aesthetic push towards the 'inflation of the represented', where the crisis of the action-image is played out by exaggerating the structures of the narrative violence of the action-image. By contrast, Tarantino's vulnerable, pulpy bodies suggest a conflict between a cinema which is self-consciously postmodern (in the sense that it depends on previous cinematic knowledge), and the desire to provoke an immediate affect based in contemporary anxieties around violence.

The pool of blood that builds up around Orange's body is as self-consciously artificial as the gangster's black and white suits, and is directly reminiscent of Godard's self-reflexive images of brutality in *Le Weekend* (1968) or *Pierrot Le Fou* (1968). The striking hue of the blood that splatters the gangster's white shirts, and that Orange drowns in, also recalls Godard's famous saying that 'It's not blood it's red'.[35] Deleuze argues that Godard's idea is another example of the specificity of cinema and relates to what he calls, the 'colour-image':

> *This is the absorbent characteristic. Godard's formula, 'It's not blood its red' is the formula of colourism. In opposition to a simply coloured image, the colour-image does not refer to a particular object, but absorbs all that it can: it is the power which seizes all that happens within its range, or the quality common to completely different images. There is a symbolism of colours, but it does not consist in a correspondence between a colour and an affect (green and hope...). Colour is on the contrary the affect in itself, that is, the virtual conjunction of all the objects it picks up. Thus Ollier is led to say that Agnes Varda's films, notably Le Bonheur, 'absorb', and absorb not only the spectator, but the characters themselves, and the situations, in complex movements affected by the complementary colours.*[36]

In Deleuze's reading of Godard's formula, he places the emphasis on the sensual and active materiality of the colour itself. Colour moves through the light in a way which infiltrates and absorbs the objects in the *mise en scène*, and this in itself is its affect, rather than any symbolic meanings the colours might have. But if in one sense the screen colour produces this material affect from itself, then colour in the white cultural imagination is also linked indexically to racial identity in both the cinematic and extracinematic worlds. The excessive redness of Tarantino's blood absorbs the white genre characters it splatters and drowns the viewer, but the real time it takes to seep out of Orange's body also connects it to the 'real' blood and violence associated with images of blackness.

The redness of the blood is a key element in *Reservoir Dogs'* mimesis of the 'hood film. The messiness of Orange's bullet wound evokes memories of the blood-smeared polythene of the sofa from Ricki's dead body in *Boyz N the Hood*. The most poignant feature of this particular scene in *Boyz* is the vain attempts of Ricki's mother to protect the American Dream she has for her son. These aspirations are smeared and spoilt by the Real of seemingly random casual violence present in the 'drive-by' shooting of Ricki. The gangsters' and the undercover cop's different plans are similarly interrupted in *Reservoir Dogs*, and sudden eruptions of random meaningless violence leave a mess of blood which drowns them all. The blood is uncontrollable because it erupts from the very characteristics which they assign to the gangsta ('always saying they're gonna kill each other'). The violence which the gangsters have assigned to African Americans is the unspoken Real within their own Symbolic structures of meaning. In this sense, the gangsters are bleeding 'black blood', and the racial contagion which Ethan Edwards and Travis Bickle attempt to prevent in earlier moments of white action cinema, becomes the visceral material which the gangsters are full of.

The sudden random eruptions of violence, and the real-time it takes for the gangsters to be absorbed by the bleeding, emphasises the powerlessness of the gangsters to control the Real. There is another mimetic connection being made here with the white viewer. By coding the gangsters in terms of what the white cultural imagination associates with the gangsta, the film also attempts to evoke a sense of powerlessness in the spectator. The gangster's unknowing imitation of the off-hand casual violence and the knowing cool of the gangsta plays on the fears generated by white cultural imagination's fabrication of blackness as unknowable and meaninglessly violent. These imitations signify an attempt to reanimate the cinematic experience by drawing on contemporary images which evoke belief and immediacy within the viewer.

Moving Beyond the 'any-space whatever'

The construction of cinematic space is the final area of the film that I want to explore where 1990s' black culture is used to reanimate white genre cinema. Tarantino expresses his desire to produce a specifically cinematic affect in *Reservoir Dogs* with some comments made in interview:

To me the most important thing was that it be cinematic. Now having said that, one of the things that I get a big kick out of with Reservoir Dogs *is that it plays with theatrical elements in a cinematic form - it is contained, the tension isn't dissipated, it's supposed to mount, the characters aren't able to leave, and the whole movie's performance driven.*[37]

Tarantino draws on a number of concepts here relating to the debate concerning the ontological differences between the theatre and cinema - including the microcosmic world of the theatre stage versus the ability of the camera to cut quickly between different worlds and settings, and the 'real' presence of actors on stage as opposed to their embodiment on screen. This enclosed theatrical setting is punctuated by the eclectic use a multitude of cinematographic aesthetics which range from conventional close-up shot-reverse shots, to the Bazinian realism of the deep-focus long take, and to Scorsesean fast zoom and panning shots. The real time is also frequently interrupted by complex flashbacks which not only alter the temporal structure of the film, but allow us to occasionally move out of the enclosed space of the warehouse.

But the warehouse setting is significant beyond the theatre/cinema media crossover, and it signals another sign of the film's mimesis of the 'hood film. The closed-in nature of the warehouse and the fact that the characters are never allowed to permanently leave echoes the spatial confines of the 'hood in *Boyz N the Hood* and *Menace II Society*. A large part of the power and the immediacy of the gangsta film is its ability to work on the level of both social realism by representing the racially imposed boundaries of the ghetto, *and* on the level of strategic mimesis - as such an enclosed world evokes memories of the contained Hollywood realism of the action-image, which enabled its protagonists to act authoritatively within a well-defined and enclosed milieu. One of the differences between the gangsta and the gangster is that the latter uses violence as an ultimate action, which usually functions as a kind of cathartic release for the viewer after a build up of narrative tension or cause and effect. Within the genres of the action-image extreme violence is usually the ultimate action within the narrative cause and effect pattern, and either signals the conclusion of the narrative, or as a cause of the next sequence of linear progression. With the gangsta, the ultimate action of murder becomes a common everyday gesture. The off-hand and casually brutal violence of the gangsta takes the logic of being able to control a milieu through action to an extreme. The milieu of the 'hood is a place of confinement where the ability of the protagonists to control situations through action is ultimately limited. The warehouse of *Reservoir Dogs* functions in a similar fashion to the way the 'hood works in the gangsta film. As Mr Pink notes, the gangsters are always threatening to kill each other in order to take control and authority in this space, and like the gangsta they are not allowed to leave.

But the big difference between the gangsta film and *Reservoir Dogs* is that the latter is unable to set its action within a socially specific *mise en scène*, such as the 'hood, because of the anachronistic status of its white genre characters and the cinema of the action-image. *Reservoir Dogs* can only imitate the dynamics of such a confined *mise en scène* within a socially neutral setting. The film is caught up in the cinema of the crisis of the action-image. Gilles Deleuze argues that one of the major symptoms of this crisis is the tendency of films to set their action within the 'any-space-whatever'. White genre film can no longer depict worlds which are a global microcosm of a unified society, where the action of the individual protagonist can effect a positive and decisive change. According to Deleuze, belief in the concept of such an organic society no longer exists in American culture, and consequently there is no longer a belief in films which manifest such a philosophy in their formal structures. In the American cinema of the crisis of the action-image settings are socially and geographically non-specific, and the action 'happens in any-space-whatever - marshalling yard, disused warehouse, the undifferentiated fabric of the city - in opposition to action which most often unfolded in the qualified space-time of the old realism'.[38]

The loss of the fixed milieux of the action-image, and the use of the any-space-whatever, was also signalled by the different movements of protagonists in the cinema of the crisis of the action-image. The generic established milieu of the West, or the Underworld, is replaced by predominance of 'the stroll, the voyage and the continual return journey'.[39] Deleuze argues that in 1970s' cinema:

> *The voyage has found in America the formal and material conditions of a renewal. It takes place through external or internal necessity through the need for flight. But it now loses the initiatory aspect that it had in...the beat journey (Dennis Hopper and Peter Fonda's Easy Rider). It has become the urban voyage, and has become detached from the affective structure which supported it, directed it, gave it even vague directions. How could there be nerve fibre or sensory-motor structure between the driver of Taxi-Driver and what he sees on the pavement in his driving mirror.*[40]

The dissipation of belief in the old limited and concrete milieux and the modern cinematic journey is a result of the new rootlessness of protagonists. In contrast to the excessively oppressive milieu of George Bailey in *It's a Wonderful Life* which, as we have seen, goes to extraordinary lengths to keep him tied to his particular cinematic world, characters of seventies 'crisis' cinema move from one space to another as they no longer belong to, or recognise, one milieu from another. As we have also seen, this idea of the rootless protagonist on a voyage through the urban landscape is a central feature of *Falling Down*. But this film attempts to reanimate the affective structures between the protagonist and the viewer by making DFens act as if geographically and socially familiar milieus can still be controlled by the white protagonist. But a further reason to suggest why *Falling Down* is a regressive film is the way that it encourages the viewer to mourn the loss of security which comes with the failure to recognise, and be recognised by, particular milieus.

The voyage through the 'any-space-whatever' is also a common feature of the *mise en scène* of the Hollywood postmodern blockbuster. Endless chases through open drains, disused factories and other indistinguishable urban landscapes feature heavily in blockbusters such as the *Terminator* films, and the *Lethal Weapon* series. Even in the fixed but faceless corporate block of *Die Hard* (McTiernan 1988), Bruce Willis is constantly on the move, from office, to lift shaft, to air-conditioning duct. But as we have also seen, the postmodern film seeks to nostalgically replicate the authority of protagonist over milieu, and in this sense, it does so through the exaggeration of the hero's powers. The 'over-the-top' spectacle of the body count and the excessive muscularity of the bodies of Schwarzenegger, Stallone and Willis inflate the ability of the individual protagonist to exert their control over any space and milieu.[41]

Reservoir Dogs uses the any-space-whatever of the warehouse to a different effect than both seventies cinema and postmodern cinema. The gangsters are powerless to leave, and no single one of them is able to exert any decisive action which does not result in the disintegration of the gangster milieu and/or death. Authority and power shift too quickly and violently, and the ability of a single protagonist to control the space is negated. First we have the struggle between Pink and White over what action must be taken after the disastrous heist; then we have the entrance of Blonde and another fight begins between him and White which is only prevented from ending in death by Pink's intervention; then Nice Guy Eddie enters and exerts a semblance of the patriarchal order that had previously been the contingent central structure of authority within the gangster's milieu; as soon as the other gangsters leave to recover the loot, Blonde then exerts the ultimate physical control of the space in his torture of the cop, but again this is only temporary until Orange wakes from his semi-comatose state and exerts his authority by shooting Blonde; finally we have the three-way shoot-out where White, Joe and Nice Guy Eddie all seek to impose their authority, a struggle which White 'wins', only to be told by Orange that he is an undercover cop, and is shot dead by the police. Attempts to exert control over the cinematic space are only temporary and end in death, and there is no escape through the stroll or the voyage. But unlike the 'hood film *Reservoir Dogs* must still use a socially neutral space - except for graffiti-covered wall scenes with Holdsway - in order to be taken seriously.

Conclusion

The use of the warehouse in *Reservoir Dogs* is ultimately another sign of the film's desire to reanimate a particular kind of cinematic affect. The concrete ties between the white gangsters and their milieu echo that of the gangsta and the 'hood, and they also produce a similar mimetic affect in the viewer. At the end of the last chapter, I argued that the confinement of the gangster in the 'hood evoked the temporary incarceration of the cinema viewer as she or he takes up a seat in the darkened auditorium of the theatre. The warehouse functions like this in *Reservoir Dogs,* and is also filled with bodies which are packed with the affective qualities of the 'dangerous' black body of the gangsta. The film produces an affect that is particular to the cinema in miming this enclosed temporal and spatial structure. As Thomas Elsaessar notes:

> *...in the cinema we are subjected to a particularly intense organization of time, experienced within a formal structure which is closed, but in a sense also circular: we are 'captured' in order to be 'released', willingly undergoing a fixed term of imprisonment.*[42]

Elsaessar suggests an essentially masochistic specificity of the cinema, where the viewer willingly subjects themselves to what Carol Clover calls 'the reactive gaze', and Noel Burch calls 'structures of aggression'.[43] Tarantino seeks to attain this affect within the postmodern era where we are bombarded by images from a multitude of different media sources. But where these images are perhaps glanced at, Tarantino's films attempt to reanimate a cinematic experience which captures the full attention of the viewer's body as well as consciousness. *Reservoir Dogs* mimes images of blackness which produce bodily affect in the white cultural imagination in order to privilege the cinema as a space where belief and the real are still obtainable, and which is beyond the surface simulation of postmodernity. In many ways *Reservoir Dogs,* like Fredric Jameson, equates affect with bodily depth. Tarantino's cinema desires the cinematic and viewer's body to be one of fleshy depth, rather than what Scott Bukatmen calls the fractal body.[44] The simulations and erosion of meaning which postmodernity has come to symbolise in theory and culture is equated with a trashy and empty, artificial white popular culture. The authority to see the differences between appearance and reality, surface and depth is granted to black culture.

The political and cultural ramifications of this mimesis are complex and there are no easy answers to the question raised by *Reservoir Dogs* construction and use of 1990s' black culture. Spike Lee has raised objections to Tarantino's appropriation of African-American culture because it fetishises blackness as a desirable other, which in the words of Michael Rogin, is based on 'the power to make African-Americans stand for something besides themselves'.[45] Tarantino's construction of African-American culture as both 'hip', authoritative, and more 'real' than white culture may well be guilty of this. But in the last chapter, I used Michael Taussig's work to suggest that mimesis makes the fetish a transformative phenomenon which provokes new ways of seeing the world. *Menace II Society,* for instance, imitates white cinematic genres to expose the racial rage at the heart of the white cultural imagination. *Reservoir Dogs'* use of black culture is more mimetic than appropriative in the sense that destruction of the film's characters is revealed to emanate from the characteristics that the gang assigns to gangsta culture. The film is about the destruction of the white self rather than the black other, and as such, it is filled with aesthetics of masochism rather than voyeurism. Most importantly, *Reservoir Dogs* does not approach African American culture from a position of white authoritative knowledge in the same way as *Falling Down* does. In this film codes of contemporary African-American culture are used to provoke affective responses in the viewer, but ultimately blackness comes to symbolise naivety, primitivism and psychosis. *Falling Down* encourages the viewer's voyeurism in that it appears to grant the viewer a position of knowledge perceived as lacking in black culture. *Reservoir Dogs* is different from *Falling Down*, as one of the main consequences of its mimesis of the affective power of black culture on the white cultural imagination is to reanimate the masochistic, bodily experience of the cinema, and expose the viewer to the 'assaultive gaze'. This necessarily puts the viewer in a position where established cultural knowledge, such as the stability and authority of white cultural identity, are open to question, and the film does not seek to provide any definitive answers to these questions.

In the next, final chapter, I will be looking at three more new-brutality films as evidence that the American Africanism and confusion of rap culture with cinematic affect in *Reservoir Dogs* is not an isolated case. The construction of the white American cultural imagination as a space of confused, empty, dead artifice, and African Americanism as an affective, real, and knowing domain is present, in various ways, in *Pulp Fiction* (Tarantino 1994), *Strange Days* (Bigelow 1995), *Se7en* and *Fight Club* (Fincher 1995 and 1999), all of which might be described as belonging to a post-Tarantinian moment in American cinema.

Notes

1. Nearly all of the reviews of *Reservoir Dogs* and *Pulp Fiction* - favourable or not - celebrate the dialogue. Derek Malcolm for example notes that 'Tarantino is clearly a brilliant screenplay writer' *The Guardian* (20 October 1994: 11).

2. As Richard Shusterman notes, 'Artistic appropriation is the historical source of hip-hop culture and still remains the core of its technique and a central feature of its aesthetic form and message' Shusterman, *New Literary History* 22 (1991: 614).

3. This mimesis of African-American culture and idiom is also evident in James Ellroy's *L.A. Quartet* crime novels, and particularly in the rhythmic prose of *White Jazz* (1993). The title of the book alludes to this and the characters of the novel are, like Tarantino's, coded as 'black', or as what being black symbolises in the white cultural imagination. There is some potential in exploring the fact that Tarantino's films and Ellroy's novels have emerged at the same historical moment.

4. Taubin, *Sight and Sound* 2 (1992: 5).

5. *ibid.*

6. Butler (1994: 212).

7. *ibid.* (212-4).

8. Morrison (1993: 52).

9. Mailer (1968: 273-76).

10. The most striking example Mailer gives of mimicking the authority of white cultural codes is his anecdote of a black man in conversation with a white woman at a middle-class party in New York. Mailer observes the woman discussing an intellectual topic which Mailer claims the African-American would know nothing about. Yet the man is able to give the appearance of being knowledgeable through picking up on the language structure of the woman's argument and intervening in the right places with appropriate non-specific questions and signs of agreement. See *ibid.* (276).

11. *ibid.* (270). This motif of movement and drifting can also be seen in other counter-cultural works of the 50s and 60s. Jack Kerouac's seminal novel, *On the Road* (1957), is perhaps the most famous example.

12. The gangster turned gangsta is much more overt in the Tarantino-scripted *True Romance* (Scott 1992) with Gary Oldman giving an extraordinary performance as a black-faced and black-tongued Rastafarian drug dealer.

13. Tarantino himself mentions LA's diner culture in relation to the opening scene of *Pulp Fiction*. He notes that:

    Everything in Los Angeles revolves around restaurants. You get together with your friends at restaurants, you have dates at restaurants, business meetings at restaurants. In many other cities you have to be of a certain wealth to go to restaurants, but in Los Angeles we have coffee shops that are open all night long. So you can not have pot to piss in and still afford to go to a coffee shop and hang out. Sight and Sound 4 (1994: 16).

14. Examples range from, Jimmy Cagney in *The Public Enemy* (Wellman 1931) to Lee Marvin's hitman in Don Siegel's version of *The Killers* (1964), to the postmodern irony of the suits in *The Blues Brothers* (Landis 1980).

15. Diawara (1993: 23). For a feminist reading of the narrative importance of fathers see Wiegman in Cohan & Hark (1993: 173-93).

16. Tarantino, *Sight and Sound* 4 (1994: 10).

17. Zizek (1991: 13-15).

18. Zizek (1989: 167).

19. For instance, at the outset of the movie the gangsters attempt to work out the meaning of the lyrics of Madonna's 'Like a Virgin'.

20. Jameson (1991: 174-5).

21. Jameson (1991: 20).

22. I have already explored this to some degree through one of the blueprints for the postmodern blockbuster, *Blade Runner* (Scott 1982). In the last chapter (following Steven Shaviro) I argued that this film 'presents simulation as the loss of the real'. The overt world of simulation and pastiche presented in this science fiction world is permeated with a sense of loss for a time and cinematic place where, what is simulated in the film, once inspired belief.

23. Dyer (1993: 141).

24. Morrison (1993: 59).

25. Burch (1981: 124).

26. West (1993: 12).

27. Tarantino, *Sight and Sound* (1994: 17).

28. Williams, *Film Quarterly* (1992: 14).

29. There are many articles which document Tarantino's self-confessed admiration for proclaimed auteurs such as Jean-Luc Godard and Howard Hawks. See for instance his interview with Adrian Wootton, reprinted in extract in *The Guardian G2* (4 February 1995: 3).

30. There are also numerous articles which attempt to impose this contemporary auteur image on Tarantino including Biskind, *Premiere* (US) (November 1994: 94-102).

31. According to an article in *The Guardian*, Tarantino's desire to make the viewer dress as the characters worked in the UK. Alex Bellos interviewed five 'self-confessed Dogs' outside the Prince Charles cinema in London where the film had a thrice-weekly showing - largely due to the BBFC delay of the film's release on video. He writes: 'Not since *The Rocky Horror Picture Show* in the seventies and *The Blues Brothers* in the eighties has a movie become so much a cult that fans will go again and again, dressing up like the characters and mimicking the dialogue' *The Guardian* (17 September 1993: 3).

32. Dargis, *Sight and Sound* 4 (1994: 9).

33. Beasley-Murray *Iris* 23 (1997: 39).

34. Dargis, *Sight and Sound* 4 (1994: 9).

35. Deleuze (1986: 118).

36. *ibid.* (118).

37. Tarantino in Smith, *Film Comment* (July/August 1994: 34).

38. Deleuze (1986: 207).

39. *ibid.* (208).

40. *ibid.*

41. See Chapter 3 of Tasker (1993: 54-73) for a discussion of whether the overblown bodies of the blockbuster represent 'the body in crisis or the body triumphant'.

42 Elsaesser in Bennett, Boyd-Bowman, Mercer and Woollacott eds. (1981: 270-82).

43. Clover (1992: 166-231). See also Studlar (1988) for a psychoanalytic account of the pleasures of masochism in the cinematic experience.

44. Bukatman (1993). Bukatman argues that:

   The body is now an infinite set of surfaces - a fractal subject - an object among objects. The dissolution of boundaries, the 'end of borders and frontiers', the waning of affect, the erosion of meaning and representation, the rise of spectacle and simulacra - all of these familiar tropes are played out upon the physical manifestation of the subject - the body. (246).

45. Rogin, *Critical Inquiry* 18 (1992: 417).

Chapter Five

Trashing Whiteness:
Pulp Fiction, *Se7en*, *Strange Days* and Articulating Affect

What I feel about the audience - particularly after the eighties, where the films got so ritualized, you started seeing the same movies over and over again - intellectually the audience doesn't know they know as much as they do. In the first ten minutes of nine out of ten movies...the movie tells you what kind of movie it's gonna be. It tells you everything you basically need to know...you just know what's gonna happen. You don't know you know, but you know. Admittedly there's a lot of fun in playing against that, fucking up the breadcrumb trail that we don't even know we are following, using an audience's own subconscious preconceptions against them, so they actually have a viewing experience, they're actually involved in the movie. Yeah I'm interested in doing that just as a storyteller. But the heartbeat of the movie has to be a human heartbeat.[1] Indirectly express many of the characteristics of the new-brutality film that I explored in the last chapter. The desire to produce movies with a 'human heartbeat' sounds oddly humanistic coming from a director who has been celebrated, or derided, by critics as the ultimate postmodern Hollywood filmmaker. But the language Tarantino uses here expresses something of the desire - seen in *Reservoir Dogs* in the last chapter - to produce a Hollywood action-cinema that can provoke an affective, physical shock, rather than the habitually perceptive and ritualistic response generated by the blockbuster movies of the 1980s and 1990s. This desired viscerality is based in a conception of the body as one of depth rather than the multi-surfaced, 'fractal' body, cited as the dominant representation of the body within postmodernity.[2] Meaningful or 'human' affect is equated here with bodily and emotional depth, and this also echoes Fredric Jameson's argument that the cultural productions of postmodernity, with their emphasis on pastiche and artifice, have led to a waning of affect. Like Tarantino's audience, who have absorbed the cinematic images of postmodernity to the degree where they don't know that they know the moves that the blockbuster is going to make, Jameson's postmodern subject has been colonized by postmodernity to the degree that there is no longer an unconscious or Real outside of its discourses and images.[3] But new-brutality films such as *Reservoir Dogs* seek to reanimate a particular cinematic affect, working on the assumption that the audience can still be taken by surprise with images that destabilize existing cultural and political discourses through the reaction they incite, affecting the body first and foremost.

What is left unsaid by Tarantino's comments is that this desire to reanimate and privilege the physical shock of the cinematic experience - in the wake of the constant bombardment of viewers by postmodernism's proliferation of different images - is based in a mimesis of 1990s' African culture (and especially rap and the 'hood film). The analysis of *Reservoir Dogs* in the previous chapter suggested that the film depends on an association of black culture with both an authentic, authoritative cultural knowledge and an affective depth. Black culture stands in contrast to the film's construction of white popular culture as a space of surface, simulation, chaos and emptiness. In other words, the tropes of the postmodern are associated with white culture, while black culture is associated with the affect that culture lacks. Yet these films are also fascinated with the possibilities that black culture may re-energise white audiences by means of the affective shock that (so constructed) it provides them.

The aesthetics of rap also display these constituents of postmodernity, and new-brutality films also suggest that rap and contemporary African-American culture have a self-reflexive awareness and knowledge of the artifice and chaos of postmodernity. By contrast, the white cultural identity, displayed, for instance, by *Reservoir Dogs'* gangsters is shown to be still under the illusion that it can impose Symbolic structures of meaning which can repress the immanent violence of the white cultural imagination. Such films also suggest that the white cultural imagination has defined the boundaries of white identity by attempting to draw lines of demarcation between itself and the anarchic, violent and primitivised state it constructs as the nature of blackness; they suggest that white cultural identity, also, has at root the same characteristics (but repressed) as that which has been constructed as black.

But perhaps the most overt reason for the coding of black culture in this way is the affective charge that images associated with black violence provide. The 'coolness' constructed around contemporary black culture and the fears provoked by black violence are mimicked by to provoke an affective shock to the viewer. Thus Tarantino's films grant contemporary black culture the power to achieve a body-first reaction which conflicts with pre-existing cultural knowledge. Throughout both *Reservoir Dogs* and *Pulp Fiction*, there is a contradictory construction of African-American culture as both having the cultural authority to see through the artifice of postmodernity and white cultural identity *and* as a sign of an unknowable, substantive and visceral, savage Real.

This chapter will argue that these kinds of 'American-Africanism' are also present - to varying degrees - in films which might be categorized as belonging post-*Reservoir Dogs* moment of American cinema. *Pulp Fiction*, *Se7en* and *Strange Days* all attempt to bring into play 'the structures of aggression' which Noel Burch identifies as immanent to the cinematic experience.[4] These films are also self-reflexively aware that this attempt to 're-privilege' the cinema as a specific affective space, is taking place at a time when traditional Hollywood narrative techniques (what Gilles Deleuze in his two cinema books terms the cinema of the 'action-image') is in crisis, and when even film that explores this crisis of the action-image have become full of clichés or parodies of clichés. The cinema of the action-image portrays characters in an organic relationship to the milieux in which they find themselves, such that the milieu and the actions they undertake reciprocally condition and are logically connected to each other through narrative; this cinema is in crisis once this relationship appears to be broken. New-brutality films take their cue from African American genres such as the gangsta film (and so-called New Black Realism, typified by *Boyz N the Hood* and *Menace II Society*), which have taken the clichés of this 'action-image' cinema and recharged them with affective and political meaning.

There are differences in the way these films attempt to negotiate the mimetic dynamic between contemporary white action cinema, white constructions of African-American culture, and contemporary black culture. *Pulp Fiction* is similar to *Reservoir Dogs* in its equation of black culture and a contemporary cinematic affect, and 'hipness'. The film also fetishises African-Americans as having the knowledge and cultural power to negotiate the empty simulation of postmodernity, which it also equates with white cultural identity. *Se7en* tends to provoke an affective shock by imitating the aesthetics of genres like 'True-Crime' TV programmes which play on the anxieties and paranoia evoked by the perceived, immanent violence of black masculinity. Yet it too suggests that blackness is a state of cultural knowledge that can penetrate the simulations of the postmodern city to arrive at the reality that lies beneath. *Strange Days* produces a similar fabrication of African-American culture as culturally powerful, particularly in the figure of Mace (Angela Bassett). Yet, this film is also much more self-reflexive than either of the other white new-brutality films in suggesting the way that white identity and culture has come to be perceived as a place of emptiness and simulation, which needs to seek affective and authentic experiences in images of black violence and black rage.

Pulp Fiction: Recycling, Violence and Superficiality

Pulp Fiction (like *Reservoir Dogs*) attempts to reanimate artefacts of the popular cultural past with an immediacy and affective power, missing from the nostalgia of postmodern film, and neglected by the critical discourses when these artefacts were produced. Trash culture from America's past is recharged in such a way that it produces a response which is immediate and bodily. Sharon Willis notes this tendency in Tarantino's output in her suggestion that, throughout the films, images of shit and waste metaphorically allude to past popular culture.[5] The other predominant metaphor, according to Willis, is the transformation of this meaningless waste into something of value. The most obvious example of this in *Pulp Fiction* is 'The Gold Watch' sequence, where Christopher Walken plays a returning Vietnam vet, giving a small boy his dead father's watch. The fact that Walken hid this object in his arse while in a Vietnamese prison camp suggests an association of shit with value. Willis notes that this metonymy runs throughout the film and argues that it signals the film's own attempts to produce an affective charge by reclaiming objects from popular culture which were perceived as trash by established critical authority. These observations are in keeping with Tarantino's own conception of the film's aesthetic aims: Tarantino talks about trashy popular culture, like pulp fiction novels, as 'sneaking through the gaps' and evading critical scrutiny; he discusses his own appropriation of this kind of material in terms of finding 'diamonds in the dustbin'.[6] As Willis notes, the idea of reconstituting a forgotten popular cultural past as something of value and meaning is also to question the branding of such material as trash in the first place: 'To redeem a previous generation's trash may be, metaphorically to turn its shit into gold, and to posit a certain reversibility of cultural authority in the process.'[7] Willis also argues that Tarantino's films turn to African-American culture as a prime source of this reversal in cultural authority. She goes on to produce a psychoanalytic reading of *Pulp Fiction* which identifies an oedipalised relationship between Tarantino and black culture. But I am more interested in the way that this American Africanism is played out in the context of the aesthetic crisis of white cinema and white cultural identity, discussed throughout this book.

As I suggested in the chapters on *Boyz N the Hood* and *Menace II Society*, the 'hood or gangsta film imitates the cinema of the action-image and the crisis of the action-image. This mimesis reanimates these cinemas by playing on the affective shock which images of the dangerous black body provoke, and by revealing the white racial rage which lies at the heart of white American cultural identity. This white racial rage is replaced in the 'hood film by a politicized black rage which assaults the certainties and authority of white cultural identity and the American Dream. The mimetic transformation of white iconic images gives the films of New Black Realism an immediacy and contemporaneity missing from the postmodern blockbuster's nostalgic and exaggerated attempts to restore the action-image cinema's relations of positive action and affect between their protagonists and milieus.

Pulp Fiction is equally concerned with providing a contemporary immediacy, which is why many of the film's intertextual references allude towards the more obscure and trashy objects of the popular cultural past. The fact that such artefacts might have been 'missed' the first time round gives them a modernist tone in the sense that they cannot operate as objects of nostalgia. But like *Reservoir Dogs*, the film also sets up a dualistic structure where the white culture is revealed as a blank, empty and meaningless space, and African-American culture is fetishised as both knowing the meaning and value of popular culture, *and* as a space of affective depth. And like *Reservoir Dogs*, *Pulp Fiction* equates the cinematic experience with the power of African-American culture to provoke a response in the body which is capable of providing a shock to conscious thought. This opposition is most present in the way that the film sets up a space of a potentially affective and meaningful real beyond its own dazzlingly overloaded intertextual play.

Pulp Fiction, like *Reservoir Dogs* and the cinema of the crisis of the action-image, is self-reflexively aware of the clichés of narrative, protagonist and situation in the Hollywood action cinema. The film reiterates old Hollywood narratives to the point where the various narratives of the film are no longer central, and are replaced by the 'moments of dramatic intensity', characteristic of the films of Martin Scorsese. But like the cinema of Scorsese, *Pulp Fiction* repeats and stresses the familiarity of the action-image cinema, in order to draw attention to the clichés themselves. Tarantino notes the standard nature of the three main narratives of *Pulp Fiction*:

> *The thing that was cool about it is that what I wanted to do with the three stories was start off with the oldest chestnuts in the world. You've seen them a zillion times. You don't need to get caught up with the story because you already know it. The guy takes out the mob guy's wife - 'but don't touch her'. And what happens if they touch? You've seen that triangle a zillion times. Or the boxer who's supposed to throw a fight but doesn't - you've seen that a zillion times too. The third situation isn't an old familiar story but an old familiar situation. The story starts with Jules and Vincent going to kill some guys. That's like the opening five minutes of every Joel Silver movie - a bunch of guys show up and pow pow pow kill somebody and then the credit sequence starts and then you see Arnold Schwarzenegger. So let's extend that whole little opening, let's hang out with them for the rest of their day and the shenanigans that follow.*[8]

Tarantino recognises the constitutive intertextuality and recurrence of narratives of the postmodern action film, in his references to Silver and Schwarzenegger. *Pulp Fiction* also displays knowledge of the crisis of the action-image, and this self-reflexive awareness is nowhere more apparent than in the relations between the milieu of Los Angeles and the protagonists.

The LA of *Pulp Fiction* is also predominantly a space of 'rootlessness', with no visibly present central milieu or individual protagonist. LA is shown as what Deleuze would call an 'any-space-whatever' in both temporal and spatial terms. Characters appear to drift in and out of neutral, non-definable spaces, like coffee-shops, motel rooms, bars and apartments. The protagonists appear to have no concrete relations with these spaces, and stroll, like Deleuze's nomad from one to another. The sense of instability is compounded by the non-definable era of these spaces. We travel from the contemporary space of the apartment block, to *The Big Combo's* boxing ring backstage, to the Godardian motel room where Butch and Fabienne play out their interminable love scene. Characters wander in and out with what on first viewing, seems to be no definable purpose or reason. Unlike the well-defined and tightly structured space of the 'hood, this LA seems to be a space of surface, and postmodern interextuality, with no concrete sensory-motor relations between protagonists and milieu. But again there is also the voicing of a desire here to move beyond the clichéd situations and narratives of the action-image - which the blockbuster repeats. In contrast to films like *Die Hard* and *The Terminator*, *Pulp Fiction* does not use familiar situations and spaces in order to evoke nostalgia for the concrete sensory-motor relations of action between the protagonist and milieu, characteristic of the action-image. Instead, the film supplies such a density of intertextual allusions to both familiar and obscure cultural artefacts of the past that the viewer's attempts to keep up provides its own kind of distraction.

In other words, the world of *Pulp Fiction* is so dense with intertextuality that any attempt to use a reference as a sign of any unified structure of meaning behind the film leads to yet another citation. A prime example of this is the much discussed briefcase, which Jules and Vincent are on their way to pick up for their gangster boss, Marsellus Wallace (Ving Rhames), in the opening sequence. The briefcase is opened twice (once in the apartment by Vincent, where the two hoods go to retrieve the case for their boss, and the second time in the final scene where Pumpkin, played by Tim Roth, attempts to take the case from Jules in a hold-up). Each time, a bright golden light absorbs the opener's face and the screen. Yet, unlike the screen characters, the viewer never gets to see the source of this golden light. The unseen contents of the briefcase thwart attempts to read it as containing some symbolic deep structural meaning. But the briefcase and golden light are caught up in a dense network of intertextual references, and at least two of these citations are direct. Both *Kiss Me Deadly* (Aldrich 1955) and *Raiders of the Lost Ark* (Spielberg 1981) feature boxes with an unseen object emanating golden light. In the narrative of both films this light is associated with the ultimate in violent destruction. The box in *Kiss Me Deadly* contains radioactive material which is opened at the end of the film (and the *film noir* cycle), leaving the world facing nuclear holocaust. The opening of the chest containing the tablets, bearing the Ten Commandments in *Raiders of the Lost Ark*, unleashes the wrath of God Himself (in fact, the gold light in *Raiders* is probably a reference itself to *Kiss Me Deadly*).

If we read the briefcase in *Pulp Fiction* as an allusion to these two films, it is possible to argue that the golden light operates as a symbol of violence itself. This reading gains more credibility in the context of golden flashes which absorb the frame during Vincent's execution of the small-time criminals who had originally stolen the case. But this interpretation still remains at the level of the surface, prompting another series of unanswerable questions. If the golden light *does* symbolise violence, what kind of violence is being suggested? Does the light mean cinematic violence or does it extend to the extracinematic violence of experiential reality? Does the golden light point towards the many journalistic discussions of screen violence provoked by Tarantino's films? The huge amount of questions and different directions prompted by the citational status of the suitcase makes it impossible to read as indicative of any single underlying deep truth. The allusions become a surface network that only has meaning in their relation to other images caught up in the same grid.

Affect, Race and the Fantasy of Depth in the Image

These futile attempts to find meaning in the briefcase suggest that it is the golden glow itself which produces the affective reaction in the viewer. Like the self-conscious red of the blood that seeps from Orange during the course of *Reservoir Dogs*, the golden glow functions as another example of the Deleuzian colour-image in the sense that it 'does not refer to a particular object, but absorbs all that it can'. The golden light fills the screen and 'seizes all that happens within its range' and is 'the affect in itself,' absorbing 'not only the spectator, but the characters themselves and the situations...'[9] Before any speculation around the origins of the intertextual allusions generated by the briefcase, the viewer's body is caught and absorbed by the rays of golden light. Steven Shaviro argues that this state between the literal physicality and the viewer's attempt to assign meanings to images provides the ontological specificity of the cinematic experience:

> *The image is not a symptom of lack, but an uncanny, excessive residue of being that subsists when all should be lacking. Images are banally self-evident and self-contained, but their superficiality and obviousness is also a strange blankness, a resistance to the closure of definition, or to any imposition of meaning...*[10]

With its unusually dense intertextuality, *Pulp Fiction* does more than most films to thwart closure and the imposition of meaning. Yet, the curiosity evoked by the unseen nature of the briefcase's contents suggests the *possibility* of depth and meaning as the viewer strains to see the object producing the golden light. There is something in the image which is beyond the surface, which invites the viewer to give it significance beyond its literal physical appearance. The unseen space of the briefcase evokes the idea that there is something beyond the superficiality and obviousness of the images themselves which is contained within the image. The imagined bottom of the briefcase suggests that, beyond the surface play of references to other images, there is a depth which is impossible for the viewer to see (which does not stop him or her from trying).

This fantasy of the cinematic image's depth could be one of the cinema's constitutive elements. Even the most knowing films of postmodernity, which depend on cultural knowledge and nostalgic simulation, suggest that this depth is associated with the physical properties of the body. *Total Recall* (Verhoeven 1988) is a film which confuses the boundaries of the real and artifice to a degree where it is almost impossible for the viewer to work out the diegetic reality. But in one particular scene, the confusion is cleared up as we and Arnold Schwarzenegger know they are dealing with the real, because of a bead of sweat that drops from an enemy's forehead. The desire for depth and the real in postmodern cinema might be demonstrated even more clearly by looking at the photoscan sequence in *Blade Runner*.

As I argued in Chapter 3, *Blade Runner* has been cited as the archetypal postmodern film in its nostalgia for a 'real' beneath the simulated world it creates. The opposition between surface and depth is used as a metaphor in this film to express this nostalgia. On the outside the replicants seem real in their anthropomorphic form, but are revealed to be artificial and constructed through their implanted memories. But beneath these signs of artifice, the replicants are also revealed to be capable of 'real', physical emotions, in the tears that Roy Batty (Rutger Hauer) sheds for Kriss (Daryl Hannah), and those shed by Rebecca for her 'lost' childhood. But Deckard's electronic search for clues in a photograph of a room demonstrates more clearly the desire for a cinematic image which has depth beyond its literal and obvious surface.

A photograph from one of the replicant's rooms is inserted into an electronic enhancer which converts the image into a digitialised grid. Sections of this grid are fractionalized further, and magnified to the point where the smallest details (replicant snake scales) become central. This visualization of the electronically altered photographic image as a grid can be read as a metaphor for the cinema screen and its images, as two dimensional and obvious. But the most striking and memorable aspect of this sequence is that it shows Deckard doing the impossible. He discovers the vital clue he is looking for by going 'behind' the image. The clue is hidden by a wall in the room, and in any image, whether electronically enhanced or not, it is impossible to see around corners - which is essentially what Deckard does. The absurdity of this image points towards a desire for depth in both this film, and I would suggest, in cinema as a whole.[11]

The difference between the desire for depth in the image in the postmodern action film and that expressed by *Pulp Fiction* lies in the latter's imaging of African-American culture. As I suggested above, the film fabricates African-American bodies and culture as a space which is somehow beyond and more real than the surface simulation of postmodernity, which it equates with white American identity. But more than this, the film suggests that the mimesis of what it perceives as the unknowable and knowing depth of African-American culture is also a means by which the cinema can be reanimated as an affective experience.

As Sharon Willis also notes, beneath the surface flow and 'never-never land' texture of the film, there is an, often unseen, centre, present in the omnipotent figure of the black gangsta figure of Marsellus Wallace (Ving Rhames). Like the black cop, Holdsway in *Reservoir Dogs*, Marsellus hovers over all the narratives and functions as the one concrete link between the protagonists and the milieu of the LA Underworld. He is constructed as the authoritative and controlling centre of the movie's narrative, in the sense that it is Marsellus who is the one who can get things done, and it is Marsellus who functions as the limit of what the other characters can and cannot do. Though he is featured centrally as on-screen presence in only one of the four narratives ('The Gold Watch'), throughout he maintains an invisible, ambient and all-knowing gaze over the other characters, controlling and motivating their actions. Marsellus is characterised as a godlike and fatherlike figure, outside of the Symbolic realities of the other characters, but at the same time controlling them. Of course Marsellus' position within the film as the mythical 'big gangster boss' makes him a direct citational descendant of boss figures in every other gangster movie: yet the fact that Marsellus is black also intimately associates him with the film's drive towards depth and affective immediacy. Marsellus and the other black character of the film, Jules (Samuel L. Jackson), are both figured as being connected to a space of the unknowable Real, beyond the simulations which constitute the diegetic reality and make-up of the other characters.

The other main characters of the film - Vincent (John Travolta), Mia (Uma Thurman), Butch (Bruce Willis), Fabienne (Maria de Medeiros) and Winston Wolf (Harvey Keitel) - are all constructed as citations of generic movie characters, without either psychological or bodily depth. There is nothing to be discovered beyond their intertextual surface. They are cinematic bodies where, as Bukatman puts it, 'the 'depth' of subjectivity continues to be denied'.[12] Vincent is the small-time gangster hood: Mia, the boss's wife; Butch, the aggressive all-American, Ralph Meeker-like, bonehead; Fabienne, the Godardian, ethereal New Wave heroine; and Winston Wolf, the Hawksian 'auteur'. The two black characters of the film are, on the surface, similarly composed of intertextual allusions to other stock cinematic figures: Marsellus the generic gangster boss, complicated perhaps by a few nods in the direction of rap culture; Jules an amalgam of small time gangster hood, blaxploitation figure, and bible-quoting black gospel preacher. But unlike the white genre figures, both Marsellus and Jules are constituted and linked to a 'thing' beyond postmodern simulation. In Jules' case this is perhaps most marked when he moves on from being a simulation of a Baptist preacher, spouting Ezekial because it was 'just a cool thing to say to a motherfucker 'fore you popped a cap in his ass'. In his conversion, Jules is shown to be cognizant of a place beyond this simulation, which, in this case, the film constructs as God. In the case of Marsellus, this beyond is directly linked to the film's attempt to reanimate the specificity of the cinematic image, restore bodily affect to the image, and construct a fantasy of depth in the image.

A hint of the film's construction of whiteness as pure artificial surface, and blackness as a knowing, contradictory space between postmodern artifice and unknowable, affective depth, is detectable in the first on-screen appearance of Marsellus. In the opening sequence of 'Vincent Vega and Marsellus Wallace's Wife', there is a two minute long take, where an unseen voice is instructing an expressionless and motionless Butch to throw a boxing match. The rest of this scene features shot-reverse shots between the back of a black head (which we later know to be Marsellus'), partially covered with a band-aid, and Butch/Willis' non-reaction to the situation. Almost from the start of the film, Marsellus is configured as unknowable depth. Throughout the scene the viewer is straining to see the face and physical site from which the diegetic voice is emanating. This curiosity becomes an affective, tactile contact between the image and the viewer's body, because of the length of time we are denied access to this physical site/sight. The shot of the back of Marsellus' head increases the divide between a visible, simulated and surface whiteness, and an unknowable, 'deep' and body-centred blackness. The band-aid stuck across the back of Marsellus' head is the pinky tinge which white people call flesh-coloured, but which obviously stands out in contrast to Marsellus' black flesh. The juxtaposition of Marsellus' head and the plaster, evokes the film's construction of the whiteness as artificial, while the black flesh underneath is unseen and unknowable.

But it is the torture and rape scene of the film which equates the unknowable depth of blackness with the affective potential and 'depth' of the cinematic experience. It is also this scene which is most suggestive in discerning the way that *Pulp Fiction* also constructs the gangsta film as a cinematic genre where affect is still possible. In the build-up to this scene we have a self-reflexive playing out of the racialised construction of the random meaningless violence of the black gangsta. The shots fired by Marsellus at Butch which hit an innocent bystander echo white paranoiac fears around the urban black body as a site of random, unpredictable violence - even though the viewer knows that Marsellus has very good narrative reasons for shooting Bruce Willis. After the randomness of this violence and the banal, nomadic 'any-space-whatever' setting of the chase, the film places Butch, Marsellus and the viewer within the confines of the torture basement. The spatial co-ordinates of the torture room, like the warehouse in *Reservoir Dogs*, evoke the space of the 'hood as one which is limited and constrained, and from which there is no escape. The two protagonists are literally tied into the milieu as they sit tied to their chairs by their hillbilly captors, Zed and Maynard. The space and situation of the protagonists again also echoes that of the cinematic apparatus, where the affect of the cinema comes from the assault of the images as we sit in a darkened auditorium bombarded by image. But as well as place of affective visual assault, the torture chamber, through intertextual association, suggests that the space of the urban 'hood and the black body are spaces of the Real and of unsymbolisable bodily depth. Through its use of depth-of field and slow-motion the scene presents the viewer with a series of spaces which, like Butch we want to see, but cannot. Eventually most of these spaces are opened up to our voyeuristic view - with the exception of one. The camera cannot move into the body of Marsellus. The interior of the body of Marsellus presents a barrier to representation and therefore a space of unsymbolisable affect, beyond white cultural knowledge. Unlike the photoscan scene in *Blade Runner* the viewer is ultimately unable to go deeper into the image.

The way that blackness and the black body becomes a barrier to the viewer's curious gaze in this scene is reminiscent of the titillating but obstructive language of rap, as it is used in the 'hood film. As I noted in chapter two, the difficulty that white audiences have in understanding rap occurs at the time when the desire to find meaning in the dialogue in the 'hood film is at its most intense. Mark Winokur notes that our 'own ignorance of black codes are being signified - our desire to be titillated is turned against us'.[13] The rape of Marsellus works in a similar fashion. Once the door to the torture room is opened by Butch, our desire to see behind it is replaced by the shock of the rape. Our voyeuristic gaze is turned back onto us in a manner which is similar to the 'reactive gaze' that Carol Clover notes assaults the viewer in many horror films. [14] Not only is Marsellus' body a space where the desire to see depth in the image is thwarted, but it is also the source of an affective shock.

The fact that Marsellus's body being penetrated by redneck hill-billy's - straight out of movies like *Deliverance* (Boorman 1972) and *The Hills Have Eyes* (Craven 1977) - is also significant here, in terms of identifying *Pulp Fiction*'s construction of blackness. Carol Clover suggests that the figure of the hillbilly has become a kind of repository of all the racist features reserved in the Classical Hollywood for the African-American. Like the African-American in action-image cinema, hillbillys are represented as a site of unpredictable violence, sexual deviancy, and as fool-type figures with a lack of sophistication or moral code. Clover argues that films like *Deliverance* appeal to both white and black audiences because of these rural figures' association with the unsophisticated racism of the Ku Klux Klan. Hillbillys are easy targets because they are other to the sophisticated urban white or black viewers.[15] But the hillbillys in *Pulp Fiction*, while functioning in this way, also point towards the more complex issues of the construction of white culture as surface, discursive blankness, and blackness as a substantive bodily source of affective depth. The self-conscious citationality of the film's portrayal of Zed and his friends also reveals the American-Africanism which saturates *Pulp Fiction*. White culture as embodied by these cinematic figures is a surface space of random and meaningless intertextuality which constructs blackness as desirable bodily substance, depth and affect.

Se7en and the Contagion and Knowledge of Blackness

we wanted to do something immediate and simple. We started with Cops, the television show - how the camera is in the backseat peering over people's shoulder, like the runt following after the pack, a vulnerable position.[16]

David Fincher's comments, like those of Tarantino quoted at the beginning of this chapter, express the desire for a cinema of immediacy that would assault the viewer. Like *Pulp Fiction* the film invites the search for depth in the images it presents and at key moments turns this gaze back on the viewer. On one level, the film's structures of aggression are visible in the mutilated bodies of the victims of the serial killer, John Doe (Kevin Spacy). As Amy Taubin notes, 'There's an across the board revulsion for the body in this movie...'[17] From the grotesquely overweight corpse of Gluttony laid out on the slab in the morgue to the barely alive Sloth, tied to his bed, the viewer is invited to look at abject representations of the body, which repulse as much as they encourage voyeurism. This kind of shock to the viewer is also a key feature of the serial-killer genre to which *Se7en* belongs. In film's like *Silence of the Lambs* (Demme 1991) and *Henry, Portrait of a Serial Killer* (McNaughton 1986), the viewer is forced to confront the nature of their voyeurism by the horror of the images she or he strains to see. As Carol Clover notes of *Silence of the Lambs*, 'as much as any film I know, it is 'in our face', aiming knife-stabs, gunshots, Lecter's lunges and indeed Lecter's insinuating stares straight into the camera and straight at us'.[18]

But key aspects of *Se7en*, marking its difference from previous examples of the serial-killer genre include both its mimetic engagement with both the desire and anxiety which the white cultural imagination associated with images of 1990s' black culture, *and* its fabrication of African-American culture as a space where there is knowledge of the powerlessness of the individual protagonist within the postmodern urban, cinematic milieu. Although *Se7en's* mimesis of African-American culture is less directly overt than the *Pulp Fiction's* construction of blackness and rap as a source of affect, the film provokes immediate responses similar to those generated by 'hood film. One of the places where this affectivity is most marked is in *Se7en's* imitation of the aesthetic styles of the contemporary media images which were both a cause and symptom of the perception of African-American culture as immanently violent in the 1990s. In many of its scenes and formal techniques, the film has allowed itself to be 'infected' by images of blackness, which action-image films like *The Searchers* and *It's a Wonderful Life* fought so hard to repress. This mimetic contagion can be explored through an analysis of *Se7en's* innovative (for a Hollywood production) camerawork and film-processing, dialogue, the urban setting, and the character's relations to the milieu in which they are situated.

Amy Taubin suggests that the cinematography of *Se7en* is a key element in producing a kind of abject affect in the viewer. The viewer is both attracted and repulsed by what she can and cannot see in the frame and, according to Taubin, this in-between state is produced by the film's use of shallow focus:

The extremely shallow focus is a way of controlling the viewer's eye, making you look at what you don't want to see and suggesting that there's something worse that you just can't get a grip on lurking on the periphery.[19]

The idea that shallow-focus lends the image a kind of ambivalence is in marked contrast to the notions of cinematic realism proposed by Andre Bazin. One of Bazin's central arguments is that extended use of depth of focus 'tends to give back to the cinema a sense of the ambiguity of reality'. The viewer can focus on the background depth of an image, instead of being forced to watch what is foregrounded by the director. According to Bazin, depth in the image empowers the audience and 'brings the viewer into a relation with the image closer to that which he enjoys with reality'.[20] Bazin's ideas are based on the premise that, in reality, the viewer has time to survey the visual field they encounter, and select what they want to focus on. A film which uses deep-focus gives them the same kind of opportunity. What is interesting about Bazin's comments in relation to *Se7en* is that shallow-focus is associated with the comparatively new medium of video, and it is video footage which was associated with realism in the 1990s cultural imagination. Shallow focus produces the feeling that there is something lurking in the background or offscreen which could visually assault the viewer at any moment. This anticipation of being bombarded by images without warning is much more in tune with the idea that postmodern reality is marked by an excess of images and visual information which colonizes the postmodern subject.

It is the expectation of being visually assaulted by images that gives true-crime TV programmes, such as *Cops*, their immediacy. Much of the running time of the 'video camera on the fender' sequences is spent patrolling at night in a 'prowler', encountering suspects and victims, whose identity is often hidden by pixilated blackouts and whose voices are obscured by bad acoustics or editorially imposed bleeps for bad language. As I noted in Chapter One, nothing much happens in terms of narrative action, but there is always the fear that some violence will leap out of the shallow-focus frame, or from the obscured protagonists. As Fincher notes in the comments above, *Se7en* uses similar technique to provoke affective suspense. In addition to the shallow focus, the film stock of *Se7en* was processed through silver-retention which, as Taubin suggests, 'produces more luminosity in the light tones, and more density in the darks'.[21] This visual effect, again produces the effect of density in the image, from which violence could erupt at any given moment.

The temporal structure of the film increases the affect of impending violence. As I noted in chapter four, Deleuze argues that the specificity of contemporary cinema is dependent on the way the time-image has replaced the action-image as the chief source of cinematic affect. The viewer's position in relation to the time it takes for a film to unfold is an immanent, physical one, and *Se7en* accentuates this corporeal connection by presenting long periods of waiting for the next grotesque victim to turn up. Indeed the fact that this is a movie about time, rather than action, is emphasized by the swinging pendulum of the timepiece which stands by Somerset's (Morgan Freeman) bed, and the intertitles of the days which structure the narrative week of the film. Having said this, what is significant about the temporality of *Se7en* is that waiting around for things to happen is also a key element of programmes like *Cops*. Like the true-crime TV programme, not much happens in *Se7en* in the way of action - with the exception of one chase through John Doe's apartment, which ends in the narrative non-action of the killer *not* shooting Mills (Brad Pitt).

Se7en's imitation of a television genre to produce a cinematic affect also incorporates the particular racially organized field of the visual which is essential to the immediacy of programmes like *Cops*. As I suggested in chapter one, these programmes were able to generate affect by suggesting that the predominantly black suspects encountered by the police are always ready to erupt with violence. The black body is seen with an immediacy and paranoia by the white cultural imagination, and the mimesis of the 'True-Crime' programmes by *Se7en* plays on this to produce its own shocks. But as well as provoking an affective shock by playing on the white anxieties around black violence, the film also produces a more direct mimesis of New Black Realism. This imitation is very striking in the urban milieu the film presents. The city in *Se7en* is a faceless and nameless place, despite the fact that the majority of the film was actually shot in downtown Los Angeles.[22] The dark streets and brightly lit corridors of the film are (again) the epitome of the Deleuzian 'any-space-whatever'. But the characters who populate this city are not nomadic in the Deleuzian sense, in that they suffer the same sense of confinement and ties to their violent milieu as do the protagonists in the 'hood film. At the outset, Somerset is determined to leave the world of his career as a detective, and is unable to do so by the end of the film, as he realizes in the final scene that there is no escape from the violent world he inhabits - even in the sepia-lit countryside which stages the film's conclusion. Indeed, even in this setting, the industrial pylons which cover the open ground of the final scene seem to cage the protagonists as much as the dark streets and buildings of the city.

The confinement of the protagonists to their milieu is also suggested by the oppressive rain that constantly falls throughout the film. Rain-drenched urban streets are a staple aspect of *noir*, and like the 'hood film, *Se7en* seeks to reanimate the affective potential of the genre. But, unlike in *Blade Runner*, the rain in *Se7en* does not function as a 'simulation of the real'. In *Blade-Runner*, the rain, like everything else in the film, seems artificial, while at the same time evoking nostalgia for *noir* films like *The Big Sleep* (Hawks 1946), and the belief that audiences were able to take these films seriously. *Se7en* moves, by contrast, beyond such pastiche as the rain provokes a similar affect to the shallow-focus and processing of the film-stock in that it prevents the viewer from being able to see into the depth of the image, while evoking the feeling that there is something, potentially violent behind the sheets of water that drench the images of protagonists and city.

The sound of heavy rain that permeates the soundtrack is also partially responsible for the muffled sound of the film. From the outset, the film makes it difficult for the viewer to hear what the protagonists are saying to each other. This effect is again reminiscent of the 'True-Crime' TV programme. As I noted above, much of the dialogue in these programmes was obscured by the bad sound from the camcorder and editorial censorship. But the 'hard to hear' dialogue in *Se7en* also has the same affect of confusion as the contemporary African-American idiom of the 'hood film. As the viewer's desire to know the narrative moves of the film is heightened, voyeurism is also thwarted by the non-audible words of the protagonists. However, whereas the 'hood film combined this affect with a political signifyin' of white culture, any overt reference to racial politics, and the specificity of African-American culture, is missing in *Se7en*.

The film seeks to deny its mimesis of both the affect of black violence on the white cultural imagination and the 'hood film, by never referring directly to race, even though one of its main protagonists is black. The Mills family, and the rest of the characters in the film are colour-blind in their dealings with Somerset - despite the fact that the former have arrived from a predominantly white small-town America. On one level this colour-blindness is part of the film's and Hollywood's liberal attempt to be non-racist. After a long history where black actors were denied any screen presence at all in Hollywood action films, and where in more recent films like *Die Hard* and *Lethal Weapon* (Donner 1987), 'black characters act as supportive figures for the white hero', it is still unusual for a black actor to play the central role in a Hollywood thriller.[23] But *Se7en* does more than grant Somerset the leading role in the central 'buddy' relationship between himself and Mills. It also makes him a figure of knowledge, who knows the reality of what's going on, even if he is ultimately powerless to prevent Doe's violence. Like Caine in *Menace II Society*, he is aware of the nightmare violence of the city, but also like Caine, he ultimately realises there is no escape or action which can prevent the horror which unfolds before him. In this sense Somerset is in stark contrast to Mills, who is the epitome of the action-image hero who, like the protagonists of the action-image, believes he can make a concrete impact on the milieu in which he finds himself. But, by the end of the film, Mills finds that the only action he can take, in shooting Doe, only perpetuates the serial killer's plans.

As in *Reservoir Dogs* and *Pulp Fiction*, the construction of African-Americans as figures with a priveliged knowledge of the milieu helps define *Se7en's* American Africanism. The black characters in these three films are able to see through the simulations of the milieux they inhabit, and detect the violent reality which lies underneath. Here, Somerset is shown to be grounded in both reality and knowledge, while Mills is naïve in his readiness to act at every turn. What is interesting about Somerset though is that the knowledge that this movie grants the black character has its source in a humanistic tradition which has predominantly been perceived as white. His knowledge of Dante and other classics in the humanist canon is in stark contrast to Mills' simulated learning, gained from a set of 'Cliff Notes'. Again, as in Tarantino, blackness is associated with depth and knowledge, and whiteness with empty futile action, and simulated knowledge. The real in *Se7en* is shown to consist of a cultural knowledge which is aware that the concrete ties of action between milieu and knowledge can no longer exist, while the white action-image hero, embodied by Brad Pitt, desires a relation where his actions can still affect his milieu.

Strange Days and the Politics of White Rage

The association of blackness with a substantive authenticity, as opposed to a whiteness which is perceived in terms of empty simulation, is also visible in Kathryn Bigelow's *Strange Days*. This film brings together many of the ideas this book has discussed concerning the white cultural imagination's immediate reaction to blackness and the new-brutality film's equation of cinematic affect with this reaction. But more than many of the other films in this book, *Strange Days* is also self-reflexively aware of the affective charge which images of blackness have, and contemporary action cinema's dependence on this immediacy. This is implicit in the way the film recognises the crisis of the cinema of the action-image. *Strange Days* presents a cinematic world where milieux are constantly shifting and disintegrating. At the same time it also plays out the nostalgia for a cinema where the sensory-motor relations between protagonist and milieu are concrete and where the protagonist can both affect the reality they exist in and where that world can affect them. The film employs this nostalgia, but in a manner which is more akin to parody than the pastiche of the blockbuster. *Strange Days* is also guilty of the American Africanism identified in Tarantino's films and *Se7en* in that it fabricates African-American people and culture as a place where there is a knowledge of a reality underneath the surface simulation of white Symbolic structures. Having said this, *Strange Days*, like the 'hood films, is not afraid to present this black knowledge as a politicized black rage against the meaningless racial rage which lies under the surface of white cultural identity. The mimesis of black culture and the fear of black violence played out in Tarantino's films and *Se7en* is depoliticized to the extent that no direct mention is made of the racialised political violence of 1990s' America. This does not necessarily mean that these films do not engage with the questions of race and cinema, but it serves to point up the fact that, by contrast, *Strange Days* puts these issues at the forefront.

Perhaps more than any other white film discussed in this book, *Strange Days* displays a cinematic world where the structures of action and recognition between protagonist and milieu have broken down. The dystopian *mise en scène* of a disintegrating Los Angeles, where Santa Claus is mugged on the street and individuals can only travel in armoured cars is reminiscent of the chaotic city presented in *Blade Runner*, as well as the fragmented city that DFens encounters on his travels in *Falling Down*. The similarity with *Blade Runner* is also apparent in *Strange Days'* setting of the action in the not-too-distant future and its *noir*-like plot of an individual caught between the ambiguous forces of law and order and criminality. But in *Strange Days* the destabilizing of narrative as the central binding characteristic of action-cinema is emphasized to a degree where attempts to make sense of the film by following the narrative are almost futile. The convoluted plot of the film is directly reminiscent of *noir*. But whereas in a classic *film noir*, such as *The Big Sleep*, the viewer is still able to grasp the 'big picture' of the plot in terms of the distinction between the forces of evil (Eddie Mars) and good (Marlowe), and gain narrative satisfaction from the film's conclusion, the narrative of *Strange Days* is a 'ragged chaos in which the story itself seems to break up and split off into a multitude of endings'.[24]

In this sense the film is comparable to blockbusters (such as *Total Recall* and *The Terminator* series) in that narrative and the relations between protagonist and milieu are de-emphasized in favour of spectacular action set-pieces and large-scale sets. As we have seen, *Total Recall* in particular has a narrative which is almost impossible to follow or make sense of in any unified way. *Strange Days'* emphasis on the spectacular rather than unified narrative may be due partially to the influence of James Cameron, the film's scriptwriter and director of *The Terminator* series and *Aliens* (1986), as well as Bigelow's own sense of the grandiose visual presence of the contemporary action film, apparent in films like *Blue Steel* (1990) and *Point Break* (1991). Yet *Strange Days* demonstrates distinct differences from both the postmodern blockbuster and one of its archetypes, *Blade Runner*. Many of these differences stem from *Strange Days'* willingness to suggest that questions of 'race' and racial rage have been major causes for the crisis of the cinema of the action-image. As suggested above, *Blade Runner* and many blockbusters present the uncertainty of the relations between individual and milieu, and the real and artificial, as a kind of nostalgic mourning for an imaginary time when the cinema of the American Dream was believed in by audiences - to the extent that the ambiguities and cracks which appeared in *noir* were shocking because they displayed the beginning of the breakdown of that cinema. *Blade Runner* replays *noir* as a 'simulation of the real' but *Strange Days'* mimesis of *noir* intensifies the crisis of the action-image. Through its mimesis of 1990s' images of racial violence, the film stresses the white racial rage which simmers beneath the surface of classic *noir*, and which begins to seep through the cracks in the cinema of the crisis of the action-image.

Throughout the film there is the suggestion that the white milieu of the law is underpinned by racial rage. This is most apparent in the sequences where the rap singer, 2K, is brutally gunned down by the two cops. The massacre of 2K and his companions by the side of a freeway directly evokes the Rodney King beating. Much of the plot of the film rests on the suspicion that the entire milieu of the L.A.P.D. is corrupt and filled with racial rage. The film does finally back down from this position by blaming the racial violence committed against 2K on two individual rogue cops, and the final scene of the film shows the white-haired, fatherly, 'good' Chief of Police striding through a riot scene in order to rid society of these two corrupt individuals. But what is most noticeable about this scene is the sense of artificiality and the feeling that it has been tacked on. In comparison to the affective power of the violent beating of Mace (Angela Bassett) and the ensuing riot (which also directly evokes the LA Rebellion which followed the acquittal of Rodney King's beatings) the individualized conventional ending is self-reflexively false. This feeling of falsity evoked by the ending is partially because the film seduces us into desire for the violence of the riot - the savagery of Mace's beating makes the viewer want the predominantly black crowd to forcefully intervene. By encouraging this desire, the film reverses the white cultural imagination's fear and anxieties around black violence, and reveals the appetite for violence which, this book has argued, lies at the heart of white American national and cultural identity. At the same time, the falsity of the ending also highlights the way that Hollywood cinema has sought to repress this desire with narrative closures which emphasize the tendency of white Symbolic structures to repress violence through symbols of white authority (the John Wayne-like intervention of the police chief).

The synthetic tone of this last scene and the police chief's appeal for racial harmony after the riot, also evokes the hollow question asked by Rodney King in a statement to the press during 1991 LA Rebellion: 'Can we all get along?'[25] As Elaine Kim notes, these words have 'been depoliticized and transformed into a Disneyesque catchphrase for Pat Boone songs and roadside billboards in Los Angeles'.[26] Intentionally or not, the counterfeit nature of this last scene evokes attempts to smother and repress the racial tension and white rage which underlies white cultural identity and its cinema, while simultaneously suggesting the precarious nature of these attempts - something which is also exposed by the 'hood films' mimesis of *noir*.

The construction of whiteness as empty simulation with a desire for a physical affective violence, and blackness as a self-aware state which negotiates the immanent violence of American culture is most visible in the relationship between the two main protagonists, Lenny Nero (Ralph Fiennes) and Mace (Angela Bassett). Throughout the film, attention is drawn to the fact that Lenny is a pale imitation of the action-image protagonist, and has lost any ability to act decisively within the disintegrating milieu which surrounds him. Apart from mourning the loss of his ex-girlfriend, Faith, he has no connection to this milieu. The affective ties which connect the action-image protagonist have gone, leaving only an image-based nostalgia for those ties. Lenny is incapable of any action, except to plug into the SQUID machine's recorded memories of his relationship with Faith. He is the embodiment of the way the film constructs whiteness as a space of surface simulation where images are everything and any bodily substance is gone. As Mace describes him, Lenny is the 'Teflon man' who is untouched by the world around him, and gets off on the 'porno for wireheads' he pedals to his clients. In his empty simulation of a life, Lenny is in stark contrast to Mace who is the embodiment of the hipness that black culture signifies, and someone who knows the difference between 'playback' and real life and 'real-time'. As Lizzi Francke notes, Mace is 'part Angela Davis, part Cleopatra Jones...a woman of extraordinary mettle who keeps a concerned eye on him and a perspective on the disordered world around him'.[27] In an ironic twist, Mace is the embodiment of the attributes of the action-image protagonist with her ability to act decisively, and her strong connections to the strongly-defined milieu of her family life and love for Lenny.

The most significant aspect of this contrast between the embodiment of white culture as empty artificiality and blackness as an authentic space with a knowledge of what is substance and what is image, is the film's own self-reflexive exploration of both the visceral power of images, and the cinema viewer's desire for that visceral affect. More than any other film in this book, *Strange Days* is a film about the action-cinema's structures of aggression and the viscerality of the cinematic experience. *Strange Days* could be described as the nineties equivalent of *Peeping Tom* (Powell 1960) in the sense that it sets out to explore what Carol Clover calls the 'assaultive' and 'reactive' gazes of the viewer, and the implicit sadism and masochism which forms the cinematic experience. As Clover notes, '*Peeping Tom*...should be taken as a commentary...on the symbiotic interplay of the sadistic work of the filmmaker, and the masochistic stake of the spectator'.[28] From its opening shot of an eye which can be read as either producing an assaultive voyeuristic gaze, or waiting to be assaulted by the images it sees, to the final episode when Mark impales himself on his own camera, *Peeping Tom* is an open commentary on the 'most often psychic pain, but sometimes physical pain as well' which 'can be considered part of an aesthetic experience' in watching film.[29] *Strange Days* is equally engaged with the essentially masochistic desire, immanent to the cinematic experience, and the fact that viewer's willingly place themselves in a position where they are subject to a physical and psychic assault by the images which unfold before them. From the start, the film suggests that the consumption of images involves a high degree of physical involvement as, like *Peeping Tom,* we are presented with an image of an eye, before being subjected to a jolting, steadicam-dominated, first-person view of a restaurant robbery and chase. At the end of the sequence we are made shockingly aware of the strong mimetic ties between ourselves and the images, as the character whose eyes we see the event through, tumbles sickeningly to his death after failing to jump a gap between buildings. In effect, we 'die' like the character.

If this is not enough, the connections between the SQUID device, through which we see the opening sequence and the cinema are made clear by Lenny in his attempt to sell his 'clips' to a client. Lenny describes the machine as 'not like TV only better...but a piece of somebody's life...straight from the cerebral cortex'. This description is reminiscent of the Hitchockian fantasy of transmitting the affective power of images directly to the viewer's brain, discussed in the introduction, and the film makes clear throughout that viewers are willing to submit to this sadism on the part of the film and filmmaker.[30] In doing so, the film also suggests that the voyeuristic position which much psychoanalytic film theory has been engaged with is only a step towards the final masochistic position of the viewer.[31]

This suggestion is made concrete in the much-discussed rape scene of the film. The scene where Iris is raped and murdered provoked condemnation from critics like Todd McCarthy who wrote, 'ironically for a film directed by a woman, more than a few women will have problems with these scenes' implying that male viewers will be titillated voyeuristically rather than physically shocked by the brutality of the scene.[32] But the scene itself prevents any identification with the sadism of the serial killer by self-reflexively alluding to the assaultive and reactive viewing positions of the viewer. The twist in this scene is that the serial killer has rewired the SQUID machine so that the victim is placed in the position of rapist, and rapist in the position of victim. The victim can see and feel what is happening to her from the rapist's point of view and vice versa. The assaultive and reactive viewing positions are confused to the point where sadism becomes masochism and masochism sadism. The overall affect of this confusion is a distraction in the viewer which is as violently affective as Lenny's reaction in the Limo as he realises what is happening. The viewer is forced to confront both the sadistic, voyeuristic and masochistic nature of the cinematic experience.

Carol Clover has argued convincingly, through psychoanalysis, that the desire for masochism in the cinematic viewer suggests a blurring of gender in the horror film, where the predominantly young male audience desires to be incorporated within a position of femininity, not traditionally associated with film viewing. Clover's analysis of *Peeping Tom* could be applied to *Strange Days*, in the sense that the film works to reveal the masochistic desire at work in film viewing. But what is more pertinent in the context of this book is the way that the film suggests that the masochistic desire for physical shocks and affect is a feature of the contemporary white cultural imagination. This is most obvious on the level of representation where it is only white males who are seen as desiring the affective thrills that the SQUID has to offer. The corporate lawyer, looking to spice up his sex life without tarnishing his wedding ring, the amputee who is given the opportunity to run along a beach, and Lenny himself, all turn to the visceral thrills the machine has to offer, because the milieu they exist in can no longer offer these 'real' experiences. The film seems to suggest through this that the (male) white culture is an empty, dead state where affect is no longer possible. The film also implicates the viewer in this, suggesting further that the cinema viewer seeks to satisfy the masochistic desire for affective shock through the perception of black violence as a source of immediacy. As I noted above, some of the most affective moments of the film are the images of racial violence in the murder of 2K, the beating of Mace by the L.A.P.D, and the subsequent riot on the eve of the millennium. This affect is also partially caused by the way that both of these characters are composites drawn from the moments of black American culture, which have been constructed as hip and cool, with 2K as the politicized gangsta rapper, and Mace the Black Pantherite, blaxploitation heroine. As I also suggested, blackness is also signified in the film as having the authority and substance missing from white culture, which is embodied in the way that Mace is figured as a mimesis of the action-image protagonist.

Conclusion

The analysis of these three new-brutality films reveals a complex mimetic dynamic at work in their attempts to move beyond the nostalgia and spectacular-based pleasures of the blockbuster. The suggestion throughout the chapter and the book has been that these films are distinct from cinema of the action-image, the crisis of the action-image and the blockbuster, because of their mimetic engagement with the American-Africanism(s) of the white cultural imagination. Blackness is figured as a combination of cool, cultural authority and affective power, and in contrast to whiteness as an empty artificial state, floundering within the chaos of postmodern culture. All of these films use these images of blackness to reanimate the visceral affective power of the cinematic experience. In this sense these films do not stand as isolated examples, but constitute a wider movement in Hollywood to go beyond the ritualized familiarity and nostalgia of the blockbuster. Other examples that could have been explored to illustrate the mimetic dynamic between Hollywood action film and black culture include, Walter Hill's *Trespass* (1992), where the structure of the warehouse setting mimes the aesthetic and affective power of the 'hood, *The Matrix* (Wachowski 1999) where it is Laurence Fishburne (in a mimesis of his performance as Furious Styles in *Boyz N the Hood*) who is the character who can tell the difference between reality and simulacra, and *Bulworth* (Beatty 1999) where the mimesis of black culture is at its most direct in Warren Beatty's performance. This mimesis involves both aesthetic and political issues concerning the history of Hollywood film and the way that questions of race have governed the affective power of this cinema.

Notes
1. Tarantino in Smith, *Film Comment* (July/August 1994: 42).

2. Bukatman (1993: 246).

3. Jameson (1991: 10). See the whole chapter for the elaboration of this thesis.

4. Burch (1981: 124).

5. Willis (1997: 190-93).

6. Tarantino, *Sight and Sound* 4 (1994: 10).

7. Willis (1997: 193).

8. Tarantino, *Sight and Sound* 4 (1994: 10).

9. Deleuze (1986: 118).

10. Shaviro (1993: 17).

11. The development and implementation of cinematographic techniques such as deep-focus photography, and depth of field, would seem to support the notion of a desire for depth in the cinematic apparatus. See Bukatman (1993: 130-37) for an in-depth analysis of the photoscan scene in *Blade Runner*.

12. *ibid.* (261).

13. Winokur, *The Velvet Light Trap* 35 (1995: 26).

14. Clover (1992: 191-202).

15. *ibid.* (135). Clover writes:

> *If 'redneck' once denoted a real and particular group, it has achieved the status of a kind of universal blame figure, the 'someone else' held responsible for all manner of American social ills. The great success of the redneck in that capacity suggests that anxieties no longer expressible in ethnic or racial terms have become projected onto a safe target - safe not only because it is (nominally) white, but because it is infinitely displaceable onto someone from the deeper South or the higher mountains or the further desert.*

16. Fincher in Taubin, *Sight and Sound* 5 (1995: 24).

17. *ibid.*

18. Clover (1992: 233).

19. Taubin, *Sight and Sound* 5 (1995: 24).

20. Bazin (1967: 37 & 35).

21. Taubin, *Sight and Sound* 5 (1995: 24).

22. Fincher in Taubin, *Sight and Sound* 5 (1995: 24).

23. Tasker (1993: 4 & Chapter 2). See also Bogle (1992) for a comprehensive survey of the representations of African Americans in Hollywood film.

24. Francke, *Sight and Sound* 5 (1995: 9). This distinction in narrative clarity between the two films can be made, despite the fact that there are a number of loose ends at the conclusion of *The Big Sleep*. The most famous of these involves the identity of the murderer of the chauffeur which starts Marlowe on his quest. The confusion surrounding this plot detail, amongst the filmmakers and authors is noted by Fredric Jameson in his retelling of the famous story of the argument between Bogart and Hawks: '...very late, after much drinking, during the filming of The Big Sleep the two men argue about the status of the dead body in the Buick in the ocean off the Lido pier: murder, suicide or some third thing? They finally phone Chandler himself, still awake and drinking at that hour; he admits he can't remember either' (Jameson in Copjec ed. 1993: 33).

25. King, *Los Angeles Times* (2 May 1992: 3).

26. Kim in Gooding-Williams ed. (1993: 228).

27. Francke, *Sight and Sound* 5 (1995: 9).

28. Clover (1992: 179).

29. Burch (1981: 124).

30. Spoto (1984: 440).

31. Slavoj Zizek also suggests that the sadism which psychoanalysis has argued accompanies voyeurism is just a stage on the path to a position of masochism in Zizek ed. (1992: 220-22).

32. The name Iris has obvious connotations with the visual, but also evokes the Jody Foster character in *Taxi Driver*.

Conclusion

As a writer reading I came to realise the obvious: the subject of a dream is the dreamer. The fabrication of an Africanist persona is reflexive; an extraordinary meditation on the self; a powerful exploration of the fears and desires that reside in the writerly unconscious. It is an astonishing revelation of longing, of terror, of perplexity, of shame, of magnanimity. It requires hard work not to see this....What became transparent were the self-evident ways that Americans choose to talk about themselves through and within a sometimes allegorical, sometimes metaphorical, but always choked representation of an Africanist presence.[1]

Toni Morrison's initial difficulty in identifying the dependency of the white literary imagination on an Africanist presence, and her ultimate realisation that American-Africanism was 'everywhere' in the development of American literature and white cultural identity has many parallels with the processes involved in understanding the affective power of the new-brutality film. These films are dependent on their mimetic relations with African-American culture, the immediate shock that images of black bodies provoke, and fabrications of blackness as a site of cultural authority and authenticity. Yet, it is precisely because the new-brutality film connects the white cultural imagination's dependence on African-American culture and American Africanism to the reanimation of an affective contemporary action-cinema that issues of 'race' and white identity are not always immediately obvious.

With the exception of *Strange Days*, the 'white' films discussed in this book are incapable of narrativising the centrality of American Africanism and contemporary African-American culture and film to their own aesthetics. In other words, race is not an organising central aspect of the narratives of these films, and therefore it is not something which is easily identified as part of the film's meaning. Race is central to these films because of the way that blackness is used to provide images of bodily affect which are experienced as outside of meaning. This lack of direct discourse about race in this cinema of the 1990s is mainly due to the fact that the old narrative structures of Hollywood film had undergone a crisis. The cinema of the action-image, where narratives are constituted by the relations of action between protagonist and milieu, is now hard for viewers to take seriously and believe in.

In Chapter One, I explored the reasons for, and consequences of, this crisis, citing after Deleuze, the crisis of the American Dream and the 'rising consciousness of minorities' as two of the major causes of the loss of belief in action-image cinema. The 'individuated' narratives of the action-image depend on belief in the American Dream's narrative of an undivided community full of individuals who can achieve wealth and happiness through a paradoxical combination of individual action and responsibility towards the milieu they inhabit. The cinema of the action-image requires belief in the possibility of a situation where the individual actions of protagonists can affect the milieu and where that milieu can affect the protagonist. This belief is no longer possible because the growing influence of African-American culture and film points towards a divided American identity which can no longer be repressed by the marginalising and oppressive elements of the American Dream.

According to Deleuze, the crisis of the action-image led to the emergence of a cinema where narratives became dispersed, a situation illustrated in Martin Scorsese's cinema where the emphasis is on moments of 'dramatic intensity' and the breakdown of relations between protagonist and milieux. This crisis is both denied and accentuated by the postmodern blockbuster. Films like *Die Hard* and *The Terminator* demonstrate nostalgia for an imagined time when viewers believed in, and were affected by, the narratives of action between individual and milieu of the action-image cinema in their superhuman heroes and overblown situations. Yet, the exaggerated nature of the situations and the protagonists in the postmodern blockbuster play their own part in revealing the crisis. In addition, the spectacular nature of these films, their dependence on the visceral thrills of the special effect, and the self-reflexive artificiality of stars like Schwarzenegger and Stallone tend to de-emphasise the importance of narrative. The narratives of the blockbuster are repetitive and ritualised to the point where they are secondary to the viewing experience. The decentralising of narrative and the loss of affect of the narratives of the action-image meant that the new-brutality film had to find different means to express the dependency of the white cultural imagination on African-American culture and American Africanism, if it was to also reanimate the affective power of the action cinema.

In the opening chapter I explored the 'cynical' way *Falling Down* negotiates both the crisis of the action-image and the impact of 1990s' African-American film on the white cultural imagination. The film attempts to overcome the loss of belief in the narratives and aesthetic structures of the cinema of the action-image by imposing a viewing position of cynical realism. The film persuades the viewer to believe they have seen the truth of urban reality and the fragmentation of milieux through a series of shifts in identification and focalization. The first of these is an immediate identification with the frustrations and actions of DFens, as he is confronted by the banal, everyday nuisances of urban living. This spontaneous identification quickly becomes one of nostalgia where the viewer is encouraged to mourn the loss of a social situation and cinema where individuals were imagined to be capable of exerting control over their milieu. Through DFens' quest, the film mimes the discourses of the jeremiad and populism found in *film noir*. *Falling Down* shows what happens when the American Dream has failed by presenting the struggles of an individual attempting to regain his rightful position as founder and protector of what makes America 'great'. Nostalgia for the imagined time when *noir* could be taken seriously is a key aspect of *Falling Down's* ability to make audiences cheer DFens' actions.

This nostalgia for a time, when the individual was also recognised as key to America's success, is quickly pathologised by the film as DFens' actions become more psychotic and violent. As the film develops the action is viewed more and more through the eyes of Prendergast, and DFens' actions, and inability to understand why he can no longer control the milieux he moves through, are ultimately constructed as childlike and naïve. Prendergast knows the American Dream has broken down but carries out his duties as a policeman as if he is still on the side of 'right'. He knows the 'truth' as it is defined by DFens but refuses to condone any actions which challenge the continuing illusions of the American Dream. His is a position of 'cynical reason' in the sense that he is 'well aware of a particular interest hidden behind an ideological universality, but still...does not renounce it'.[2] The film turns this cynical reason into a cinematic cynical realism because it attempts to impose on the viewer the cultural knowledge to see 'the way things really are, not the way they should be' - or at least the way the film sees things as they really are.[3] *Falling Down* achieves this cynical realism through its inability to grasp the complex affects of contemporary black film. The film attempts to narrativize the affective power of black rage, by equating it with the psychotic and childlike naivety of DFens. DFens is not so much a mimesis of the protagonists of the 'hood film as an appropriation, contextualised in a discourse of a contingent but authoritative white cultural identity. In this sense the film demonstrates its own lack of sophistication. *Falling Down* was aware that it was in competition with the 'hood film, but did not understand the complexities of the action cinema's dependence on African-American culture and the American Africanisms it constructs.

The 'hood or gangsta film reanimated Hollywood action cinema and deepened the crisis of 'white' films, by provoking the kinds of affective power missing from action-image cinema and the postmodern blockbuster. The release of *Boyz N the Hood* initially sparked paranoia concerning the imagined naivety of black audiences, and fears that they would confuse the images of black violence in the film's trailer with extracinematic life. I noted that this paranoia was produced by the white cultural imagination's own tendency to see images of blackness as immediate and containing an immanent violence which threatened to spill out from the screen. Anxiety around black masculinity is experienced as immediate, but produced by a 'racial disposition of the visible'.[4] This is the response that *Falling Down* seeks to both imitate and distance itself from. A more complex affect of the 'hood film is the way it recasts the old Hollywood genres and more recent forms of image-making to reveal the white racial rage which lies at the heart of the white American cultural identity. *Boyz N the Hood* and *Menace II Society* both reveal how the white US cultural imagination has been unable to symbolize white

US cultural identity's dependence on images of blackness. *Menace II Society*, in particular, accentuates US white cultural identity's inability to articulate its dependency on constructions of black culture by preventing the white viewer from assuming a comfortable voyeuristic insight into the 'hood. For instance rap and black idiom is used in these films to frustrate white viewers at the point when they are most titillated. In this context black culture becomes an alternative Symbolic system of signification rather than an unsymbolisable Real.

The 'real' unspoken revealed by these films is the racial rage which drives white cultural and cinematic production. The gangsta's mimesis of the gangster and *film noir* evokes the way that this racial rage took the form of the marginalisation of African-American bodies and culture in the cinema of the action-image. *Menace's* imitation of the cinema of Scorsese also exposes the way that the repression of racial rage begins to produce cracks in late action-image films, (such as *It's a Wonderful Life* and *The Searchers*) until the structures of action between protagonist and milieu are finally ruptured in crisis films like *Mean Streets* and *Taxi-Driver*. Finally, in its mimesis of 1990s' genres and mediums labelled as 'realist' (such as the 'True-Crime' show and video), *Menace* also lays bare the way that this rage has been transformed into an American Africanism which constructs the black body as immanently violent, but also as a sign of the real and authenticity. *Menace* is a film which suggests a Hollywood cinema which depends on racial rage and the mimetic relations between white and black popular culture and cinema.

The 'hood films also emphasise the way that black cinema and its politicized black rage can produce affective responses in white audiences. Black rage is implicitly connected to the physical aspects of the cinematic experience itself, and this is particularly marked in the mimetic connections between the confined space of the 'hood and the constraints temporarily imposed and desired by the film viewer, tied to her or his chair in a darkened theatre for the duration of the film. The fact that the relationship of action and confinement between the 'hood and its protagonists mimics the spatial coordinates of action-image's sensory-motor relations between protagonist and milieu stresses the impotency of contemporary white cinema to produce the same affect. The narratives of white cinema (the gangsta film seems to suggest) lack the ability to articulate the ways in which the mimetic relations between 'races' is fundamental to the Hollywood action-cinema's sense of its own self.

The crisis of the old narratives is one of the reasons why the new-brutality film of the 1990s has difficulty in articulating the centrality of its reliance on Africanist images and contemporary black culture and film. This dependence manifests itself in the mimetic and affective images of these films. As we have seen, Tarantino is aware of the familiar and repetitive nature of the action-cinema's narratives and his films turn to the affective power which images of blackness possess to produce shock in his films. The torture scene in *Reservoir Dogs* is shocking, not because the film directly narrativizes its dependence on contemporary African-American culture and the immediacy and anxiety which black violence and black bodies provoke. I suggested that the shock comes because the scene imitates the white fears aroused by black violence in relation to the forces of law and order (as illustrated at a later date by the Rodney King episode and trial), and embodies the same traits of anarchic, savage and 'meaningless' violence in a white figure, intertextually linked to the iconic figure of the white gangster. The scene evokes the involuntary realisation of the white viewer that her or his very identity is inextricably entwined with images of blackness which are either fabricated as immediate in white American Africanism, and/or those produced by contemporary black film and culture.

Reservoir Dogs and the other new-brutality films connect these affective images to the cinema's immanent 'structures of aggression' and the viewer's masochistic desire to be viscerally assaulted by the cinema screen. *Reservoir Dogs*, *Pulp Fiction*, *Se7en* and *Strange Days* all mime the affective power of images of blackness to reanimate the potential of the cinema to produce body-first shocks. But this mimesis is not cynical in the way that *Falling Down's* appropriation of the 'angry' political narratives of the 'hood film is. *Falling Down* wants to have it both ways in the sense that it wants to capture the immediacy and affective impact of the 'hood film, but position this shock within the terms of a discourse which reaffirms the certainties and distinctness of white cultural identity - despite introducing a degree of contingency within that authority.

There is a different kind of American Africanism at work in *Reservoir Dogs*, *Pulp Fiction* and *Se7en* in the sense that they fabricate African American culture as space of cultural authority and the real, amidst the simulation and violent chaotic flux of cultural identity and cultural productions characterized as the postmodern in the 1990s. The uncertainties of cultural identity and feelings of powerlessness caused by the proliferation of images and media within postmodernity are coded as white in these film. Blackness, on the other hand, is a space where it is possible to know the difference between the real and the simulation, and where it is possible to produce an affect which is linked with the notion of the body and the image which has depth.

In the discussion of *Pulp Fiction* and *Se7en*, we saw how these questions were connected to the symbiotic interplay between the voyeuristic and masochistic impulses of the viewer. Even at its most archetypal postmodern moment, the cinema has suggested that there is a depth to the image, beyond its surface obviousness. This was literalised in *Blade Runner* in the 'impossible' images of the photoscan sequence. The new-brutality film connects this question of the desire to see depth in the image with the masochistic desire to be assaulted by what is found lurking there. Moreover it makes this issue of bodily affect a racial one with its construction of blackness and the black body as both a barrier to the voyeuristic curiosity of the assaultive gaze, and the site where that gaze is turned back on the viewer. *Reservoir Dogs*, *Pulp Fiction* and *Se7en* all use images of blackness, or what the white cultural imagination fabricates as the immanent violence of blackness, to affect the viewer. This Africanism is constructed within the context of the action-image cinema's inability to directly narrativize its dependence on black culture in its making and self-definition.

The most affective moments of *Strange Days* are also reliant on an American Africanist presence and the affective power of blackness. But the film is also a self-reflexive meditation on the mimetic relations between African and white American cinema and culture. Moreover it makes the question of white desire for both affect and authenticity central to its narrative and representations. In this sense the film marks a turning point in the new-brutality film. The dependence of American cinema and the white cultural imagination on black culture, in making and defining its own self is made narratively central in this film. In this sense the mimetic relations are understood as a discourse rather than evoked through the shock of the affective and mimetic image.

This narrativization of white cinema's necessary engagement with African-American culture and images of blackness is apparent in films which have been released since the new-brutality moment. One of the reasons why this book has not discussed *Jackie Brown* as a new-brutality film is that the pleasures of this film depended as much on cultural discourses and knowledge of the importance and hipness of black culture as they do on the affective impact that images of blackness have on the white cultural imagination. For this reason *Jackie Brown's* American Africanism is a lot more blatant and easy to grasp as a key constitutent of the film's meaning. There *are* moments in the film when shock is caused because of the mimesis of the immanent violence the white cultural imagination associates with blackness. The scene where Ordell (Samuel L. Jackson) shoots a suspected stool pigeon is again reminiscent of the Rodney King episode, in both the camera's long take, and the way it moves up to assume a position of distance from the event. But the film explicitly depends on a cultural knowledge of blaxploitation, and Tarantino's own fetishisation of black popular culture. The white cultural imagination's reliance on constructions of black culture for affect is openly articulated in the iconic figure of Pam Grier, from the moment she is filmed moving along the escalator in the title sequence (reminiscent of *The Graduate* (Nichols 1967)) to the sequence where she is filmed driving to the accompaniment of Randy Crawford's 'Streetlife'.

American cinema and culture's reliance on hip-hop culture is even more explicitly narrativized in *Bulworth*. The film's narrative places the mimesis of the affective power of black culture right at the heart of the USA's political structures. The initial shock of the film is provoked by a 60 year old American presidential candidate speaking and moving like a 'boy from the 'hood'. And this shock is transformed into discourse by the film's liberal political engagement with the way that blackness is an essential constituent of what it is to be American. The most striking aspect of this film is that the mimesis of blackness is overt in the narrative, and in contrast to the latent imitations in the affective images of the earlier new-brutality film. This open narrativization of the dependency of American cinema on African-American film and culture in *Bulworth* meant that the moment of the new-brutality film passed very quickly. The fact that this film articulates the centrality of constructions of blackness as fundamental to the way that American identity and culture is constituted and organised could signal the white American cultural imagination's readiness to admit the importance of black cultural film and production.

Toni Morrison's project was to detect the signs and contradictions in American literature which revealed the way the importance of black culture was hidden and submerged within the text. She was also concerned with the way that the white literary imagination constructed black culture in imaginary terms as a violent, real and sublime space within the context of its apparent repression and omission. The emergence of the 'hood film and the widescale commerical success of rap in general meant that the importance of black culture can no longer be invisible in white cultural productions and a film like *Bulworth* might suggest that predominantly white cultural institutions like the Hollywood studios are prepared to make African-American film production a central part of their output. The fact that Miramax, Tarantino's once independent production company, has been bought by Disney, and is producing films like *Pulp Fiction* and *Jackie Brown*, that could be described as black, might also point towards this admittance.[5] In this context the new-brutality could be construed as an important phase in white culture's realisation that 'Africanism is inextricable from the definition of Americanness - from its origins on through its integrated or disintegrating twentieth-century self'.[6]

But the reality is that this realisation has not materialised in a marked increase in mainstream black cinematic production. Indeed, African-American Hollywood film production has been sparse since the initial wave of 'hood films - with some notable exceptions such as *Dead Presidents* (Hughes 1996), *Panther* (Van Peebles 1995), *Higher Learning* (Singleton), and Spike Lee's output[7] In this context, Spike Lee's comments around cultural property, and the opportunistic appropriation of black culture by white film, retain a compelling validity in the sense that the importance of African-American culture in the constitution of white American cultural identity can only be fully realised through the strong visible presence of an African-American cinema. This book has argued that it was the black-produced images of the 'hood film which provided the source of the new-brutality films aesthetic drive, and other 'mainstream' black images may produce another aesthetic shift in Holllywood.

In spite of this, the new-brutality film and its affective images may still prove to be a significant staging post in the continuous reshaping of American national and cultural identity. It is because these films and their mimetic images operate at the level of affect that the meaning of what it was to be an American at the end of the twentieth century was destabilised. The fact that this cinema does not directly politicise, or put into discourse, the dependence of Hollywood cinema and white culture on fabrications of blackness and the mimesis of African-American culture means that definitions of white cultural identity and white cinema remain uncertain. The ramifications of the cinematic and cultural shock caused by the affective mimetic image are on-going and it remains to be seen what the final significance of the new-brutality film will be in terms of the production of future cinema and the constitution of American cultural identity. But this book argues that reading the images of 1990s' American cinema in terms of mimesis, affect and 'race' is crucial in determining the future shape of American cultural and cinematic identity.

Afterword - The Aesthetic Globalisation of American Cinema

This book has argued implicitly that American Hollywood cinema can be read as a history of that institution's intentions and capacity to reanimate its affective power. The new-brutality film represented a certain shift in Hollywood's attempts to produce a cinema of affect. The new-brutality film eschewed individuated narratives and mimed the affective power of black culture in the white cultural imagination, while suggesting that the immanent violence of the US lies within white American cultural identity. This is perhaps played out in its' most literal form in David Fincher's 1999 film, *Fight Club*. The aesthetics of masculine masochism which permeate the film and its critique of the simulations of US consumer culture, suggest that the only authenticity to be found is in physical pain and guilt. Such introspection is more difficult in the 'post 9/11' moment and the resulting attempt by the American government to redefine the nation's role as policeman of the world.

Paradoxically, while its government is seeking to pursue the fantasy of controlling the world and its cultures, Hollywood cinema has never been more infected by images from other national and global cinemas. The re-emergence of the musical in Hollywood is one genre affected by this. A film like *Moulin Rouge* (Luhrmann 2001) owes as much to the visual and bodily spectacles of Bombay or Bollywood cinema as it does to the stop-start narratives and glaring technicolour of a Minnelli musical of the 1950s. The globalisation of aesthetics in Hollywood film is particularly interesting in relation to post new-brutality films. The *Matrix* trilogy and Tarantino's *Kill Bill Vol. 1* (2003) qualify for this category in that they share the desire to reanimate the affective power of American cinema in ways which are connected to questions of American cinematic identity, and yet do not depend on the individuated narratives of the action-image. The main argument of this book is that the new-brutality film sought to produce affect through its mimesis of images of blackness that the white cultural imagination experienced as immediate in the cinema. Moreover these attempts rested on the assumption that black culture and people have access to a reality and authenticity missing from white postmodern culture. The *Matrix* series and *Kill Bill Vol. 1* share many of these attributes, and at the same time tend to mime the aesthetic styles of Hong Kong cinema in their action scenes.

The Matrix in particular associates black bodies and culture with the real. The film creates urban corporate America as a computer programme or matrix populated by images and surfaces which can change at the click of a button, whereas the real world is a post-holocaust, dirty industrial milieu where the worst excesses and disruptions of modernity and postmodernity have resulted in the near-extinction of the human race. In some ways the cinematic world of *The Matrix* is the ultimate milieu of the cinema of the crisis of the action-image. The city in the first film goes beyond Deleuze's 'any-space-whatever' in that it does not exist as a geographically known place. Yet, within this space Morpheus (played by Laurence Fishburne, reprising his role as Furious Styles in *Boyz N the 'Hood*) is the Good Father who knows the truth and real substance of the world as opposed to the blank space which is Keanu Reeves in his role as Neo/Andersen.[8] The interesting aspect of this is that Morpheus leads Neo to this truth through the body and the highly visual martial arts medium. The combination of the non-narrative spectacularity of this kind of choreographed action and the black body as a site of affect seems to me to be symtomatic of the post new-brutality films' concerns with a drive towards a new kind of affective, non-national Hollywood cinema.

The miming of the aesthetics of Hong-Kong action Film suggests that the images in films like *The Matrix* are not subordinate to the individuated narratives which dominated the Hollywood action-image. David Bordwell argues that Hollywood-style scenes of violence typically consist of rapid editing which tends to cut away from the scenes of violence and pain to keep the narrative moving. By contrast Hong Kong action cinema (most notably the films of John Woo) tend to have what Bordewell, calls a 'pause-burst-pause' rhythm that dwells on images of violence which do not necessarily emphasise the narrative progress and actions of main protagonists.[9] Hong Kong Cinema in general (at least since the 1970s) tends to emphasise the affective power of the cinematic image itself rather than individuated narratives which dominated the action-image. Ackbar Abbas makes this point especially in relation to the 'New-Wave of Hong Cinema' and its concerns with Hong Kong cultural identity in the wake and aftermath of the 1997 handover to China. For Abbas, the cinema in Hong Kong is hugely important in its imaging of its own cultural identity. The visualisation of Hong Kong, in films like *Rouge* (Stanley Kwan 1998) *The Blade* (Tsui Hark 1995), *Once Upon a Time in China* (Tsui Hark 1990), *Chungking Express* (Wong Kar-Wei 1994) and *In the Mood for Love* (Wong Kar-Wei 2000), could never be in terms of narratives which were individuated on the one hand but which made the local act as the global on the other as in the structures of Hollywood action-image. Hong Kong always had to see itself as a locality within a global stage both because of its colonial past and the handover to China, and also in terms of its position as a center of finance within global capital and information flows. The Hong Kong experience and identity is one of transience and fragmentation because amongst other things much of the population consists of refugees and expatriates. Abbas remarks that Hong Kong cinema 'investigates the dislocations of the global where the local is something unstable that mutates right in front of our eyes...It is by being local in this way that the new Hong Cinema is most international'[10] Consequently this is a cinema which is not set on being both a national and global cinema (in the way that Classical Hollywood was), and it is also a cinema that focuses on the detail of the image and uses this to produce affects which ultimately provoke a sense of the encounter and disappearance of all that is stable.

The new-brutality film was one of the symptoms of the instability of US cultural and national identity in the 1990s and is the inheritor of the cinema of the crisis of the action-image. The Hollywood action-image of the American Dream is no longer possible as an affective cinema because of reasons this book has charted. Yet, Hollywood cinema's drive to reanimate its affective power in the twenty-first century has moved on from the mimesis of an internal 'other' in the form of African-American to an imitation of other cinemas which have never been able to be 'national' and 'global' in the Hollwood sense of a totalising narrative. There seems to be a drive in contemporary action film to find an affective American cinema not defined in terms of narrative and not defined in terms of a unified well-defined place or national identity which is quintessentially American.

Kill Bill Vol. 1 perhaps exemplifies this most clearly. The central protagonist of film, The Bride (Uma Thurman) is not individuated in the sense of psychological depth or realism. The character works more as an emblematic figure of revenge in a similar fashion to many female characters in 1970s' martial arts and samurai movies, rather than a figure of psychoanalytical identification for the viewer. The Bride's body is constantly in 'the act of becoming' rather than a stable entity through which the viewer can comfortably assume a voyeuristic position. The emphasis in *Kill Bill Vol. 1* (as with such films as The Shaw Brothers 1970s' *Kungfu* films, *Lady Snowblood* (Fujita 1973) and *The Lone Wolf and Cub* series) is on the spectacular set-pieces of highly stylised action and violence. Yet it is not the representation of violence in the scenes of bloodletting that provokes affect, but rather the self-conscious manipulation of images that are produced through the mimesis of cinematic styles and a soundtrack which are 'un-American' in their composition and history. *Kill Bill Vol. 1* is a film that, like the new-brutality film, is concerned with the dynamics of sadism and masochism in the viewing experience. This self-reflexivity is clear from the outset where the titular character Bill speaks the lines 'Do you find me sadistic?...No kiddo, this moment, this is me at my most masochistic' as, offscreen, he prepares to shoot the beaten and bloodied face of Uma Thurman. The slow-motion close-up of the bullet heading towards the screen and viewer works as a rather clumsy attempt to signify that the ability of film to provoke affect through shock is under the spotlight in this film. Such images are prevalent throughout *Kill Bill Vol. 1* right up to the climactic chapter, 'Showdown at the House of Blue Leaves', where The Bride dispatches 88 gang members as well as the first name on her vendetta, O-Ren-Ishi.

The fact that many of these attempts to reanimate the affective power of the cinematic image in *Kill Bill Vol. 1* take their cue from cinemas which do not have a straightforward relationship to the question of national cultural identity (including Hong Kong Martial Arts cinema, Japanese Samurai films, John Woo, the Spaghetti Western and, less obviously, Wong Kar-Wei), raises again the question of what a Hollywood cinema's relationship is with American cultural identity in the early twenty-first century. The issues arising from this question are the subject for another book but I suggest that even a cursory analysis of the post new-brutality film indicates a story of cultural globalisation that is a good deal more complex than narratives of cultural appropriation and the immanent authority of US cultural identity and production. The language of mimesis with its emphasis on the undermining properties of contamination, infection and tactility seems a more productive route through which to explore the affective and political power of Hollywood in its contemporary moment.

Notes

1. Morrison (1993: 16-17).

2. Zizek (1989: 29).

3. Joel Schumacher, director of *Falling Down* in Fuller, *Interview* 23 (1993: 112).

4. Butler in Gooding-Williams, Robert ed. (1993: 18).

5. Wyatt in Neale, S. & Smith, M. eds. (1998: 74-91).

6. Morrison (1993: 65).

7. Lott in Neale, S. & Smith, M. eds. (1998: 211-29).

8. Keanu Reeves is almost the embodiment of what is surface and non-substantial about white American culture, particularly when one recalls his early role in *Bill and Ted's Excellent Adventure* (Stephen Herek 1988).

9. Bordwell in Yau ed. (2001: 73-95).

10. Abbas (1997: 190).

Bibliography

Abbas, A., *Hong Kong: Culture and the Politics of Disappearance,* Minnesota: University of Minnesota Press (1997).

Aumont, M., Bergala, A., Marie, M., & Vernet, M., *Aesthetics of Film,* trans and revised Richard Neupert, Austin: University of Texas Press (1992).

Baker, Houston A., *Black Studies, Rap and the Academy,* Chicago IL: University of Chicago Press (1993).

Baudrillard, J., *Simulations,* New York: Semiotext(e) (1983).

Bauer, E., 'The Mouth and the Method: Interview with Quentin Tarantino' *Sight and Sound* 8:3 (1998: 8-9).

Bazin, A., *What is Cinema? Volume 1,* trans. Hugh Gray, Berkeley CA: University of California Press (1967).

Beasley-Murray, J., 'Whatever Happened to the Neorealism? Bazin, Deleuze, and Tarkovsky's Long Take' *Iris* 23 (1997: 37-53).

Bellos, A., 'Movie Director Taps a Reservoir of Suits and Guns Cultists' *The Guardian* (17 September 1993: 3).

Benjamin, W., 'The Work Of Art in the Age of Mechanical Reproduction' in Mast, G. Cohen, M. & Braudy L. *Film Theory and Criticism* 4th ed., Oxford: Oxford University Press (1992: 665-82).

Benjamin, W., *Illuminations,* trans. Harry Zohn, Hannah Arendt ed., London: Cape (1970).

Benjamin, W., *One Way Street and Other Writings,* trans. Edward Jephcott & Kingsley Shorter, London: Verso (1985).

Bennett, T., Boyd-Bowman, S., Mercer, C. and Woollacott, J. eds., *Popular Television and Film,* London: BFI Press (1981).

Bhabha, H., *The Location of Culture,* London: Routledge (1994).

Biskind, P., 'An Auteur is Born' *Premiere* (US) (November 1994: 94-102).

Bogle, D., *Toms, Coons, Mulattoes, Mammies and Bucks,* New York: Continuum (1992).

Bogle, Donald & Goldstein, Bruce 'Blaxploitation' *National Film Theatre Programme Guide* (August 1996: 5-9).

Bordwell, D., Staiger, J. & Thompson, K., *The Classical Hollywood Cinema: Film Style and Mode of Production to 1960,* New York: Columbia University Press (1985).

Bordwell, D., 'Aesthetics in Action: *Kungfu,* Gunplay and Cinematic Expressivity' in Yau, Esther ed. *At Full Speed: Hong Kong Cinema in a Borderless World,* Minnesota: University of Minnesota Press (2000: 73-95).

Botting, Fred & Wilson, Scott 'The Tarantinian Ethics' *Theory, Culture and Society* 15:2 (1998: 90-112).

Boundas, Constantin V. ed., *The Deleuze Reader,* New York: Columbia University Press (1993).

Boyd, T., 'Put Some Brothers on the Wall: Rap, Rock and the Visual Empowerment of African American Culture' in Carson, Diane and Friedman, Lester eds. *Multicultural Media in the Classroom,* Chicago: University of Illinois Press (publication forthcoming at time of writing).

Brennan, T., 'Off the Gangsta Tip: A Rap Appreciation or Forgetting about Los Angeles' *Critical Inquiry* 20:4 (1994: 663-693).

Brennan, T., 'Rap Redoubt: The Beauty of the Mix' *Critical Inquiry* 22:1 (1995: 159-61).

Brunette, P., 'Singleton's Street Noises' *Sight and Sound* 1:4 (1991: 4).

Bukatman, S., *Terminal Identity: The Virtual Subject in Post-Modern Science Fiction,* Durham NC: Duke University Press (1993).

Burch, N., *Theory of Film Practice,* Princeton NJ: Princeton University Press (1981).

Butler, J., 'Endangered/Endangering: Schematic Racism and White Paranoia' in Gooding-Williams, Robert ed. *Reading Rodney King, Reading Urban Uprising,* London: Routledge (1993: 15-23).

Butler, J., *Bodies That Matter: On The Discursive Limits of 'Sex',* London: Routledge (1994).

Carson, Diane and Friedman, Lester eds., *Multicultural Media in the Classroom,* Chicago: University of Illinois Press (Forthcoming at time of writing).

Carter, M., 'Spike Lee, Quentin Tarantino - 'Now it's Your Turn, Baby'' *The Independent* (3 December 1998: 32).

Charney, L., 'The Violence of a Perfect Moment in Slocum', J. David ed., *Violence and American Cinema,* New York: Routledge (2001).

Chion, M., *Audio-Vision,* New York: Routledge (1994).

Clover C., *Men Women and Chainsaws,* London: BFI Press (1992).

Clover, C., 'White Noise' *Sight and Sound* 3:8 (1993: 6-9).

Cook, Pam ed., *The Cinema Book*, London: BFI Press (1985).

Copjec, J. ed., *Shades of Noir,* London: Verso 1992.

Copjec, J., 'The Phenomenal Nonphenomenal: Private Space in *Film Noir*' in Copjec, Joan ed., *Shades of Noir,* London: Verso (1993: 167-99).

Corrigan, T., *A Cinema Without Walls: Movies and Culture after Vietnam,* London: Routledge (1991).

Dargis, M., 'Pulp Instincts' *Sight and Sound* 4:5 (1994: 6-10).

Darke, C., 'Sibling Rivalry' *Sight and Sound* 3:7 (1993: 27-8).

Davies, J., 'Gender, Ethnicity, and Cultural Crisis in *Falling Down* and *Groundhog Day*' *Screen* 36:3 (1996: 214-32).

Davis, Jude & Smith, Carol R., *Gender, Ethnicity and Sexuality in Contemporary American Film,* Keele: Keele University Press (1997).

Davies, M., *City of Quartz: Excavating the Future in L.A.,* London: Verso (1990).

Davis, M., *L.A. Was Just the Beginning: Urban Revolt in the United States*, Los Angeles: Open Magazine Pamphlet Series (August 1992).

Deleuze, G. & Guattari, F., *Anti-Oedipus: Capitalism and Schizophrenia,* trans. Robert Hurley, Mark Seem & Helen R. Lane, Minneapolis: University of Minnesota Press (1983).

Deleuze, G., *Cinema 1: The Movement-Image,* trans. Hugh Tomlinson & Barbara Habberjan, London: Athlone (1986).

Deleuze, G. & Guattari, F., *A Thousand Plateaus: Capitalism and Schizophrenia,* trans. Brian Massumi, Minneapolis: University of Minnesota Press (1987).

Deleuze, G., *Foucault/Gilles Deleuze,* trans. and ed. Sean Hand, London: Athlone (1988).

Deleuze, G., *Cinema 2: The Time-Image*, trans. Hugh Tomlinson & Robert Galtea, London: Athlone (1989).

Deleuze, G., *Masochism,* trans. Jean McNeil, New York: Zone Books (1991).

Diawara, M., 'Black American Cinema: The New Realism' in Diawara, Manthia ed. *Black American Cinema,* London: American Film Institute/Routledge (1993: 3-25).

Diawara, M., 'Noir by Noirs: Towards a New Black Realism' in Copjec, Joan ed. *Shades of Noir,* London: Verso (1993: 261-79).

Diawara, Manthia ed., *Black American Cinema,* London: American Film Institute/Routledge (1993).

Douglass, P., 'Deleuze and the Endurance of Bergson' *Thought* 67:264 (1992: 47-61).

Dyer, R., *Heavenly Bodies,* London: BFI Press/Macmillan (1987).

Dyer, R., *White,* London: Routledge (1997).

Dyer, R., *A Matter of Images,* London: Routledge (1993).

Dyer, R., *Stars,* London: BFI Press (1979).

Dyson, M., 'Between Apocalypse and Redemption: John Singleton's *Boyz N the Hood*' *Cultural Critique* 21:3 (1992: 121-41).

Easthope, Antony ed., *Contemporary Film Theory*, London: Longman (1993).

Eco, U., 'Casablanca: Cult Movies and Intertextual Collage' in Lodge, D. *Modern Criticism and Theory,* London: Longman (1988: 449-56).

Eisenstein, S., *The Film Sense*, trans. & ed. Jay Leyda, London: Faber & Faber (1986).

Ellis, Brett E., *American Psycho,* New York: Vintage (1991).

Ellison, R., *Invisible Man,* New York: Vintage Books ed. 1972 (1947).

Ellroy, J., *White Jazz,* London: Arrow (1993).

Elsaesser, T., 'Narrative Cinema and Audience-Orientated Aesthetics' in Bennett, T., Boyd-Bowman, S., Mercer, C. and Woollacott, J. eds. *Popular Television and Film*, London: BFI Press (1981: 270-82).

Faludi, S., *Backlash: The Undeclared War Against Women,* London: Chatto (1991).

Fanon, F., *The Wretched of the Earth,* New York: Grove Press (1966).

Fanon, F*., Black Skins, White Masks,* New York: Grove Press (1967).

Farred, G., '*Menace II Society*: No Way Out For the Boyz N the Hood' *Michigan Quarterly Review* 35:3 (1996: 475-92).

Farred, G., 'No Way Out of the Menaced Society: Loyalty Within the Boundaries of Race' *Camera Obscura* 5 (1995: 7-23).

Francke, L., 'Virtual Fears' *Sight and Sound* 5:12 (1995: 6-9).

Francke, L., 'Twister' *Sight and Sound* 6:8 (1996: 65).

Fuery, P., *New Developments in Film Theory,* Macmillan, London (2000).

Fuller, G., 'About Everything that Drives You Nuts' *Empire* 49 (1993: 74-78).

Gabriel, J., 'What Do You Do when Minority Means You? *Falling Down* and White Masculinity in the 1990s' *Screen* 37:2 (1996: 129-51).

Gaines, J., 'Films That Make You Want to Fight Back (And Why White People Fear Them)' (1994 article unpublished at the time of writing).

Gates, Henry L., 'Blood Brothers: Albert and Allen Hughes in the Belly of the Hollywood Beast' *Transition: An International Review* 63 (1995: 164-77).

Gates, Henry, Louis ed., *Black Literature and Theory,* London: Routledge (1984).

Gilroy, P., *The Black Atlantic: Modernity and Double Consciousness,* London: Blackwell (1993).

Gooding-Williams, Robert ed., *Reading Rodney King, Reading Urban Uprising,* London: Routledge (1993).

Guerrero, Ed., *Framing Blackness,* Philadelphia: Temple University Press (1993).

Hansen, M., 'Early Cinema, Late Cinema: Permutations of the Public Sphere' *Screen* 34:3 (1993: 197-210).

Harrigan, R., 'Sweet Sweetback's Baadasssss Song' *Film History* 6:4 (1994: 383-404).

Himes C., *A Rage in Harlem,* Garden City NY: Doubleday (1957).

Himes, C., *Black on Black: Baby Sister and Selected Writings,* New York: Doubleday (1973).

Himes, C., *Cotton Comes to Harlem,* Garden City NY: Doubleday (1953).

Himes, C., *If He Hollers Let Him Go,* Garden City NY: Doubleday (1945).

Himes, C., *My Life of Absurdity,* New York: Doubleday (1976).

Himes, C., *The Quality of Hurt,* New York: Doubleday (1976).

'Fear of Violence Haunts Exhibitors as Curtain Goes Up On *Boyz*' *The Hollywood Reporter* 318:6 (12 July 1991: 9,16. no named author).

hooks, bell *Outlaw Culture: Resisting Representations,* London: Routledge (1994).

Jameson, F., *The Geopolitical Aesthetic,* London: BFI Press (1992).

Jameson, F., *The Cultural Turn: Selected Writings on the Postmodern,* London: Verso (1998).

Jameson, F., 'The Synoptic Chandler' in Copjec, Joan ed. *Shades of Noir,* London: Verso (1993: 33-57).

Jameson, F., *Signatures of the Visible,* London: Routledge (1990).

Jameson, F., *Postmodernism, or the Cultural Logic of Late Capitalism,* London: Verso (1992).

Jones, J. & Doherty, T., 'Two Takes on *Boyz N the Hood*' *Cineaste* 18: 4 (1991: 16-19).

Kelley, Robin D., 'Kickin' Reality, Kickin' Ballistics: "The Gangsta Rap and Postindustrial Los Angeles"' in Perkins, Eric ed. *Droppin' Science: Critical Essays on Rap Music and Hip Hop Culture,* Philadelphia: Temple University Press (1995: 85-105).

Kelley, Robin D., *Race Rebels: Culture, Politics, and the Black Working Class,* New York: Routledge (1994).

Kennedy, B., *Deleuze and Cinema: The Aesthetics of Sensation,* Edinburgh: Edinburgh University Press (2000)

Kennedy, L., 'Alien Nation: White Paranoia and Imperial Culture in the U.S.' *The Journal of American Studies* 30:1 (1996: 87-100).

Kim, Elaine H., 'Home is Where the Han is: A Korean Perspective on the Los Angeles Upheavals' in Gooding-Williams, Robert ed. *Reading Rodney King/Reading Urban Uprising,* London: Routledge (1993: 215-36).

King, A., 'Columbia Backing up its Boyz' *The Hollywood Reporter* 318:17 (15 July 1991: 1,6).

King, A., 'Outcry of Support for *Boyz* in Aftermath of Gunplay' *The Hollywood Reporter* 318:18 (16 July 1991: 1,122).

King, R., 'Rodney King's Statement' *Los Angeles Times* (2 May 1992: 3).

Kirby, L., 'Male Hysteria and Early Cinema' *Camera Obscura* 17 (1988: 112-31).

Kracauer, S., *Theory of Film: Redemption of Physical Reality,* London: Oxford University Press (1960).

Kristeva, J., *Powers of Horror: An Essay on Abjection,* New York: Columbia Univesity Press (1982).

Kroker, A. & Kroker, M. eds., *Body Invaders: Panic Sex in America,* New York: St Martin's Press (1987).

Krutnik, F., *In a Lonely Street: Film Noir, Genre, Masculinity,* London: Routledge (1991).

Lacan, J., *The Four Fundamental Concepts of Psycho-Analysis,* trans. Alan Sheridan, New York: Norton (1978).

Lacan, J., *Ecrits: A Selection,* trans. Alan Sheridan, New York: Norton (1977).

Laplanche, J., *The Language of Pyscho-Analysis,* trans. Donald Nicholson-Smith, New York: Norton (1973).

Lawson, M., 'And the Crowd Went Wild' *The Independent* (14 February 1995: 28).

LeBeau, V., *Lost Angels: Psychoanalysis and Cinema,* Oxford: Blackwell (1991).

Lewis, Jon ed., *The New American Cinema,* Durham NC: Duke University Press (1998).

Lodge, D., *Modern Criticism and Theory,* London: Longman (1988).

Losa, Steven Alvarez, Milo, Santiago, Josefina, Moore, C., 'Los Angeles Gangsta Rap and the Aesthetics of Violence' *Selected Reports in Ethnomusicology* Los Angeles CA: Sriela (1994: 149-61).

Lott, T., 'Hollywood and Independent Black Cinema' in Neale, S. & Smith, M. eds. *Contemporary Hollywood Cinema,* London: Routledge (1998: 211-29).

McDowell, Deborah E., 'Pecs and Reps: Muscling in on Race and the Subject of Masculinities' in Stecopoulos, Harry and Uebel, Michael eds. *Race and the Subject of Masculinities,* Durham NC: Duke University Press (1997: 361-85).

Mailer, N., *Advertisements For Myself,* London: Panther (1968).

Malcolm, D., 'Cheap Thrill a Minute' *The Guardian* (20 October 1994: 11).

Maltby, R. & Craven, D., *Hollywood Cinema: An Introduction,* Oxford: Blackwell (1995).

Massood, P., 'Mapping the Hood: The Genealogy of the City in *Boyz N the Hood* and *Menace II Society*' *Cinema-Journal* 35:2 (1996: 85-97).

Massood, P., '*Menace II Society*' *Cineaste* 20:2 (1993: 44).

Massumi, B., 'The Autonomy of Affect' in Patton, Paul ed. *Deleuze: A Critical Reader,* Oxford: Blackwell (1996: 217-240).

Mast, G. Cohen, M. & Braudy, L. eds., *Film Theory and Criticism,* 4th ed. Oxford: Oxford University Press (1992).

Maxwell, W., 'Sampling Authenticity: Rap Music, Postmodernism and the Ideology of Black Cinema' *Studies of Popular Culture* 14:1 (1991: 1-15).

McArthur, C., *Underworld USA,* London: BFI Press (1972).

McKelley, J., 'Raising Caine in a Down Eden: *Menace II Society* and the Death of Signifyin(g)' *Screen* 39:1 (1998: 36-52).

Metz, C., *Psychoanalysis and Cinema: The Imaginary Signifier,* London: Macmillan (1982).

Morrison, T., *Playing in the Dark: Whiteness and the Literary Imagination,* London: Picador (1993).

Mulvey, L., 'Visual Pleasure and Narrative Cinema' reprinted in Antony Easthope ed. *Contemporary Film Theory,* London: Longman (1993: 111-25).

Neale, S. & Smith, M. eds., *Contemporary Hollywood Cinema,* London: Routledge (1998).

Nichols, Bill ed., *Movies and Methods: An Anthology,* Berkeley: University of California Press (1976).

Pascaroli, L., 'Steel in the Gaze: On POV and the Disclosure of Vision in Kathryn Bigelow's Cinema' *Screen* 38:3 (1997: 232-46).

Patton, C., 'Authenticity and African-American Culture' *College Literature* 23:2 (1996: 177-80).

Patton, Paul ed., *Deleuze: A Critical Reader,* Oxford: Blackwell (1996).

Peary, Gerald ed., *Quentin Tarantino: Interviews,* Jackson MS: University of Mississippi Press (1997).

Perkins, Eric ed., *Droppin' Science: Critical Essays on Rap Music and Hip Hop Culture,* Philadelphia: Temple University Press (1995).

Pfeil, F., *White Guys,* London: Verso (1993).

Pfeil, F., 'From Pillar to Postmodernism: Race, Class, and Gender in the Male Rampage Film' in Lewis, Jon ed. *The New American Cinema,* Durham NC: Duke University Press (1998: 146-86).

Pines, J. & Willeman, P., *Questions of Third Cinema,* London: BFI Press (1989).

Place, J. A. & Peterson, L. S., 'Some Visual Motifs of Film Noir' *Wide Angle* 10:1 (1974: 30-35).

Polan, D., 'Powers of Vision, Visions of Power' *Camera Obscura* 18 (1988: 106-19).

Prelinger, R., *Ephemeral Films CD Rom,* London: Voyager (1992).

Pulver, A., 'The Movie Junkie' *The Guardian G2* (19 September 1994: 8-9).

Quinn, M., 'Never Shoulda Been Let Out of the Penitentiary' *Cultural Critique* 34 (1996: 65-89).

Reid, M., *Redefining Black Film,* Berkeley CA: University of California Press (1995).

Rodowick, D. N., 'Reading the Figural' *Camera Obscura* 24 (1990: 90-121).

Rodowick, D. N., *Gilles Deleuze's Time-Machine,* Durham NC: Duke University Press (1997).

Rodwick D. N., 'The Difficulty of Difference' *Camera Obscura* 15 (1982: 4-15).

Rogin, M., 'Blackface, White Noise: The Jewish Jazz Singer Finds His Voice' *Critical Inquiry* 18 (1992: 417-453).

Ropars-Wuilleumiar, M., 'The Cinema, Reader of Gilles Deleuze' *Camera Obscura* 18 (1988: 120-26).

Rose, B., 'The Last Stand of the Capra Hero' *The Journal of Popular Film and Television* 6:2 (1977: 79-93).

Rose, T., *Black Noise: Rap Music and Black Culture in Contemporary America,* Hanover NH (1994).

Salaam, Mtume ya., 'The Aesthetics of Rap' *The African-American Review* 29:2 (1995: 303-15).

Salisbury, M., '*Falling Down*: Joel Schumacher and Michael Douglas' in *Interview* 23:3 (1993: 110-15).

Scarry, E., *The Body in Pain: The Making and Unmaking of the World,* Oxford: Oxford University Press (1985).

Schwarz, T., *Hollywood Genres,* New York: Random House (1981).

Schwarz, Vanessa & Charney, L., *Cinema and the Invention of Modern Life,* Berkeley: University of California Press (1995).

Seydor, P., 'Sam Peckinpah' *Sight and Sound* 5:10 (1995: 18-24).

Shaviro, S., *The Cinematic Body,* Minneapolis: University of Minnesota Press (1993).

Shusterman, R., 'The Fine Art of Rap' *New Literary History* 22:3 (1991: 613-32).

Shusterman, R., 'Critical Response: Rap Remix: Pragmatism, Postmodernism, and other Issues in the House' *Critical Inquiry* 22:1 (1995: 151-158).

Silverman, K., *The Subject of Semiotics,* Oxford: Oxford University Press (1983).

Silverman, K., *The Acoustic Mirror: The Female Voice in Psychoanalysis and Cinema,* Bloomington: Indiana University Press (1988).

Silverman, K., *Male Subjectivity at the Margins,* London: Routledge (1992).

Simms, Holt, G., 'Stylin' Outta the Black Pulpit' in *Rappin' and Stylin' Out: Communication in Black America,* Urbana: University of Illinois Press (1972: 189-204).

Singer, B., 'Modernity, Hyperstimulus, and the Rise of Popular Sensationalism' in Schwarz, Vanessa & Charney, L., *Cinema and the Invention of Modern Life,* Berkeley: University of California Press (1995: 72-99).

Smith, G., 'When You're in Safe Hands' *Film Comment* July/August (1994: 32-36, 38, 40-43).

Slocum, J. David ed., *Violence and American Cinema,* New York: Routledge (2001).

Spoto, D., *The Dark Side of Genius: the Life of Alfred Hitchcock,* Boston MA: Little, Brown (1984).

Stecopoulos, Harry and Uebel, Michael eds., *Race and the Subject of Masculinities,* Durham NC: Duke University Press (1997).

Stern, L., *The Scorsese Connection*, London: BFI Press (1995).

Studlar, G., *In the Realm of Pleasure: Von Sternberg, Dietrich, and the Masochistic Aesthetic,* Urbana: University of Illinois Press (1988).

T.R.U.T.H, '*Menace II Society*' *Artrage* February/March (1994: 13).

Tallack, D., *Twentieth Century America: The Intellectual and Cultural Context,* London: Longman (1991).

Tarantino, Q., 'On *Pulp Fiction*' *Sight and Sound* 4:5 (1994: 10-11).

Tarantino, Q., 'My Heroes' *The Guardian* (4 February 1995: 3).

Tasker, Y., *Spectacular Bodies: Gender, Genre and the Action Cinema,* London: Routledge (1993).

Taubin, A., 'The Men's Room' *Sight and Sound* 2:8 (1992: 5-7).

Taubin, A., 'Girl N the Hood' *Sight & Sound* 3:8 (1993: 14).

Taubin, A., 'The Allure of Decay' *Sight and Sound* 5:12 (1995: 23-24).

Taussig, M., *Mimesis and Alterity: A Particular History of the Senses,* London: Routledge (1994).

Taylor, C., 'Black Cinema in the Post-Aesthetic Era' in Pines, J. & Willeman, P. *Questions of Third Cinema,* London: BFI Press (1989: 90-110).

Telotte, J. P., 'Definitely Falling Down: *81/2, Falling Down* and the Death of Fantasy' *The Journal of Popular Film and Television* 24:1 (1996: 19-25).

Toop, G., *Rap Attack Two: African Rap to Global Hip-Hop,* London (1991).

Toop, G., *The Rap Attack: African Jive to New York Hip-Hop,* London (1984).

Vernet, M., '*Film Noir* on the Edge of Doom' in Copjec, J. ed. *Shades of Noir,* London: Verso (1992: 1-33).

Walker, John ed., *Halliwell's Film Guide 1997,* London: Harper Collins (1996).

Wallace, D. & Costello, M., 'Signifying Rappers' *The Missouri Review* 13:2 (1990: 7-26).

Warshow, R., *The Immediate Experience,* New York: Atheneum Books (1970).

Washington, P. & Shaver, L., 'The Language Culture of Rap Music Videos' in Adjaye, Joseph & Andrews, Adrianne ed*., Language, Rhythm and Sound: Black Popular Culture into the Twenty-First Century,* Pittsburgh PA: University of Pittsburgh Press (1997: 164-77).

Watts, C., 'Thinking *Disclosure*: Or the Structure of Post-Feminist Cynicism' *Women: A Cultural Review* 6:3 (1995: 275-86).

West, C., *Race Matters,* New York: Beacon Press (1993).

White, A., 'Flipper, Purity and Furious Styles' *Sight and Sound* 1:14 (1991: 8-13).

Wiegman, R., 'Feminism, "The Boyz" and Other Matters Regarding the Male' in Cohan, S. & Hark, Ina Rae ed. *Screening the Male,* London: Routledge (1993: 173-93).

Williams, J., 'Frank Capra and the Cinema of Populism' in Nichols, Bill ed. *Movies and Methods: An Anthology,* Berkeley: University of California Press (1976: 65-78).

Williams, L., *Hard Core: Power, Pleasure and the Frenzy of the Visible,* Berkeley CA: University of California Press (1989).

Williams, L., 'Film Bodies, Gender, Genre, Excess' *Film Quarterly* VXLIV:4 (1992: 2-13).

Willis, S., *High Contrast: Race and Gender in Contemporary Hollywood Film,* Durham NC: Duke University Press (1998).

Winokur, M., 'Marginal Marginalia: The African-American Voice in the Nouvelle Gangster Film' *The Velvet Light Trap* 35 (1995: 22-32).

Wood, J., 'You're Sayin' a Foot Massage Don't Mean Nothin', and I'm Sayin' it Does' *The Guardian* (12 November 1994: 31).

Wright, R., *Native Son,* New York: New American Library 1964 (1940).

Wyatt, J., *High Concept - Movies & Marketing in Hollywood,* Austin: University of Texas Press (1994).

Wyatt, J., 'The Formation of the "Major Independent": Miramax, New Line and the New Hollywood' in Neale, S. & Smith, M. eds. *Contemporary Hollywood Cinema,* London: Routledge (1998: 74-91).

Yearwood, G., 'The Hero in Black Cinema: An Analysis of the Film Industry and Problems in Black Cinema' *Wide Angle* 5:2 (1982: 42-50).

Yau, Esther ed., *At Full Speed: Hong Kong Cinema in a Borderless World,* Minnesota: University of Minnesota Press (2001).

Zizek, S., *The Sublime Object of Ideology,* London: Verso (1989).

Zizek, S., *Looking Awry: An Introduction to Jacques Lacan Through Popular Culture,* Cambridge MA: M.I.T. Press (1991).

Zizek, Slavoj ed., *Everything You Always Wanted to Know About Lacan But Were Afraid to Ask Hitchcock,* London: Verso (1992).

Zizek, S., 'In His Bold Gaze, My Ruin is Writ Large' in Zizek, Slavoj ed. *Everything You Always Wanted to Know About Lacan But Were Afraid to Ask Hitchcock,* London: Verso (1992: 211-273).

Filmography

Title	Country of Origin	Director	Year Released
Angels With Dirty Faces	US	Michael Curtiz	1936
Bad Lieutenant	US	Abel Ferrara	1992
Basic Instinct	US	Paul Verhoeven	1992
Batman Forever	US	Joel Schumacher	1995
Battleship Potemkin	USSR	Sergei Eisenstein	1925
The Birth of a Nation	US	D.W. Griffith	1915
Blade Runner	US	Ridley Scott	1982
The Blues Brothers	US	John Landis	1980
Blue Steel	US	Kathryn Bigelow	1990
Body Heat	US	Lawrence Kasdan	1984
Bonny and Clyde	US	Arthur Penn	1967
Boyz N the Hood	US	John Singleton	1991
Bulworth	US	Warren Beatty	1999
Casablanca	US	Michael Curtiz	1942
Casino	US	Martin Scorsese	1995
Chungking Express	HK	Wong Kar-Wei	1994
Cleopatra Jones	US	Jack Starret	1973
Clockers	US	Spike Lee	1995
A Clockwork Orange	UK	Stanley Kubrick	1971
Dead Presidents	US	A. & A. Hughes	1996
Deliverance	US	John Boorman	1972
Die Hard	US	John McTiernan	1988
Die Hard 2	US	Renny Harlin	1990
Die Hard With a Vengeance	US	John McTiernan	1995
Dillinger	US	Max Nosseck	1945
Disclosure	US	Barry Levinson	1994
Do the Right Thing	US	Spike Lee	1989
Falling Down	US	Joel Schumacher	1992
Farewell My Lovely a.k.a. *Murder, My Sweet*	US	Edward Dymtryk	1944

Farewell My Lovely	US	Dick Richards	1975
Fatal Attraction	US	Adrian Lyne	1987
Flatliners	US	Joel Schumacher	1990
Foxy Brown	US	Jack Hill	1974
The Godfather	US	Francis F. Coppola	1972
The Godfather Part Two	US	Francis F. Coppola	1974
The Godfather Part Three	US	Francis F. Coppola	1990
Higher Learning	UK	John Singleton	1995
Kill Bill Vol. 1	US	Quentin Tarantino	2003
The Killer	HK	John Woo	1989
The Killers	US	Don Siegel	1964
Gone With the Wind	US	Fleming/Cukor/Wood	1939
Henry: Portrait of a Serial Killer	US	John NcNaughton	1990
The Hills Have Eyes	US	Wes Craven	1977
Hoop Dreams	US	Steve James	1994
In the Mood For Love	HK/Fr	Wong Kar-Wei	2000
It's A Wonderful Life	US	Frank Capra	1946
King of New York	US	Abel Ferrara	1990
Jackie Brown	US	Quentin Tarantino	1997
The Jazz Singer	US	Alan Crosland	1927
Juice	US	Ernest Dickerson	1992
King of Comedy	US	Martin Scorsese	1983
Kiss Me Deadly	US	Robert Aldrich	1955
Last Year at Marienbad	Fr/It	Alain Resnais	1961
Lethal Weapon	US	Richard Donner	1987
Lethal Weapon 2	US	Richard Donner	1989
Lethal Weapon 3	US	Richard Donner	1992
Live and Let Die	US	Guy Hamilton	1973
The Maltese Falcon	US	John Huston	1941
The Matrix	US	A.Wachowski	1999

Matrix Reloaded	US	Wachowski	2003
Mean Streets	US	Martin Scorsese	1973
Menace II Society	US	A. & A. Hughes	1993
Miller's Crossing	US	Joel Coen	1990
The Naked City	US	Jules Dassin	1948
Near Dark	US	Kathryn Bigelow	1987
North By Northwest	US	Alfred Hitchcock	1959
Once Upon a Time in America	US	Sergio Leone	1983
Once upon a Time in China	HK	Tsui Hark	1998
Out of the Past	US	Jacques Tourneur	1947
Panther	US	Mario Van Peebles	1995
Pat Garrett and Billy the Kid	US	Sam Peckinpah	1973
Peeping Tom	UK	Michael Powell	1960
The Picture of Dorian Gray	US	Albert Lewin	1945
Pierrot Le Fou	Fr/It	Jean-Luc Godard	1968
Point Blank	US	John Boorman	1967
Point Break	US	Kathryn Bigelow	1991
Predator	US	John McTiernan	1987
Psycho	US	Alfred Hitchcock	1960
The Public Enemy	US	William Wellman	1931
Public Hero Number One	US	J.Walter Ruben	1935
Pulp Fiction	US	Quentin Tarantino	1994
Raging Bull	US	Martin Scorsese	1980
Raiders of the Lost Ark	US	Steven Spielberg	1981
Rally Round the Flag Boys	US	Leo McCarey	1958
Rambo: First Blood Part Two	US	George Cosmatos	1985
Reservoir Dogs	US	Quentin Tarantino	1991
Rio Bravo	US	Howard Hawks	1959
Rock, Rock, Rock	US	Will Price	1960
The Running Man	US	Paul Michael-Glaser	1987

Le Sang Des Betes	Fr/It	Georges Franju	1949
Scarface	US	Howard Hawks	1931
The Searchers	US	John Ford	1956
Se7en	US	David Fincher	1995
Shaft	US	Gordon Parks Snr	1971
Shaft in Africa	US	John Guillermin	1973
She's Gotta Have It	US	Spike Lee	1986
The Silence of the Lambs	US	Jonathan Demme	1991
Speed	US	Jan de Bont	1994
Straight out of Brooklyn	US	Matty Rich	1991
Strange Days	US	Kathryn Bigelow	1995
Superfly	US	Gordon Parks Jnr	1972
Sweet Sweetback's Baadasss Song	US	Melvin Van Peebles	1971
The Swimmer	US	F.Perry & S.Pollack	1968
Taxi Driver	US	Martin Scorsese	1976
The Terminator	US	James Cameron	1984
Terminator II	US	James Cameron	1991
Total Recall	US	Paul Verhoeven	1988
Trespass	US	Walter Hill	1992
True Romance	US	Tony Scott	1992
The Truman Show	US	Peter Weir	1998
Uncle Tom's Cabin	US	Edwin Porter	1903
Le Weekend	Fr/It	Jean-Luc Godard	1968
White Heat	US	Raoul Walsh	1949
The Wild Bunch	US	Sam Peckinpah	1969
The Wizard of Oz	US	Fleming/Vidor	1939
Les Yeux Sans Visage	Fr/It	Georges Franju	1959

Index

A

Abbas, Akbar 192, 193; 'New Wave of Hong-Kong Cinema' 191

Acousmatic sounds 7, 45, 83, 103

Action-cinema 13, 52, 73, 159, 175, 177, 183, 186

Action-image, the (Deleuze) 3, 21, 23, 36, 39, 43, 53, 61, 62, 66-7, 69, 73, 80, 82, 84-7, 91, 93-4, 96, 99, 100, 102, 109, 112-3, 119, 121, 128-31, 143, 150, 152, 164, 169, 170-1, 173-4, 176-7, 183, 185-6, 188; aesthetics and philosophy of 90; certainties of cinema of 122; clichés of 50, 51, 161; cracks in 54, 110, 175; crisis of 19, 24, 32, 34-35, 37, 47, 49, 51, 52, 56, 59-60, 78-9, 101, 116-8, 125, 127, 132, 135 76n, 150, 153, 161-3, 179, 184, 191, 192; Deleuze and 19, 23, 34, 47, 49, 50-52, 59, 79-80, 85-6, 90, 99, 101, 109, 113, 131, 135 73n 76n, 153, 161

Aesthetics 8, 20, 24, 33, 36, 49, 53, 81, 85-86, 90, 94, 111, 148, 156, 161, 183, 190-191; appropriation of black 139; cinematic 15; cinematographic 152; of race 9; of rap 37, 100, 137, 160

Affect: pp1-193; abject 170; and American Africanism 29, 37, 156; autonomous 11; of blackness 123; bodily 8, 12, 108, 125, 132, 155, 167, 183, 188; cinematic 8, 12-13, 16, 18, 24, 26, 34, 36-7, 76, 85, 116, 137, 146-7, 151, 154, 156, 159, 161, 171-2, 174; 'human' 159; and masculinity 26; and cinematic immediacy 8, 22,109; and cultural knowledge, tensions 13; as intensity 10; and milieu 57, 91, 99, 117, 162, 184; and meaning 9, 32-3, 145, 146; and meaning/knowledge 9, 32-3, 145-6; primacy and autonomy of (Massumi) 10; unsymbolisable 87, 169

African-American (culture) pp.8-192: affectivity of culture 30; as anarchic 29, 36, 76, 92, 93, 101, 102, 115, 132, 141, 160;bodies. See Black bodies; cultural authenticity 33; figure of the 'gangsta' 26, 27, 93, 94, 100, 111, 149; masculinity 27, 28, 104; popular culture 33; as sexually licentious 138; street slang/vernacular 87, 88, 96 n11, 138; white culture's dependency on 31, 32, 34, 186

Aggression 12, 23; 'Structures of aggression' (Burch) 14, 24, 125, 146, 155, 160, 170, 177, 187

Aldrich, Robert 50, 125, 164

Altman, Robert 50

Alienation 20, 128, 141

All the President's Men (Pakula) 25

American Africanism (Toni Morrison) 3, 29-30, 32, 35, 37, 59, 68, 76, 92, 133, 137, 141, 146, 156, 162, 173-4, 183-8; and affect 29; as alternative aesthetic 34; as reflexive 30

American dream 20, 35, 39, 57, 61, 62, 66, 67, 85, 89, 91, 99, 100, 105, 113, 116, 140, 151, 162, 175, 183, 184, 185, 192; corruption of 36, 56, 110; gangsta mimesis of 103; as poor copy of 106, 107; ideology of 73, 90, 93, 110, 112; myth of 49, 93, 130; unspoken violence in 102-3

American popular culture 8, 33, 34

American populism 57, 135

American Psycho (Brett Easton Ellis) 19

Amplification 10

Angels With Dirty Faces (Curtiz) 90, 135

'Any-space-whatever' (Deleuze) 19, 24, 51, 53, 153, 154, 163, 168, 172, 191

Architecture, Benjamin on 17

Assaulted viewer. *See* Cinematic experience *and* Viewer.

Audience: pp7-186; black audience 36, 58, 74, 76-7, 94, 99, 169, 185; white audiences 28, 74, 77, 79-80, 88, 91, 99-100, 111-2, 126, 160, 169, 186

Aura (Benjamin) 16, 17, 21, 86, 107, 108, 133 dissolution of 16; of 'the original' 16,17, 86; withering away of 16

Authenticity 35, 58, 73, 81, 101, 188; Benjamin on 16

black body/blackness as sign of 28, 58, 59, 60, 76, 100, 111, 112, 123, 137, 142, 145, 147, 174, 183, 186, 191; and black cultural authority 32,

33, 37, 73, 85; and cinematic 103, 142; immediacy and 35, 61, 86, 89, 90, 92; video ('live) and 123-5

B

Basic Instinct (Verhoeven) 47, 54

Bassett, Angela 161, 176

Baudrillard, Jean, 25, 40; and hyperreality 25

Bazin, Andre 12, 39, 152, 180; on depth in image 171

Beasley-Murray, John 5, 23, 40, 149, 158

Bellour, 64

Benjamin, Walter 18, 28, 39, 52, 96, 107, 133 30n, 149; and aura 16, 17, 21, 86, 107, 108, 133; auratic presence 108; and commodity fetish 106; concentration and distraction 16; notion of cinematic shock 16, 18, 93; and optical unconscious 108, 109

Big Combo, The (Lewis) 21, 163

Bigelow, Kathryn 8, 37, 156, 174, 175

Big Sleep, The (Hawks) 48, 172, 175, 180

Birth of a Nation, The (Griffith) 38 3n

Biskind, P. 157

Black bodies 13, 59, 68, 74-5, 77, 86, 95, 100, 118, 123, 125, 131, 147, 183, 191; affective power of 93, 99, 101, 110 126; Rodney King 25, 26, 27, 28, 176, 187, 188; sign of real and authenticity 32-3, 37, 73, 85, 186; Surplus symbolic value of (Rogin) 8

Black cinema 73, 111, 126, 186

Black culture 8, 30, 31, 35, 40, 41, 68, 93, 104, 106, 126, 132, 134, 142, 146, 147, 156, 161, 162, 170, 174, 177, 179, 186, 188, 189, 190; as affective depth 160, 168, 169, 174; as desirable cool 32, 91-2; as desirable 'other'155; as site of affect 34, 44, 191; re-energise white audience 160; black separatism 84, 91, 94; used to reanimate white cinema 151

Black masculinity/Black male bodies 26, 27, 29, 73, 75, 95, 113, 161, 185; anxieties and paranoia around 28; fetishisation of violent 106, 148; imagined primitivism of 28; threat of 28

Blackness 3, 8, 28, 32, 34, 35, 37, 38, 40, 58, 59, 60, 104, 109, 111, 112, 113, 123, 125, 126, 134, 137, 141, 145, 146, 147, 148, 151, 156, 160, 161, 167, 168, 169, 170, 176, 177, 179, 185, 186, 187, 188, 189, 190; and anxiety 31; as (substantive) authenticity 174, 183, 191; as source of affective violence 29; as 'cool' 32; as desirable 'other' 155; and disavowal 31; as excess 29; fears and anxieties around 30; and fetishism 31; imitation of 26; and paranoia 30; structured by the symbolic order 29; in white literary imagination 29; tropes of 110, 133 36n; as symbol of 'the Real' 29, 119, 132

Black on black violence 36, 99, 104

Black nihilism 105, 109, 129

Black rage 102

Black violence 26, 30, 36, 59, 75-6, 80, 94, 99, 104, 109, 126, 131, 134, 160-1, 172-4, 176, 179, 185, 187; media images of 28

Blade, The (Hark) 192

Blade Runner (Scott) 21, 22, 79, 102, 114, 157, 166, 169, 172, 175, 180, 187

Blaxploitation 35, 80, 81, 82, 139, 145, 147, 167, 179, 188; and black males as action heroes 80; heroine 177, 179

Blockbuster. *See* Postmodern blockbuster

Blood 18, 19, 23, 52, 119, 165; black 151; and colour-image (Deleuze) 150

Blues Brothers, The (Landis) 157 14n

Blue Steel (Bigelow) 175

Blue Velvet (Lynch) 12, 22, 38

Body Heat (Kasdan) 102

Body, the 10-12, 28, 38, 75, 86-7, 107-8, 148, 154, 158-9, 163, 165, 169-70, 187, 191; assault on body of the viewer 8; cinematic body 8, 9, 14, 147, 149; physicality of bodies 23; and thought/body 14, 15; vulnerability of 22

Body-first (reaction) 11, 28, 34, 37, 38, 44, 47, 84, 86, 107, 125, 145, 160, 187; to black male bodies 28; way of knowing 10; *See also* Black bodies

Bogle, Donald 95, 180

Bonny and Clyde (Penn) 118

Bollywood (Bombay) cinema 190

Boorman, John 51, 169

Bordwell, David 39, 191, 193; and Hong-Kong action film 191

Boss figure 143

Boyd, Todd 76, 95, 158

Boyz N the Hood (Singleton) 3, 35-6, 57, 58-9, 68, 73, 76-7, 80-2, 84, 85, 86-8, 90-5, 99, 100-2, 104, 111, 128-9, 143, 151, 161-2, 179, 185; as social realism 103, 126, 148, 152; Oedipal trajectory of 78; as rite of passage movie 78, 103; as 'safe' film for white audiences 74, 79, 112

Brennan, T. 96

Brunette, Peter 81, 95

Bukatman, Scott, 167, 179; 'fractal body' 155, 158 n44, 180 n11

Bulworth (Beatty) 25, 38, 179, 188, 189

Burch, Noel, 39, 49, 69, 134, 157, 180, 181; 'structures of aggression' 14, 24, 125, 146, 155, 160, 170, 177, 187

'Burden of representation' (Gilroy) 101

Buscemi, Steve 138, 143

Bush, George 106

Butler, Judith 27, 40, 58, 70, 95, 103, 112, 132, 156, 193; catachresis 140; on Franz Fanon 28, 75; on Rodney King 28; 'racial disposition of the visible' 31, 76, 99, 123, 185

C

Cagney, Jimmy 92, 96, 97, 134, 135, 157

Cameron, James 22, 44, 75, 175

Capra, Frank 49, 57, 113, 130, 135

Cassavetes, John 12, 51

Catechresis (Butler), and copy 140

Chungking Express (Kar-Wai) 192

Cine-literacy 126

Cinema (film): pp1- 193; of the action-image. *See* action-image; affective powers of 9; of American Dream 116, 175; of attractions 77; Black 73, 111, 126, 186; Bollywood 190; Early 15, 16, 18, 23, 39, 52; and globalisation 190; and Hip-Hop culture 188; Hollywood. *See*

Hollywood film/cinema; and language 9; and movement 83, 117; and narrative 19, 46; postmodern 10, 145, 154, 166; reanimation of 73, 86, 118, 147, 183; as sensory and affective medium 9; and time 23; and thought/body 15; and violence. *See* violence. white 30, 36, 94, 100, 111, 115, 162, 186, 188, 190

Cinema of rage 3

Cinematic body (Shaviro) 8, 9, 14, 147, 149

Cinematic experience 8, 17, 32, 62, 93, 125, 146, 151, 155, 158, 163, 165, 168, 177, 178, 179, 186; affective potential 35, 44, 137; and (kind of) affect produced 26; of assaulted viewer 11; physical shock of 160; of the Real 126; reanimation of 147; as tactile and as visceral 9; violence 18, 20, 101, 126, 148, 164

Cinematic memories 94, 100, 102, 129

Citationality. *See* Intertextual

Civil Rights Movement 116; and 'rising consciousness of minorities' 183

Charney, Leo 39, 70

Chungking Express (Kar-Wai) 192

Classic gangster film 89, 90, 91, 104, 108, 126, 127, 134, 135, 143

Classical Hollywood (film) 13, 18, 21, 24, 39-40, 46-7, 79, 82, 85, 88, 117, 126-7, 129-30, 169, 192; individualized violence of 22; representations of blackness 31

Classic spectator, the 60, 62, 63, 66, 67

Cleopatra Jones (Starret) 81, 177

Clover, Carol 37, 41, 55, 68-9, 70, 158, 169, 177, 180 15n; gender, blurring of 178; 'the reactive gaze' 155; on *Silence of the Lambs* 170

Coen, Joel 135

Colour-image (Deleuze) 150, 165

Commodity, the 107, 124

Commodity Fetishism 106, 148

Contagion 31, 151, 169; mimetic 170; racial 128, 151

Cook, Pam 89, 96, 134, 135

Coolness 33, 91, 160

Copjec, Joan 40, 41, 70, 133, 134, 180; and dead voice-over 113; and noir 114

Coppola, Francis F. 135

Cops 59, 123, 126, 169, 171, 172

Copy, the 16, 86, 102; cinematic 28; having extra dimension and power 28

Copycat 74, 76, 139; behaviour 89; violence 89

'Correspondence of time' 11

'Cowboy and Indian' 127, 128

Crisis *See* Action-image: aesthetic 32, 35, 36, 49, 111, 125, 126, 131, 162; and American Dream 49, 183; of Hollywood realism 47; (loss) of belief 19, 20, 183, 184; Oedipal 19; postmodern 19; of relation between individual and milieu 19, 49, 51, 78-9, 117, 121; in white cinema 111; of white culture 144

Cultural authority/authenticity 137, 147, 160, 162, 179, 183, 187; black bodies as sign of 32-3, 37, 73, 85, 186

Cultural identity 35, 36, 37, 38, 59, 68, 76, 84, 85, 92, 93, 94, 100, 118, 119, 132, 133, 135, 140, 146, 149, 156, 160, 161, 174, 176, 183, 186, 187, 189, 192, 193; Hong-Kong 191; white American 9, 29, 30, 32, 102, 103, 116, 162, 185, 189, 190; built on racial rage 116

Cultural knowledge 9, 19, 24, 37, 51, 78, 147, 156, 165, 174, 185; and affect 13, 28, 86, 127, 146; blackness as source of 29, 160, 161, 169, 188

Culture: pp.8-193; African-American, and white American 8, 13, 24, 27, 30-1, 33-5, 37, 38, 44-5, 59, 68, 73, 89, 93, 100, 137, 145-7, 155-6, 160-3, 166, 170, 173, 183-5, 187-90; disposable 144; American popular 8, 33, 34; white, crisis of 29, 32, 35, 100, 109, 118, 146, 193; trash 144, 161

Cynical realism 184; and reason 68, 185

D

Dangerous black body, the 3, 25, 36, 73, 92, 93, 99, 100, 108, 162

Dargis, Manhola 149, 150, 158

Davis, Angela 177

Davis, Mike,122, 123,

Darke, Chris 16

Dead Presidents (Hughes brothers) 189

Dead voice-over 111, 113, 114

Deleuze, Gilles: 9, 10, 20, 21, 38, 39, 40, 50, 52, 56, 70, 80, 85, 86, 90, 95, 96, 99, 109, 110, 133, 134, 136, 149, 158, 161, 180, 183; *See.* action-image; 'any-space-whatever' 19, 24, 51, 53, 153, 154, 163, 168, 172, 191; 'bad' 18, 19; 'good cinema' 19; on Benjamin 16; on cinematic violence 18; and colour-image 150, 165; crisis of action-image 3, 24, 32, 34, 37, 43, 47, 49, 51-2, 59- 60, 78-9, 101, 116-9, 125, 127, 132, 135, 53, 162-3, 175, 179, 184, 191, 192; on extracinematic world 49, 54, 79; and Guattari 68; 'inflation of the represented' 18, 19, 23, 131, 150; and movement-image 15, 18; on noir 48, 51, 69, 113; and nooshock 15, 18; and time-image 23, 69, 171; and white events 50, 54, 117

Deliverance (Boorman) 169

de Niro, Robert 117, 119

Depth 92, 144, 165, 166, 170, 80; affective 160, 163, 167, 169; African-American culture/blackness as 37, 145, 146, 155, 160, 163, 166, 167, 168, 169, 174; body and 159; Bazin on 171; of (cinematic) image 37, 164, 165, 166, 167, 168, 169, 170, 171, 173, 187; Jameson and 144, 145, 155; the Real and unsymbolisable bodily 168; whiteness as lack of 146, 167

Diawara, Manthia 41, 57, 70, 82, 94, 95, 96, 110, 111, 133, 143, 157; on Chester Himes 110; '*Noir* by noirs' 111

Die Hard (McTiernan) 21, 40, 52, 53, 67, 150, 154, 164, 173, 184

Dillinger (Nosseck) 134, 143

Disavowal 31, 40; and white viewers 31

Disclosure (Barry Levinson) 45, 47

Disembodiment 7, 73

Distraction 16, 17, 21, 22, 127, 132, 147, 148, 149, 164, 178

Dobson, Tamara 81

Doherty, Tom 68, 84, 92, 95, 96, 97

Do the Right Thing (Lee) 94

Double Indemnity (Wilder) 111

Douglas, Michael 35, 43, 44, 45, 46, 47, 54, 55, 64, 69, 70

Dramatic intensity 75, 117, 118, 120, 128, 163, 184

Duhamel, George 16

Duration 16, 90, 186

Dyer, Richard 31, 39, 40, 146, 157

E

Early cinema 15, 16, 18, 23, 39, 52

Eco, Umberto 11, 38, 79, 95

Ego, temporary loss of 17

Eisenstein, Sergei 15, 16, 39, 149

Ellison, Ralph *Invisible Man* 96 60n

Ellroy, James 156 3n

Elsaesser, Thomas 158

Emotion and intensity, distinction 10,

F

Falling Down (Schumacher) 3, 8, 35, 36, 37, 38, 43, 44, 45, 46, 47, 52, 53, 54, 55, 57, 58, 59, 62, 63, 67, 68, 69, 73, 74, 80, 85, 86, 94, 99, 109, 129, 132, 134, 141, 153, 156, 175, 184, 185, 187, 193

Faludi, Susan 69

Fanon, Frantz 28, 75, 95; Negro 74, 76

Farewell My Lovely (Richards) 135

Farewell My Lovely a.k.a. *Murder, My Sweet* (Dymtryk) 129

Fatal Attraction (Lyne) 45, 47, 55

Father (figure), the 140 103, 140, 142, 143; Good, the 191

Femininity 178

Femme fatale/s 47; black 111

Fetishisation 106, 107, 148, 188; of black body 148; as illusory 107

Fetish/Fetishism 16, 31, 31, 34, 35, 40, 84, 106, 107, 108, 124, 133, 139, 148, 149, 155, 161, 162, 188; Benjamin and commodity fetish 16, 106; and white viewers 31

Fiennes, Ralph 176

Fight Club (Fincher) 156, 190

Film: (pp.1-193) *See* also Cinema; gangsta 89, 90, 126, 127, 128, 129, 131, 137, 148, 152, 161, 162, 168, 185, 186;gangster 36, 81, 89, 90, 91, 101, 108, 126, 134, 135, 140, 143. *See* Film noir/noir; Hollywood. *See* Hollywood film/cinema; Hong-Kong action 191; *See* Hood film; horror 169, 178; *See* New Black Realism; *See* New Brutality; post-generic genre film (Jameson) 79; post-Screen 13; representational approaches to 139; science fiction 21, 44, 102, 144, 157; self-reflexive 7, 34, 46, 47, 67, 68, 92, 118, 137, 143, 146, 150, 160, 161, 163, 168, 177, 184, 188; temporal structure of 149, 152, 171

Film noir 48, 50, 51, 56, 61, 62, 69, 79, 101, 108, 109, 110, 113, 125, 126, 129, 164, 175, 184, 186

Film theory 9, 13, 14, 40, 46, 62, 79, 82, 88, 178; psychoanalysis 12, 127, 135, 178, 181; semiotic 9

Fincher, David 8, 37, 156, 170, 171, 180, 190

Fishburne, Laurence 57, 78, 143, 179, 191

Flashbacks 24, 138, 139, 152

Focalization 36, 45, 184

Focus, 22, 43, 83, 95, 103, 105, 109, 111, 135, 137, 152, 170, 172, 180; and depth 171; shallow 171

Ford, John 51, 119

Foxy Brown (Hill) 81

Francke, Lizzi 40, 177, 180 24n

Franju, Georges 39

Freeman, Morgan 172

G

Gaines, Jane 5, 28, 40, 77, 86, 95, 96

Gance, Abel 15

Gangsta 3, 36, 40, 59, 73, 87, 93, 94, 95, 99, 105, 108, 109, 116, 123, 124, 134, 138, 141, 149, 151, 154, 155, 157, 166, 179; African-American figure of 26, 27, 92, 93, 94, 100, 111; as copy 102, 103 (poor) 106; film 89, 90, 126, 127, 128, 129, 131, 137, 148, 152, 161, 162, 168, 185, 186; fetishisation of iconic images 107; and inability to act 129; milieu of 129, 131, 154; mimesis of the white gangster 102; violence of 100, 139,

152; Gangsta and gangster 104, 152, differences between 152

Gangster/s 3, 7, 8, 18, 19, 24, 28, 61, 73, 96, 99, 100, 106, 122, 128, 129, 139, 149, 150, 151, 152, 157, 160, 164, 167, 186; coded as African-American in *Reservoir Dogs* 27; as glamorous 89, 90; film 11, 36, 56, 81, 89, 90, 91, 101, 104, 108, 126, 127, 134, 135, 140, 143; milieu 119, 127, 128, 154; mimicry of gangsta 141; myth of 105; as white 26, 81, 92, 93, 101, 102, 138, 139, 140, 141, 142, 143, 148, 154, 187

Gaze, the 55, 62, 92; assaultive and reactive 37; voyeuristic 169, 177

German Expressionism 110

Ghetto (urban), the 74, 78, 80, 81, 83, 85, 86, 91, 92, 95, 99, 105, 107, 114, 115, 126, 130, 132, 134; black existence in 106; (utopian) escape 103, 104, 128; as *mise en scène* and milieu 102, 129; nightmarish violence of 112; racially imposed boundaries 152; as space of the Real 116

Globalisation 190, 193

God (Christian) 130, 135, 140, 164, 167

Godfather, The (Coppola) 135

Gone With the Wind (Fleming/Cukor/Wood) 38

Goodfellas (Scorsese) 114, 119, 124, 127, 139, 140, 143

Gormley, Paul *The Affective City* 132 n1

Graduate, The (Nicols) 145, 188

Great Depression, the 89

Grier, Pam 35, 81, 139, 188

Guerrero, Ed 74, 80, 82, 85, 95, 96

Guilt, white 116

H

Habitual perception 17, 20, 78; Taussig on 108

Hannah, Daryl 166

Hansen, Miriam 67, 68, 71

Hauer, Rutger 166

Hawks, Howard 48, 52, 90, 157, 172, 180

Hays Code 90

Hills Have Eyes, The (Craven) 169

Henry: Portrait of a Serial Killer (McNaughton) 170

Heinlein, Robert 144

Hero/anti-hero 20, 46, 47, 48, 53, 61, 64, 65, 66, 89, 90, 96, 114, 121, 122, 129, 130, 131, 150, 154, 173, 174; Classical 128

Higher Learning (Singleton) 189

Hillbilly, the 169

Himes, Chester 70, 110, 111

Hip-hop culture 33, 59, 109, 156, and cinema 188; and word 'nigger' 33

Hipness 32, 33, 34, 35, 92, 137, 161, 177, 188

'History', and 'truth' 124

Hitchcock, Alfred 12, 15, 63, 125; Hitchcockian fantasy, the 14

Hollywood film/cinema 8, 9, 13, 18, 19, 20, 21, 22, 23, 24, 25, 31, 35, 40, 44, 45, 48, 53, 62, 68, 78, 79, 82, 88, 109, 126, 126, 128, 131, 132, 140, 159, 176, 179, 180, 183, 186, 189, 190, 191, 193; fantasy of action-man 129; imitation of other cinemas 192; and white racial rage 116-8.

Homo marginalis 129

Homosexual 111, 138

Hong-Kong, 193; cinema 191; colonial past 192; handover 191

'Hood, the 31, 38, 48, 59-60, 67-8, 74, 79-94, 99-100, 103, 105, 112, 113-6, 125-131, 137, 143, 147-8, 151-4, 160-179, 185-191; as embodiment of the Real 114, 115, 126; physical and psychic constraints of 125, 128

Hood film/new black realism 31, 38, 41, 57, 60, 68, 74, 80, 81, 82, 84, 86, 87, 88, 91, 92, 93, 94, 95, 130, 131, 137, 147, 148, 151, 152, 154, 160, 162, 169, 170, 172, 173, 174, 176, 185, 186, 187, 189, 190; absence of nostalgia in 126-7; and father figure 143

hooks, bell 57, 70, 91, 96, 104, 105, 106, 107, 108, 109, 111, 133

Hoop Dreams (James) 95

Horror (film) 169, 178

Hughes brothers (Hughes, A. & A.) 35, 58, 70, 74, 80, 81, 94, 103, 104, 132, 189

Hyperreality (Baudrillard) 25

I

Ice Cube 78, 91, 92, 100, 138
Ice T 138
Identification 36, 45, 55, 56, 62, 63, 65, 66, 105,
   112, 113, 116, 178, 184, 192; secondary 121
Identity: pp. 9-193; cinematic 33, 34, 94, 190,
   191; cultural 9, 29-30, 32, 35-8, 59, 68, 76, 84-
   5, 92-4, 100, 102-3, 116, 118-9, 132-3, 135, 140,
   146, 149, 156, 160-2, 174, 176, 183, 185-7, 189,
   190-93; national 30, 93, 192; politics of 38;
   racial 80, 87, 150; White American cultural 9,
   29, 30, 32, 102, 103, 116, 162, 185, 189, 190;
   built on white racial rage 116; instability of
   132; white male 47
Ideology 12, 30, 33, 52, 59, 62, 64, 68, 100, 106,
   135; of American Dream 73, 90, 93, 110, 112;
   of individualism 110; racist 29
Image/s: pp.8-193; of blackness 8, 28, 30, 31, 32,
   34, 35, 37, 38, 113, 146, 151, 155, 170, 174, 179,
   185, 186, 187, 188, 191; of black violence 28,
   36, 76, 131, 161, 185; bodily impact of 9, 108;
   cinematic 9, 12, 13, 15, 16, 17, 18, 19, 20, 27,
   37, 50, 51, 93, 99, 148, 159, 165, 166, 167, 191,
   193; iconic 107, 109, 145, 148, 149, 162;
   signification of 9
Immediacy 10, 12, 13, 15, 17, 20, 23, 28, 33, 35,
   52, 59, 61, 67-8, 74, 77, 85-6, 89-90, 92-3, 100,
   123-8, 131, 137, 142, 145-8, 151-2, 161-2, 167,
   170-2, 174, 179, 187; of black body 38;
   cinematic 8, 22, 109; and distanciation 73
Immediate reality 124, 142
Inflated male bodies 131 41n, 158
'Inflation of the represented' 18, 19, 23, 131, 150
Intensity 10, 75, 92, 117, 118, 120, 128, 147, 163,
   184; as affect 10
Intertextuality (postmodern) 11, 13, 25, 33, 34,
   51, 52, 92, 93, 101, 102, 127, 137, 144, 145, 147,
   163, 164, 165, 169;
In the Mood For Love (Kar-Wai) 192
Involuntary memory (Stern) 27, 102, 93, 100,
   102;

Involuntary realization 187
Involuntary shock 100
Italian neo-realism 12
It's A Wonderful Life (Capra) 49, 57, 61, 113,
   121, 130, 131, 135, 153, 170, 186

J

Jackie Brown (Tarantino) 25, 33, 35, 137, 145,
   188, 189
Jackson, Samuel L 167, 188
Jameson, Frederic 25, 39, 40, 61, 70, 82, 92, 95,
   96, 101, 132, 144, 155, 157, 159, 180; and
   aesthetic effect 13; affect as synonymous with
   emotion 26; and post-generic genre film 79;
   'waning of affect' 92, 145
Japanese Samurai films 193
Jazz 38, 91, 137, 156
Jazz Singer, The (Crosland) 38
Jeffries, Jim 77
Jeremiad 56, 57, 61, 64, 84, 90, 91; and populism
   184
Johnson, Jack 77
Jones, Jacquie 80
Juice (Dickerson) 57, 94, 123

K

Kar-Wai, Wong 192, 193
Keitel, Harvey 117, 120, 138, 143, 167
Kelley, Robin D. G 87, 96
Kennedy, Barbara 9
Kerouac, Jack *On the Road*, 157 11n
Kill Bill Vol. 1 (Tarantino) 32
Killer, The (Woo) 149
Killers, The (Siegal) 157 14n
Kim, Elaine 176, 180
Kiss Me Deadly (Aldrich) 50, 125, 164
Krutnik, Frank 69, 134

L

Lacan, Jacques (Lacanian) 29, 63, 88, 89, 108,
   113, 135, 143, 144, 145;
Lacanian 'Real', the 88, 113; 'Thing of the Real'
   143

Lack 113

Lady Snowblood (Fujita) 192

Lang, Fritz 9, 12, 15, 21, 26, 33, 70, 78, 87, 88, 92, 105, 106, 113, 116, 120, 133, 139, 141, 144, 145, 157, 159, 169, 171, 193

LA/Los Angeles 24, 43-4, 47, 51, 54-5, 58-60, 70, 74, 78, 80-3, 95, 103, 122, 126, 142, 157, 164, 167, 172, 175-6, 180; as 'any-space-whatever' 163; Riots (1992) 123

L.A.P.D 26, 27, 176

Last Year at Marienbad (Resnais) 39

Laura (Preminger) 111

Lee, Spike 34, 94; and cultural property 189; criticisms of Tarantino 33, 155; and word 'nigger' 33

Lehman, Ernest 14

Lethal Weapon (Donner) 21, 40, 150, 154, 173

Liotta, Ray 119

Live and Let Die (Hamilton) 81

Lone Wolf and Cub, The 192

Lucas, George 11, 21, 40, 147

M

McDowell, Deborah E. 40, 41, 95

Madonna *Like a Virgin* 139

Madsen, Michael 24, 138

Mailer, Norman 71, 141, 156 fn10; hipster, the 140; white negro 57, 68, 141

Malcolm, Derek 25, 40, 156

Maltese Falcon, The (Huston) 125

Manipulation, director's 18

Masochism 12, 37, 135, 156, 158, 177, 178, 181, 190, 193

Massumi, Brian 10, 26, 28, 38, 40, 68

Matrix, The (Wachowski) 179, 190, 191

Matrix Reloaded (Wachowski) 147

Masculinity 26, 27, 28, 29, 30, 47, 69, 73, 95, 104, 113, 139, 161, 185; in crisis 46; Tasker on 70 33n, 158 41n, 180 23n

Marx, Karl 107; and commodity fetishism 106, 148

Massood, Paula 103, 112, 125, 126, 132, 133, 134

Mean Streets (Scorsese) 19, 81, 117, 118, 119, 128, 139, 143, 186

Medeiros, Maria 167

Memory 5, 94, 126, 131; Collective white cultural 92; Involuntary (Stern) 27, 93

Menace II Society (Hughes brothers) 3, 31, 35, 36, 58, 59, 68, 70, 74, 80, 81, 94, 95, 99, 100, 101, 102, 103, 104, 105, 108, 110, 112, 114, 115, 116, 117, 121, 122, 123, 126, 127, 128, 129, 130, 132, 134, 142, 146, 148, 152, 155, 161, 162, 173, 185, 186; and aesthetic crisis 125; mimesis of film noir 109, 111, 113; retrospective narrative voice-over 111

Metz, Christian 39, 63

Milieu/Milieux 19-24, 47-135, 152-4, 161-191; in action-image cinema 121; confinement and ties to 154, 172; and inability to act 121, 129; and individual/protagonist 85, 120

Miller's Crossing (Coen) 135

Mimesis/mimetic 3, 7, 13, 24, 28-55, 81-193; connection between screen and viewer 11, 49, 55, 104, 149, 151; of black culture 31, 126, 132, 174, 179; of blackness 30, 34, 147, 189; dynamics of 24; of 'hood film 152; power of cinematic image 20; processes of contagion and tactility 31; relations between cultures 31; Taussig on 106

Mimetic machines 107, 108

Mise en scène 22, 38, 68, 81, 103, 129, 131, 152, 153, 175; and 'any-space-whatever' 154; and colour 150

Montage 16, 19, 43, 124

Morrison, Toni 31, 40, 70, 103, 132, 133 36n, 157, 189, 193; American Africanism 3, 29-30, 32, 35, 37, 59, 68, 76, 92, 133, 137, 141, 146, 156, 162, 173, 174, 183-8; 'white cultural imagination', the 25-38, 40-1, 44, 58-9, 68, 73-7, 80, 84-5, 87, 89, 91, 93-4, 99, 100, 101, 102, 106, 109, 111, 113, 115-6, 118, 123-7, 131-2, 137, 141, 143, 145-7, 150-1, 155-6, 160, 170, 172-4, 176, 178-9, 183-5, 188, 190, 191; 'white American literary imagination' 29; writerly unconscious' 183

Movement 18, 157; of the camera 7, 83, 117, 120; and cinema 83, 117; and colour-image 150; -image 15

Movement-image (Deleuze) 18; moving-image 15, 19, 108; bodily impact of 107-8

Moulin Rouge (Luhrmann) 190

Mulvey, Laura 5, 46, 69, 82

Murnau, F.W 15

N

Naked City, The (Dassin)

Naming/baptism 140

Narrative: pp 7-193; accuracy (in video) 124; cause and effect (lack of) 50, 128;   closure 122; decentralization of 22; linear 10, 20, 82, 118, 129; logic of 7; Oedipal 78, 79, 95; pathological 119; of postmodern blockbuster 22, 184; realism 103, 104, 124; resolution 22; violence of Classical Hollywood 117

National identity 30, 192; white American 93

Negro (Fanon) 74, 76; White (Mailer) 57, 68, 141

Neo-realism, Italian 12

New Black Realism 35-7, 57-9, 68, 73-6, 80-9, 94, 100, 125-7, 133-4 70n, 142-3, 146, 148, 161-2, 172; ability to reanimate 137; affective power of 85; assault on white cultural imagination 131; and film noir 110; display of violence 111; and powerlessness 132

New-brutality film 3, 8-9, 12, 24-6, 31-5, 38, 57, 84, 100, 137, 156, 159-61, 174, 179, 184-93; and affect 13; and mimesis of African-American culture 183; and viscerality of image 132; white 36, 74, 89, 94.

'Nigger', the word 33, 138

Nihilism 105; black men and 105, 109

Noir (film) 21, 36, 40, 48, 50, 51, 52, 56, 57, 62, 67, 69, 79, 90, 101, 108, 112, 113, 116, 126, 129, 133, 134, 135, 164, 172, 184,
   hero 61, 114; mimesis of 109, 175, 176; retrospective narrative voice-over 111; exclusion of African Americans 110, 125, 186; white 110

Noir by noirs (Diawara) 57, 111

Nooshock (Deleuze) 15, 18

North By Northwest (Hitchcock) 14

Nostalgia 32, 40, 44-45, 57, 60, 61-67, 108-9, 126, 145-148, 161-4, 172-4, 177, 179, 184-5; and *Blade Runner* 102, 166, 175; and desire and lack 21; as white cultural phenomenon 137

O

Once upon a Time in China (Hark) 192

Optical unconscious 108, 109

'Original', the 17, 86 (Benjamin); 'deauthenticising' and 'derealising' 16

'Other', the 30-2, 62; as contagious pollutant 120, 128

Out of the Past (Tourneur) 61

P

Pain 14, 16, 64, 104, 135, 149, 177, 190, 191; and Scarry 11; and torture 7

Panther (Van Peebles) 189

Parallax View, The (Pakula) 51

Paranoia 28, 30, 36, 59, 68, 74-5, 94, 115, 118, 128, 131, 161, 172, 185

Pastiche (postmodern) 11, 25, 52, 70, 114, 144-5, 157-9, 172-4

Pat Garrett and Billy the Kid (Peckinpah) 24

Peckinpah, Sam 12, 19, 20, 126, 149; films as elegiac 24

Peeping Tom (Powell) 177, 178

Penn, Chris 19, 143

Perception 9, 54, 68, 76, 107, 127, 170, 179; habitual 17, 20, 78, 108; as racially organized system 13; white/non-white ways of perceiving 31

Pesci, Joe 119

Picture of Dorian Gray, The (Lewin) 39

Pierrot Le Fou (Godard) 150

Pitt, Brad 172, 174

Pixilation 124

Pleasure 13, 33, 37, 45-6, 53, 60, 67, 87-8, 100, 112-3, 127, 135,158, 179, 188; spectacular 44, 137; visual pleasures 22

Point Blank (Boorman) 51

Point Break (Bigelow) 175

Postmodern blockbuster 13, 21, 25, 32, 34, 37, 39 43n, 44, 52-3, 73-4, 92, 109, 131-2, 137, 147, 150, 157 22n, 162, 175, 185 and 'any-space-whatever' 154; as 'inflation of the represented' (Deleuze) 23; and *mise en scène* 154; and superhuman heroes 184; narrative of 22, 184; *Star Wars* as (Lucas) 21; *Raiders of the Lost Ark* as (Spielberg) 21; use of violence as spectacle 22

Postmodern condition 37, 49, 55; characteristics of 26, 32; 'Play' 11; 'waning of affect' (Jameson) 26 cf. 'surfeit of it' Massumi) 26

Postmodernism: intertextuality 32; referentiality 93, 101; and Tarantino 11;

Postmodernity 34, 37, 40, 137, 142, 144-5, 147, 159-61, 165-6, 187, 191; erosion of meaning 155; random nostalgia of 146; reality and artifice of 143; simulacra of 146

Post-Screen film 13

Powell, Michael 177

Powerlessness 24, 76, 113, 116, 129, 130-2, 137, 170, 187; of gangster 24, 151; of whiteness 147

Predator (McTiernan) 21

Protagonist and milieu(x), links between 48, 49, 50, 85, 118, 121, 130, 164, 174, 183, 186; breakdown of relation 128, 175

Pryor, Richard 33

Psycho (Hitchcock) 12, 63

Psychoanalysis (film theory) 12, 135, 178, 181; and mother fixation 127

Public Enemy, The (Wellman) 96, 97, 134, 157 14n

Public Hero Number One (Walter) 96

Public and private 114

Pulp Fiction (Tarantino) 3, 8, 25, 32, 34-7, 95, 100, 137, 144-6, 156-9, 160, 165, 168-70, 173, 187-89; and crisis of action-image 163; fetishises African-Americans 161, 166; intertextuality of 164; mimesis of black culture 132; and recharged trash culture 161-2

R

Race/ethnicity 1, 3, 7, 18, 24, 26, 28, 31, 33-4, 40-1, 67, 84, 110, 120, 127, 129, 135, 138, 141, 148, 165, 173-75, 179, 183, 186, 190-1; aesthetics of 9; fetishisation 188; politics of 25

Racial rage: debilitating effects 121; and paranoia 118, 128; white 102; and white American cultural identity 116

Racial tension 176; unresolved 118

Racism 40, 58, 141, 169

Raiders of the Lost Ark (Spielberg) 21, 164

Rain 172, 173

Rambo: First Blood Part Two (Cosmatos) 22, 52, 105

Rap 26, 40-1, 91-2, 95-6, 104, 106, 116, 138-9, 141, 145-6, 156, 167, 169-70, 176, 186, 189; aesthetics of 37, 100, 137, 160; experienced as bodily (aural) assault 87; soundtrack 87, 88; and white public space 87

Rape 139, 168, 169, 178

Real, the 96, 132-3, 145, 148, 151, 168; blackness as symbol of 119, 139; of cinematic experience 126; 'hood as embodiment of 114, 115, 126; in Lacan/Lacanian 29, 113, 144; primitivist 88, 89; racial 139; representation of 144; savage 115, 160; surplus of 119; 'Thing of' 143; unknowable 88, 167; unpredictable appearance of 115; urban ghetto as space of 116; violence of 143; in Zizek 88

Realism 35-7, 44-94, 100-2, 110-1, 123-153, 161-2, 171-2, 192; Cinematic 12, 82, 101, 126, 171Classic Hollywood 78, 152; contemporary 142; cynical 3, 43-5, 65, 67-8, 73, 85, 184-5; narrative 103, 104, 124; new black *See New Black Realism;* social 103, 126

'Reality', as outmoded concept 44

'Reality TV'/Media 123, 124, 126

Renaissance space 46, 82

Representation/s 18, 47, 58, 61, 79-81, 86, 101, 103-5, 115, 126, 131, 147, 158-9, 178, 183, 192; abject, of the body 170; interior of the body as barrier to 169; of the Real 144;

Representational approaches (to film) 139

Repression 31, 36, 109, 160, 170, 176, 184, 186, 189

Reservoir Dogs (Tarantino) 3, 7-8, 10-3, 18, 24-28, 31-2, 34-5, 37, 41, 100, 134, 137-40, 145-54, 159-68, 173, 187-8; aesthetics of masochism (cf. voyeurism) 156; crisis of white culture 144; mimesis of black culture 132, 152, 155; mimicry of the gangsta 141; of rap 141

Resnais, Alain 12

Rhames, Ving 164, 166

Rio Bravo (Hawks) 52

Robinson, Edward, G. 92, 96

Rouge (Kwan) 192

Roundtree, Richard 81

Rites of passage movie 78-9, 103

Rodney King 25-8, 176, 187-8; as dangerous black body 25

Rogin Michael 8, 38, 41, 155, 158

Rose, Tricia 36

Roth, Tim 142, 164

Running Man, The (Glaser) 22

S

Sadism 12, 177, 178, 181, 193; sadistic violence 7

Sang Des Betes, Le (Franju) 39

Saturday Night Fever (Badham) 149

Scarface - Shame of a Nation (Hawks) 90, 96, 104, 134, 135

Scarry, Elaine 11, 15, 38

Schumacher, Joel 8, 35, 44, 54, 55, 58, 60, 68, 70, 85, 94, 96, 193

Schwartz, Thomas 22, 39, 52, 96, 154, 163, 166, 184

Schwarzenegger, Arnold 22, 52, 154, 163, 166, 184

Science fiction (film) 21, 44, 102, 144, 157

Scorsese, Martin 12, 19, 24, 36, 50, 51, 81, 101, 109, 114, 117, 118, 119, 121, 122, 124, 126, 128, 139, 147, 152, 163, 184, 186

Scorsesean cinema 109, 117, 147

Searchers, The (Ford) 51, 119, 120, 121, 122, 127, 128, 170, 186

Second World War, the 23, 32, 49, 85, 131, 135

Self-reflexivity 7, 34, 46, 47, 67, 68, 92, 118, 137, 143, 146, 150, 160, 161, 163, 168, 177, 184, 188

Sensation 9, 13, 25, 27, 35, 74, 93

Sensory-motor link/relations 23, 48, 52, 53, 86, 99, 164, 174, 186; cracks/crisis in 109, 121

Se7en (Fincher) 3, 8, 37, 38, 156, 159, 160, 161, 169, 170, 171, 172, 173, 174, 187, 188; colour-blindness 173; mimesis of New Black Realism 172; reanimate potential of noir 172; and 'True-Crime' TV 161, 171, 173

Shaft (Parks, Snr) 80, 81

Shaft in Africa (Guillermin) 81

Shaviro, Steven 9, 21, 38, 40, 69, 102, 132, 157, 165, 180; *Cinematic Body* 8, 9, 14, 147, 149

She's Gotta Have It (Lee) 94

Shock 12-20, 25, 30-9, 74, 79-80, 84, 88, 93, 94, 100, 106, 108, 114, 124, 126, 146-149, 159-163, 169, 170-193; affective 13, 25, 30, 32, 35, 36, 37, 94, 160, 161, 162, 169, 172, 179; Benjamin's notion of cinematic 16; cinematic 16, 18, 93; exploitative 33; involuntary 100; masochistic desire for 178, 179; Nooshock (Deleuze) 15, 18; physical 159, 160; politicised 33; to thought (Deleuze) 15, 18, 84, 100, 108

Shusterman, Richard 88, 96 48n, 157 2n 88, 96, 156

Silence of the Lambs, The (Demme) 170

Signification 9, 13, 87, 89, 93, 116, 133, 186; conscious and unconscious processes of 9; cultural 13; clash of Symbolic structures of 89, 116, 117

Silverman, Kaja 130, 133, 135; and 'celestial suture' 130, 131; 'dominant fiction' 133 21n

Silver Surfer, The 143

Singleton, John 35, 57, 73, 75, 78, 81, 92, 94, 95, 189

Simulacra 146, 158 44n, 179

'Simulation of the real' 172

Simulation/surface 32, 37, 99, 102, 119, 143, 144, 146, 147, 155, 157, 160, 161, 165, 166, 167, 172, 174, 175, 176, 177, 187, 190; as intensification of the real 102; nostalgic 99, 165; as postmodern condition 32; postmodernity 155, 161; and whiteness 176

Singer, Ben 39

Siskel, Gene 75, 77, 80, 95

Skin 10, 13, 26, 29, 33, 88, 145

Sloterdijk, Peter 66, 71

Social realism 103, 126, 148, 152

Space: cinematic 55, 79, 80, 82, 151; (exertion of) control of 84, 154; extracinematic 84; renaissance 46, 82; white cinematic 74, 87

Spacey, Kevin 170

Special effects 131

Spectacular, the 22, 40, 67, 147, 175, 184, 192; emphasis on 22; spectacle of the body 154; violence as 22

Spectatorship 67; *See also* Audience *and* Viewer.

Speed (de Bont) 40, 53

Spielberg, Steven 11, 21, 164

SQUID machine/device 177, 178

Stars 13, 22, 44, 46, 52, 81, 89, 92, 138, 184; female 46

Star system,

Star Wars (Lucas) 21, 40

Staying Alive (Stallone) 149

Stern, Lesley 40, 70, 94, 97, 119, 120, 121, 134; 'dramatic intensity' 117, 128, 184; 'involuntary memory' 27, 93, 100, 102; as 'sensation of sensuous reminiscence' 27, 93

Stewart, James 49, 130

Stone, Oliver 25

Straight out of Brooklyn (Rich) 94

Strange Days (Bigelow) 3, 8, 37, 38, 156, 159, 160, 177, 183, 187, 188; dystopian *mise en scene* 175; fabrication of African-American culture 161, 174; mimesis of noir 175; reversal of fears around black violence 176; sadism and masochism in 178; similarity/differences with *Blade Runner* 175

'Structures of Aggression' (Burch) 125; as immanent to cinematic experience 160

Structures of meaning 116, 151, 160; racially organised and symbolic 118

Studlar, Gaylyn 158 43n

Sunset Boulevard (Wilder) 111

Superfly (Parks Jnr.) 80

Sweet Sweetback's Baadasss Song (Van Peebles) 80, 81

Swimmer, The (Perry & Pollack) 70

Symbolic order, the 115, 146; blackness structured by 29; immanent violence beneath 140

Symbolic (structure) 31, 114, 116, 119, 151, 160, 174, 176; boundaries 118; reality 63, 88, 89, 96, 113, 133, 144; uncertainty/instability of 139

T

Tactility 31, 107, 193

Tales of the Highway Patrol 123

Tarantino, Quentin 7, 8, 12, 25, 26, 32, 34, 37, 41, 94, 100, 132, 137, 142, 144, 145, 146, 147, 150, 151, 152, 156, 157, 158, 159, 160, 161, 162, 163, 165, 170, 174, 179, 180, 186, 188, 189, 191; and bodily impact of films 33; and fetishism 148-149, 155; and postmodernism 11; reanimation of cinematic experience 155

Tasker, Yvonne 70 33n, 158 41n, 180 23n

Taubin, Amy 39, 80, 95, 104, 105, 132, 134, 156, 170, 171, 180; on *Reservoir Dogs* 139; sado-masochistic dynamic 12

Taussig, Michael 17, 39, 40, 86, 133, 155; on Benjamin 28; and the (commodity) fetish 106, 107; and mimesis 28; on optical unconscious 108; and 'particulate sensuality' 106; and processes of contagion and tactility 31

Taxi Driver (Scorsese) 19, 51, 117, 120, 121, 122, 127, 128, 181; and (crisis) of action-image 119

Temporal bodily control 14; and Hitchcock 14

Terminator, The (Cameron) 22, 44, 154, 164, 175, 184

Terminator II (Cameron) 22, 75

'Thing, The' 143

Thought: ambivalence of 132; and the body 14, 15, 149; conscious and habitual 11, 15, 86, 93, 107, 132, 163; 'shock to thought' 15, 18, 84, 100, 108

Thurman, Uma 167, 192, 193

Tierney, Lawrence 138

Time and cinema

Time-image (Deleuze) 23, 69, 171

Total Recall (Verhoeven) 22, 44, 52, 67, 165, 175

Torture 7, 12, 13, 14, 18, 23, 24, 25, 26, 27, 28, 31, 32, 35, 145, 149, 154, 168, 169, 187; body and 11, 15; Scarry on 11

Trash culture 144, 161

Travolta, John 149, 167

Trespass (Hill) 179

True crime TV 101, 109, 123, 125, 126

True Romance (Scott) 157 12n

Truman Show, The (Weir) 62

'Truth' 65, 66, 112, 185; as outmoded concept 44; blackness as sign of 111; and 'history' 124

Tupac Shakur 138

Twister (de Bont) 22

U

Uncle Tom's Cabin (Porter) 38

Unconscious, the 139; and Jameson 144; writerly unconscious' (Morrison) 183

V

Van Peebles, Melvin 80, 81, 189

Vernet, Marc 40, 56, 57, 70, 110

Verhoeven, Paul 22, 44, 47, 52, 165

Vertov, Dziga 15

Video 27, 51, 64, 65, 115, 157, 171, 186; authority/immediacy of 'real-life' 124; effect 123; method of immediacy and authenticity 124; tape as object-token 125

Viewer, the: pp7-192; assault on body of 8, 146; body of 8, 11, 149; body-first response of 28, 145; boundary between screen and 8, 12, 14, 49, 146, 193; masochistic position/desire of 178, 179; and pain 14; 'passive state of' (Benjamin) 17; and temporary incarceration 154; vulnerability of 12; white 37, 77, 88, 89, 115, 116, 131, 151, 186, 187;

Viewing position 44-5, 54-7, 62-6, 68, 86, 126, 178, 184

Violence (and cinema): pp7-192; anarchic 36, 76, 94, 102; black male 77; black on black 36, 99, 104; cinematic 18, 20, 101, 126, 148, 164; of Classical Hollywood film 22, 117; copycat 89; eroticised 111; at heart of white culture 100; narrative 20, 117, 150; of the Real 143; sadistic 7; as spectacle (in postmodern blockbuster) 22; unspoken 102-3; white 28; and white American identity 9, 29, 30, 32, 102, 103, 116, 162, 185, 189, 190; in white cultural imagination *See* Black violence.

Viscerality 38, 59, 159; of image 38, 132, 177, 179

Visual/Visuality 13, 46, 53, 124, 126, 128, 131, 144, 168, 171, 172, 175, 181, 190, 191; effects of violence 22

Voice-over: 103, 115, 116, 118, 119; cinematic 111; dead, 111, 113, 114; unreliability of/misleading 112, 114

Voyeurism 37, 156, 170, 173, 181

Voyeuristic authority 80

W

White Heat (Walsh) 19, 97, 127, 134 72n

Washington, Booker, T. 91

Watts, Carol 5, 47

Watts Riots (1965) 123

Weekend, Le (Godard) 150

Welles, Orson 12

West, Cornell 105, 106, 107, 108, 109, 111, 133, 148, 157

Western 12, 20, 21, 25, 52, 69, 75, 79, 106, 121, 125, 126, 140, 193

'White cultural imagination' (Morrison) 25, 29, 31, 33, 34, 35, 36, 37, 38, 40, 41, 44, 58, 68, 73, 74, 77, 84, 85, 87, 89, 91, 93, 99, 100, 101, 102, 106, 111, 113, 115, 116, 123, 124, 125, 127, 132, 137, 141, 143, 145, 146, 147, 150, 151, 155, 156, 170, 176, 178, 183, 184, 185, 188, 190, 191; aesthetic crisis in 32; anxieties of around black masculinity 27; fears of (immanent) black violence in 26, 30, 36, 59, 75-6, 80, 94, 99, 104, 109, 126, 131, 134, 160-1, 172-4, 176, 179, 185,

187; powerlessness of 131; unspoken Real of 118

White: pp9-193; cultural identity 30, 35, 37, 38, 59, 68, 76, 84, 85, 93, 100, 119, 133, 146, 156, 160, 161, 174, 176, 183, 186, 187, 190; culture as empty, nostalgic 142, 177; as death (Dyer) 146; fears and desires 92; guilt 116; new brutality film 36, 74, 89, 94, 132; racial rage 36, 102, 116, 118, 162, 175, 185; racism 58, 140, 141; vulnerable body 149

White (popular) culture 145, 155, 160; as blank meaningless surface 37

White Negro (Mailer) 68, 71, 140, 141, 156-7 fn10

Whiteness 3, 29, 30, 110, 147, 159, 167, 174, 176, 177, 179; as artificial 168; as depthless simulation 146; Dyer on 31; as voyeurism and masochism 37

White viewers 13, 36, 37, 59, 80, 88, 89, 91, 99, 100, 115, 116, 123, 131, 151, 186, 187; disavowal and fetishism 31; and impact of black male body 77; and involuntary awareness/realisation 35

White racial rage 36, 102, 116, 117, 118, 162, 175, 185

Wild Bunch, The (Peckinpah) 20, 24, 149

Williams, Linda 40, 95, 135, 157; "make the body do things" 8, 38, 148

Willis, Bruce 52, 150, 154, 167,168

Willis, Sharon 161, 162, 166, 180

Winokur, Mark 87, 88, 92, 96, 97, 135, 169, 180; and 'ethnic other' 93

Wizard of Oz, The (Fleming/Vidor) 132.n9

Woman in the Window, The (Lang) 21

Woo, John 149, 191, 193

Wood, James 25, 38, 40, 120

Women 46, 69, 111, 139, 178

Wright, Richard Native Son 70, 96, 111

Z

Zizek, Slavoj 40, 61, 62, 63, 66, 70, 71, 88, 96, 133 45n, 144, 157, 181 31n, 193; Lacanian model of the Real 145